e-Business Strategies for Virtual Organizations

e-Business Strategies for Virtual Organizations

Janice Burn

Peter Marshall

Martin Barnett

Oxford   Auckland   Boston   Johannesburg   Melbourne   New Delhi

Butterworth-Heinemann
Linacre House, Jordan Hill, Oxford OX2 8DP
225 Wildwood Avenue, Woburn, MA 01801-2041
A division of Reed Educational and Professional Publishing Ltd

A member of the Reed Elsevier plc group

First edition 2002

British Library Cataloguing in Publication Data
A catalogue record for this book is available from the British Library

ISBN 0 7506 4943 7

Composition by Genesis Typesetting, Rochester, Kent
Printed and bound in Great Britain

Contents

Computer Weekly Professional Series

There are few professions which require as much continuous updating as that of the IS executive. Not only does the hardware and software scene change relentlessly, but also ideas about the actual management of the IS function are being continuously modified, updated and changed. Thus keeping abreast of what is going on is really a major task.

The Butterworth-Heinemann–*Computer Weekly* Professional Series has been created to assist IS executives keep up to date with the management ideas and issues of which they need to be aware.

One of the key objectives of the series is to reduce the time it takes for leading edge management ideas to move from the academic and consulting environments into the hands of the IT practitioner. Thus this series employs appropriate technology to speed up the publishing process. Where appropriate some books are supported by CD-ROM or by additional information or templates located on the Web.

This series provides IT professionals with an opportunity to build up a bookcase of easily accessible, but detailed information on the important issues that they need to be aware of to successfully perform their jobs as they move into the new millennium.

Aspiring or already established authors are invited to get in touch with me directly if they would like to be published in this series.

Dr Dan Remenyi
Series Editor
Dan.remenyi@mcil.co.uk

Other titles in the Series

Authors' Preface

There are dozens of books and articles arriving monthly on e-business, the Internet and telling you how to make money in the new economy. Why is this book different, and how does it stand out?

This book is not:

- a recipe for success on the Internet;
- an advertisement for a consultancy's services or methodology;
- a guide to getting venture capital for a dot-com enterprise; or
- a guide to taking a new e-business enterprise public.

This book is:

- a critical explanation of what we mean by e-business;
- a means of understanding the vital concept of virtual organizing;
- a set of strategy approaches to thinking for and about the new economy;
- helpful templates for organizing workgroups and teams thinking about change.

While it is possible to address our topics at many levels and with varying degrees of abstraction, we have chosen to pitch our text at the level of the practising manager. Our reader will have a good grounding in business concepts and some understanding of the reach of technology without needing specialist technology or network knowledge. Academics and managers at many levels are applying themselves to the areas we encompass in this book, therefore we are obliged to restrict our focus and level – and we have chosen that appropriate for graduate managers, or students choosing to study at a university at Master's level or above. While we welcome readers from outside this group, we cannot inflate the text to explain below a certain level.

We open by looking at how new information and communication technologies affect business activities – generally referred to as the new economy, or the Internet economy. To assist us in this, we look at the significant restructuring of organizations resulting from e-business. We introduce the core concepts and argue that this new business paradigm is one where core business processes may need to be rethought and redesigned, new organizational forms and interorganizational forms may need to be developed and where the emphasis will be on collaboration rather than competition within the virtual market.

Having set the scene, we move on in Chapter 2 to examine relevant aspects of the Internet, intranets, and extranets, which facilitate networks both within and between organizations. We note that this results in fundamental changes and rethinks to potential and satisfactory organizational structures, and also to the way in which organizations position themselves within their environment to compete and/or cooperate with other organizations.

From this we derive a workable notion of virtuality, and of the virtual organization, defined as 'an entity which comprises a combination of different companies or individuals that have combined to complete specific projects or business propositions and development'. This core notion will be referred to and adapted throughout the following chapters.

The idea of business models is introduced and examined in Chapter 3. Virtual organizations obviously have a need for business models, which are different from the traditional, but there is no one single business model that is appropriate to all forms of virtual enterprise. Different organizations, we argue, require different business models. These will reflect the extent and strength of their interorganizational links within their networked alliances.

In the most basic sense, a business model is the method of doing business by which an organization can best sustain itself – which in most cases means generating revenue. The selected business model will therefore be that which spells out how the organization positions itself within the value chain in order to make financial return. For this reason we introduce variations of virtual organizations early on so that readers may select appropriate forms for their economic sector or enterprise, and work through later chapters with this in mind.

Selecting the structural and strategic forms of business model will effectively set the strategic agenda for the virtual organization and define the relationships, roles, business processes and partnerships which should be exploited. Business models will be reintroduced throughout the text to extend and expand on the early exposition.

We go further, in Chapter 4, to look at the implications of interconnectedness and decreasing communications costs. In particular, we focus here on approaches to strategy formulation for virtual organizations or strategic business networks, commenting on the need for some changes in emphasis in strategy formulation, given the realities of contemporary business environment. In this context we introduce the new term, if not entirely new construct, of 'coopetition' to describe the information and resource – sharing strategies that are replacing naked aggression and competition in many business contexts.

At this stage, in Chapter 5, we have sufficient background and common terminology to examine in depth the first three underlying and major constructs that make sense of an electronic business community:

- internetworked markets;
- the Internet enabled supply chain; and
- interorganizational systems.

These concepts are complemented, in Chapters 7, 8, and 9 by the following related terms:

- integrated organizational systems;
- intelligent knowledge-based systems; and
- information-based business architecture.

But at this stage, we digress from overarching issues to integrate another stream of concern, namely that of smaller businesses and what's in e-business and globalization for them. There is much concern, in economies around the world, that globalization, alliance formation and e-business online exchanges will threaten small or locally based organizations. From a small French farmer to an Indonesian pepper merchant, legitimate concern is expressed at the potential for e-business to homogenize the world and drive out opportunities for small entrepreneurs and family businesses.

Chapter 6 specifically addresses the issue of what the new economy means for the small or medium-sized enterprise. In this chapter we suggest and explain how the availability of the Internet and web technologies provides unique advantages for SMEs to build effective global infrastructures in at least three ways:

- internet-based infrastructures are relatively cheap – requiring significantly reduced capital investments over proprietary ones;
- they provide an ever converging and rich environment for effective business networking and interorganizational process management; and
- they provide SMEs with access to a huge mass of consumers through e-business.

This means that e-business is an extremely attractive option for most SMEs, although they come bundled with admitted threats. The challenges these opportunities and threats present are not helped by the general lack of clearly defined frameworks for analysis of the entire process of strategy building, implementation and management with respect to this emerging global information economy.

This chapter attempts to address the problem by providing a holistic framework for the study and design of global information infrastructure within the organizational context of SMEs. With such analytical tools and specific e-business strategies SMEs could and should capitalize on the opportunities offered in the electronic marketplace. The framework is supported by a number of international case studies.

We strike a more esoteric note in the following chapter, as we consider the role of knowledge as capital and the value of knowledge assets to the organization. Strategies for knowledge management are reviewed and linked with strategies for change. This approach introduces virtual encounters, virtual sourcing, and virtual expertise and knowledge. Finally the issues or actual execution of strategies are considered and suggestions are made for the development of an action framework.

By Chapter 8 we are in a position to appreciate that an organization that is responsive to change and capitalizes on new alliances, better customer and supplier relationships and new markets, products and services needs to have a different strategic planning and management process in place which is associated with an effective value measurement system. We discuss these accordingly, noting where existing static value measurements based on financial returns do not reflect the holistic view of an enterprise moving towards virtual organization.

Our next topic brought to the mix is that discussed for many years under the term 'outsourcing'. We have established that, essentially, the virtual organization is an opportunistic grouping of collaborating organizations, each of which focuses on a set of core competencies or capabilities at which it excels. Traditionally the use of suppliers to provide essential processes is referred to in IS as outsourcing.

A general but acceptable definition of this concept runs: outsourcing is a decision taken to contract out or make available the organization's assets, activities and/or staff to a third party supplier. This third party, in return, provides and manages these assets (for payment) over a contracted term.

This result may be a fluid network of firms changing according to circumstances and needs. Such a network of firms is likely to be created and sustained through the processes of outsourcing and partnering/alliance formation – a virtual organization is born.

In this context we provide outside views to complement those of our own that are developed throughout. It will be helpful at this stage to look at these models or visions for the future, looking at the role of both outsourcing and partnering or alliances, and the close relationship of both these to virtual organizing and the virtual organizational form.

Moving into a fairly complex area now, as many of the threads of this book are brought together, Chapter 10 considers the issues involved in integrating front-end and back-end processes, and specifically the role of enterprise resource planning (ERP) systems as back-end support aligning with customer relationship management (CRM) systems at the front-end.

We look at the business value chain as it is affected by the new technologies; we at the consumer relationship in flux. And we examine the implications of changed communications for employee relationships. We address environmental change and organizational performance issues and the factors that empower employees to support large-scale change. In particular we look at the motivational factors influencing employees to initiate change in the face of these new realities and the implications for management of both IT and non-IT employees in the learning organization.

Finally we take a grander view, turning to the question of how and whether today's business-centric, e-business organizational forms will evolve into customer-centric e-communities.

In Chapter 11 we review cultural influences on organizations and information technology applications. This is expanded into the development of online communities where a shared culture of common practices is a key factor in effective development and maintenance.

Finally, the whole issue of global expansion is placed under the spotlight and the implications for the future are examined. What will happen? The choice is yours, and to make a choice that reflects your needs, you must be informed. Thank you for allowing us to share our thoughts, we look forward to any responses you may have to this text.

Janice M. Burn
Peter Marshall
Martin Barnett

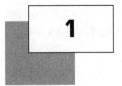

1 e-business and the virtual organization – a new rationale for 21st century organizations

> Though of real knowledge there be little,
> yet of books there are plenty.
> (Herman Melville, *Moby Dick*)

1.1 Introduction

As we enter the new millennium, there is a general feeling that there is a new social and economic reality, largely based on new communication technologies. We cannot open a book or magazine without seeing assertions, more or less supported by evidence, that we are entering a new age. In particular, this applies to the world of business, transformed as it has been by a number of powerful forces such as globalization and the advent of the Internet. There is a sense that the world of business is significantly different from even 20 years ago. This is exemplified by the prevalence of terms such as 'new economy', 'information economy', 'digital economy' and so on. These terms suggest, rather imprecisely, that we have a new business reality, and that the role of IT and the Internet are significant, or perhaps even defining features or characteristics of that new business reality.

There are two broad constructs that help to structure and make some sense of this new reality if they are defined and thought about clearly: namely the 'new economy' and the 'Internet economy.' In this chapter we shall introduce these notions as fundamental constructs for the rest of the book. There is a sense in which trends such as globalization and the effective use of increasingly more powerful and reliable IT have transformed the national economies of the USA and Europe to such an extent that when referring to, say, the contemporary US economy, we could meaningfully talk about something called the 'new economy'. A separate construct refers to the economy that is clustered around the Internet and the new electronic commerce or e-business phenomenon.

Finally, there has been a significant restructuring of organizations since e-business intensifies collaborations among multiple organizations with several complex, economic, strategic, social and conflict management issues as well as major organizational and technological factors. This new business paradigm is one where core business processes may need to be rethought and redesigned, new organizational forms and interorganizational forms may need to be developed and where the emphasis will be on collaboration rather than competition within the virtual market. Driven by such phenomena as the World Wide Web, mass customization, compressed product life cycles, new distribution channels and new forms of integrated organizations, the most fundamental elements of doing business are changing and a totally new business environment is emerging. This form of 'virtual' organization will have a considerable impact on all aspects of business strategy in the 21st century. This chapter examines these issues in turn and sets the scene for the remaining chapters in the book as we explore the nature and rationale of the virtual organization, virtual markets and strategies for coopetition, strategies for designing, transitioning and managing the virtual organization.

1.2 The new economy

The notion of the new economy is somewhat elusive to define. There is speculation that the recent sustained boom in the US economy as instanced by increased corporate earnings and profits, low unemployment, relatively high productivity, low inflation and an absolutely soaring stock market, has led to that economy being 'new', in the sense that some of the old economy rules and principles no longer apply, at least with the same force. Among such speculation is a view that stronger productivity growth now allows the US economy to grow faster without inflationary pressures. There is also the view that in the short run a trade-off between inflation and unemployment has changed so that low unemployment and low inflation can coexist. Other speculation looks at the sources of growth in the US economy and identifies factors such as computerization and globalization as driving forces changing the nature of the old economy. Indeed to some writers, IT has an especially important transformatory role. Shepard, writing in *Business Week*, claims that:

Information technology ... is, in short, a transcendent technology – like railroads in the 19th century and automobiles in the 20th century. (Shepard 1997)

Mandel, another *Business Week* writer, claims that the:

New economy – so far propelled by information technology – may turn out to be only the initial stage of a broader flowering of technological business and financial creativity. (Mandel 1998)

Connected to the pre-eminent role given to IT and its potentially transforming power, has been the important role given to knowledge as a new form of capital, and the role of knowledge management, as well as research and innovation as wealth creating factors.

Another element of the new economy construct is the increasingly important role of the service sector. We can choose to see the evolution of economies from an agrarian-based economy through an industrial economy through to a service economy and then on to the emergence of an experience economy. Each economic stage has all the elements of preceding and succeeding stages, but the focus and emphasis are different. The contemporary economies of the developed world can be seen to be new in terms of their emphasis on producing and delivering services and the emerging idea of staging complete experiences for consumers. Of course, modern, new economies examined along this plane are only different in degree from the older economies of 20 years ago, but this difference in degree could be seen as a 'strand of newness' in the 'new economy'. Thus we see that the nature of the new economy has many and varied aspects of novelty, and these are given different degrees of emphasis by different thinkers, as we shall see throughout this book.

Economists are examining the new IT-based organizations and the economic world they shape, but have come to no agreement yet on whether there are new economic laws to be discovered, or whether the old economy macroeconomic principles and technical relationships still apply. For some it is a given that, while technology may change, economic laws do not. Perhaps it is too soon to hold any definite views on this. As we shall see, the potential for new business and organizational forms resulting from a still-developing set of technologies has yet to be properly mapped out, and we are all still learning.

1.3 Is the 'new economy' really new?

Well, there are new features and emphases, but the basic macroeconomic principles seem unaltered. The mass psychology of a new economy is certainly there, with some very real non-psychological effects such as soaring stock prices and firms who continually make losses not profits being given very high stock valuations because they are 'new economy' dot-coms. However, this irrational exuberance has been seen before – for example, in the 19th century with the craze for building railways, and in the 20th century with the overvaluation of radio in its early days.

We have thus examined some of the major ideas that contribute to and thread through the notion of the 'new economy' as an economy operating on new rules and principles. This view of the 'new economy' is one that relies on the notion illustrated in Figure 1.1, of an economy transformed by IT and other factors such as globalization.

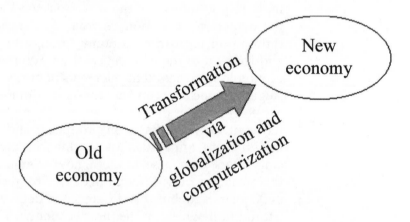

Figure 1.1

Even the terms 'information economy' and 'digital economy' are sometimes covered by the above sense of a 'new economy' arising from transformation of the old economy through various forces – IT looming large among these forces. As an example, consider Brynjolfsson and Kahin's definitions:

The term 'information economy' has come to mean the broad, long-term trend toward the expansion of information- and knowledge-based assets and value relative to tangible assets and products associated with agriculture, mining, and manufacturing. The term 'digital economy' refers specifically to the recent and still largely unrealised transformation of all sectors of the economy by the computer enabled digitisation information.

(Brynjolfsson and Kahin 2000)

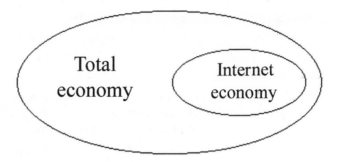

Figure 1.2

There is, however, another definition of the 'information economy', 'digital economy' or 'Internet economy'. This notion revolves around the set of Internet-based organizations, the 'dot-coms' and others involved in e-commerce. This 'Internet economy' as we shall refer to it is clearly a subset of the total economy, as shown in Figure 1.2.

1.4 Framework of e-business

The emergence of e-business has led to dramatic redefinitions of the nature of an organization. Complex business networks working together along the value chain are defined by their ability to get products to market with the widest range of consumers at the cheapest cost and fastest speed. This, in turn, has led to a completely different set of problems for the management of such structures with complex interrelationships, changing paradigms for intermediation, and an emphasis on collaborative competition. Today's business executive needs to have a framework for understanding such relationships in order to evaluate strategic opportunities in the global marketplace.

We have found that in information management projects, where there is a need to analyse or construct large systems, it is useful to structure them as a hierarchy of several levels in which the lower ones provide the support platform for the higher. In the case of e-business supporting interorganizational systems, such a hierarchy may usefully be viewed as displayed in Table 1.1.

We can use this table to view the e-business as made up of three levels:

- *technology-based infrastructure* – the hardware and software making up the ICT to deliver functionality over networks;
- *services* – all messaging activities; and

Table 1.1 The hierarchical framework of e-commerce

Meta Level	Level	Function	Examples
Products and structures	7	Electronic marketplaces and electronic hierarchies	Electronic auctions, brokerages, dealerships, and direct search markets
			Interorganizational supply chain management
	6	Products and systems	Consumer services over distance – retailing, banking, stock broking, etc.
			Information and entertainment on demand: educational services, fee-based content sites
			Supplier–customer linkages
			Online marketing
			Electronic benefit systems
			Intranet and extranet collaboration
Services	5	Enabling services	Online catalogues, directories, smart agents
			Smart card systems, e-money
			Digital authentication services
			Digital libraries, copyright protection services
			Traffic audit
	4	Secure messaging	EDI, electronic funds transfer, e-mail
Technology-based infrastructure	3	Hypermedia/ multimedia object management	World Wide Web with Java
	2	Communications utilities	Value added networks and Internet
	1	Wide area telecommunications infrastructure	Guided and wireless media networks

- *products and structures* – the provision of goods and services together with intra- and inter-organizational information sharing and the creation of electronic supply chains and marketspaces. Let us look at these in a little more detail.

1.4.1 Technology-based infrastructure

Supporting this framework are three basic levels.

The first is the global network of telecommunications networks linking public and private networks through a computer-controlled switching system. The potential for interorganizational strategies extends as far as the reach of these media. Differences in regional and national penetration of these networks is, and will be for the foreseeable future, a function of government policies, funding and control strategies together with private sector belief in their profitability in areas in which this is allowed to function.

ICT capabilities are made available for business use in two important ways. The first available system was that of privately constructed and leased networks, the value added networks (VANs). These were constructed to make available services over and above those offered by the common carriers (then almost entirely state-run and regulated monopolies, created for voice transmission), and to make a profit in the process. The second has arrived with the development of the Internet from a government sponsored and research medium into today's principal inexpensive vehicle for e-business.

The separate software-based layer of the Internet known as the World Wide Web has resulted in the possibility of a single, distributed, worldwide, hyperlinked database with password-protected and private networks (intranets and extranets) linked to it. The Web is a medium for the distribution, presentation and sale of information-based objects. As a platform-independent service it has been enhanced by recent developments in platform-independent programming languages, such as Java, further enhancing its utility. Nevertheless, it needs to be understood that as a separate and software-based layer, the Web can and may be replaced in the future by an information management mechanism that would better meet the demands of very large-scale use of the global network of networks.

1.4.2 Services

The service level provides for the transfer of messages and enabling services for business. Using a suite of protocols developed for the free sharing of information, this level is robust and inexpensive. The downside is that, unlike proprietary EDI systems, there is no inbuilt security, confidentiality, authentication and similar services demanded by commerce. This issue is currently being addressed by such means as cryptography, Internet tunnelling, and the development of protocols such as the secure electronic transaction (SET) layer issuing from credit card companies.

e-mail is the most pervasive tool of the Internet and a cost-cutting measure that is generally the first to be appreciated by business. While issues of e-mail contracts, confidentiality, evidentiary value and such like are yet to be fully resolved, this tool is expected to retain its prime position in the business repertoire.

More activity is under way in the area of enabling services: tools for searching, price comparison, customizing information delivery and receipt, together with electronic money initiatives and e-banking, are under formulation. This service area is changing too rapidly for a book to offer the latest advice: you are advised to conduct web searches on topics of particular interest. It is, however, worth briefly examining the possible implications of e-money. e-money in its various forms is expected to become a substitute for credit and debit instruments and also for bank notes and coins at considerable expense to the handling agencies such as banks, finance houses and government controlled agencies.

e-money has considerable social implications beyond this since it does not have the obvious anonymity of cash. There are also the security and legal implications and, of course, the auditing and tax implications of electronic transfers. Within the global context we must also recognize that the majority of consumers are not currently web enabled and so there may be far reaching implications for social and economic reform in the less developed countries of the world.

1.4.3 Products and structures

A lot of interest and publicity surrounds consumer-oriented applications of e-business. Companies such as Amazon (booksellers), Dell (computer retailers), CDNow (music sellers),

Discover Brokerage Direct (securities transactions) and Security First National Bank (banking services) are frequent visitors to the business and popular press. In traditional P/E ratio terms, none of these firms is exciting, yet their market capitalization during 1999/2000 suggests that Internet-based stocks are perceived, rightly or wrongly, as gaining value in other ways.

Alongside the overtly commercial sector, information for entertainment purposes (infotainment) on demand is another growing sector. From news corporations (CNN, The Times of London, etc.) to web versions of paper magazines (Hotwired) and purely electronic journals, magazines and newsletters, the Web is awash with information available in both push and pull formats. The boundaries of information and entertainment are blurring, as are those between commercial and not-for-profit sites. Unfortunately, while enthusiasm and experimentation are rampant, no clear models for success have yet emerged.

The linkages between businesses (B2B) and between business and consumer (B2C) along the traditional supply chain is perhaps clearer as well as being the fastest-growing area of e-business. This exciting area is attracting the most attention as new configurations of the supply chain model are enabled by ICT, giving rise to both the pervasive practice of implementing intra- and interorganizational networks to fashion new supply chains and to the new organisational forms which will be discussed throughout this book.

1.5 e-business

One spectacular aspect of the transforming role of IT in business has been the rise of e-business that has followed the advent of the Internet. The Internet has meant that business organizations have been connected to both other business organizations and to mass markets of consumers via computer networks. Worldwide there are over 400 million people connected to the Internet, with over 150 million of them in the USA. This connectivity has allowed goods and services to be bought and sold over computer networks. In the case of digital goods, these goods, including music, software and text, can be bought, sold, and distributed over the Internet. With other goods and services, the goods are purchased and paid for over the Internet and distributed by logistics carriers to business addresses and consumers' homes. Such online buying, selling, and paying for goods and services constitutes electronic commerce or e-business.

Planning and managing such systems requires an integrated multi-dimensional approach across the e-business and the development of new business process models.

1.5.1 e-business impact

While it captures public attention, the use of electronic tools and internet technologies to market to end users (business-to-consumers, or B2C trading) is in its infancy. This form of e-business still constitutes a very small proportion of the total economy, whichever way it is measured. Recent figures from the US Department of Commerce show that for the third quarter of 2000, online retail sales in the USA amounted to US$6.373 billion. This represented only 0.78% of total retail sales. Thus whatever the significance of e-commerce, it is not significant because of the size of the phenomenon. Furthermore, in terms of remote shopping, we have had TV shopping and catalogue shopping well before the turn of the century, but it could be argued that these forms of retailing, although similar to Internet-based retailing, captured public imagination and media attention much less than online retailing. Just why this is the case is not easy to pin down, but computers have always been seen as a modern or avant-garde technology. Professional investors' and venture capitalists' imaginations have also, many would argue, been captured by the new e-commerce possibilities. So many spectators of this phenomenon have watched with some amazement as investment dollars have poured into the new 'dot-coms' or Internet-based retailers and service providers, even as these companies continue to make not solid profits, but steady losses. After several years of hype and gravity-defying stock prices, this particular unreal strand of the 'new economy' seems to be taking a sudden and stern correction toward reality and sobriety. In fact, at the beginning of the year 2001, the question is whether the reaction to the 'dot-com' excesses of the so-called 'new economy' will in fact be an overcorrection which punishes not only lacklustre dot-coms with little or no business performance, but also some apparently healthy and indeed innovative technology-based firms.

It is from the e-commerce phenomenon that much of the language and emotion underpinning the idea of the 'new economy' originates. The 'virtual' or online business with no investment in bricks and mortar buildings and storefronts has seemingly captured the imagination of the public and investors alike. Indeed, so strong is the link, in the public and professional imagination, that the terms 'new economy', 'information economy' and so on are often used to refer to the Internet-based retailers and the set of enabling technology firms that support them.

Meanwhile the real thrust of e-business lies elsewhere, in the area of business-to-business (B2B) transactions. Within this area we may discern a thread of ideas and action that has been growing stronger in the last 20 years – that of strategic alliances and the notion of collaborative advantage. The contemporary business literature is abundant with talk of strategic networks, informal strategic alliances, collaborative advantage and the like. This strand of thinking emphasizes the benefits of core competencies – sticking to the knitting. In other words you do what you are really good at and obtain the other capabilities you need by outsourcing or forming an alliance with an appropriate business partner. Thus the full business capability for producing a good or service is exercised by a group of collaborating firms. When this becomes the mode of operating for a significant proportion of the economy then firm boundaries begin to blur, and we have the rise of a new organizational form – the boundaryless corporation, the extended enterprise, or indeed the virtual organization. This organization may have a complex set of linkages developed along the business supply chain as shown in Figure 1.3.

This new organizational form, together with the increased propensity to outsource capabilities and business processes or to partner with other organisations, is another important feature of the new economy.

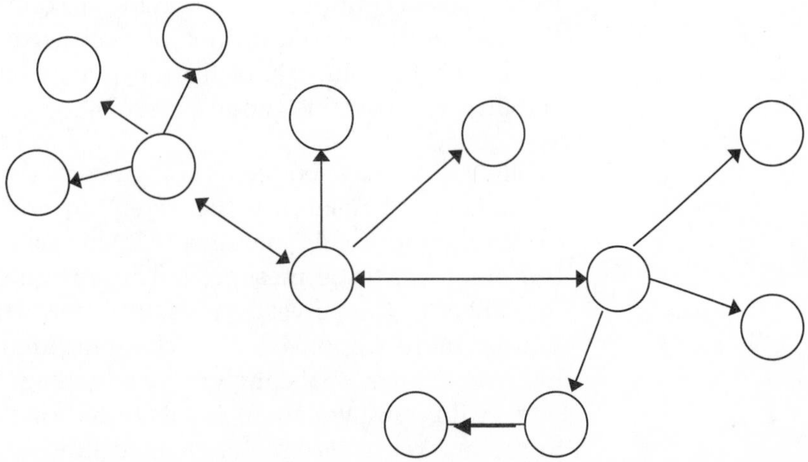

Figure 1.3

1.6 Technology as enabling virtual organizations

If we accept the notions of the new economy and/or the Internet economy, we expect that these constructs will have implications in the nature and operations of enterprises within the new economy. As the transaction cost of locating, evaluating, and interacting with other organizations drops dramatically in price (in terms of both money and time) in the new economy, we could expect to see the boundaries of an organization becoming more fluid as the distinction between work done within an organization and work prepared or processed outside, but for, the organization becomes clearer. We are seeing, it is argued, the emergence of boundary-spanning networks as a characteristic of our age in the same way as the industrial revolution gave rise to distinctive organizational forms around 200 years ago. Today's strategic challenge of doing more with less has led firms to look outward as well as inward for solutions to improve their ability to compete without adding internal resources. Viewed through this lens, we may identify three strategic options for firms to cope with increasingly competitive markets. Firms can either pool their resources with others, form alliances to exploit market opportunities, or link their organizational systems in partnerships. The value of going virtual is often espoused in the management literature but there is as yet little empirical research to show that value and virtuality are directly related. Indeed, there are so many fuzzy concepts related to virtuality that any broad statement made with regard to virtual organizations must be regarded with suspicion. It could be argued that there is a degree of virtuality in all organizations but at what point does this present a conflict between control and adaptability? Is there a continuum along which organizations can position themselves in the electronic marketplace according to their needs for flexibility and fast responsiveness as opposed to stability and sustained momentum?

While there may be general agreement with regard to the advantages of flexibility the extent to which virtuality offers flexibility and the advantages that this will bring to a corporation have yet to be measured. There is an assumption that an organization that invests in as little infrastructure as possible will be more responsive to a changing marketplace and more likely to attain global competitive advantage but this ignores the very real power which large integrated organizations can bring to the market in terms of sustained innovation over the longer term. Proponents of the virtual organization also tend to underestimate the force of virtual links. Bonds, which bind a virtual organization together, may strongly inhibit flexibility and change rather than nurture the concept of the opportunistic virtual organization. Aldridge (1998) suggests that it is no accident that the pioneers of electronic commerce fall into three categories:

- start-ups, organizations with no existing investment or legacy systems to protect;
- technology companies with a vested interest in building the channel to market products and services;
- media companies, attracted by low set-up costs and immediate distribution of news and information.

Such organizations can more easily adopt a 'virtual' structure compared to those with large physical infrastructure investments and complex operating and management hierarchies.

1.7 What do we mean by a virtual organization?

We meet the term 'virtual organization' in many contexts, and it is often not clear what sense each author attaches to this term. To add to the confusion, authors have created a variety of different terms and definitions to describe this new form of network organization, such as virtual company, virtual enterprise, virtual factory, and virtual office. To round off this chapter, we shall introduce some basic definitions to help you navigate the remainder of this book, and to orientate you in your further reading. In general when we use the term below, we shall use it to mean a partnership network, unless otherwise stated.

The different definitions of 'virtual organization' partly depend on the view taken of the concept 'virtual'. It is helpful at the outset to note that there are four different concepts of 'virtual' popularly used in the context of organizational configurations.

- Virtual means 'unreal, looking real'. It is in this sense that we talk of 'virtual reality' when talking of a simulation or depiction of a non-existent physical state of affairs or world. When this sense is used, an author simply means that a virtual organization has the appearance of a real (traditional) company for externals, but in reality this company does not exist, it is only a conglomerate of independent network partners. Examples of configurations meeting this criterion are explored in Chapter 3 below.

- Virtual means resembling or giving the appearance of a well-known physical item or object, which in fact it is not. It normally implies that the virtual object so described is supported by information and communication technology (ICT). This sub-concept of virtual means that something is only created by data. In this sense we talk readily of virtual shopping malls – in this case we are using the model of the physical shopping mall to describe a grouping of enterprises which appear to be in proximity and to form a cluster while in fact they need have no physical locations in common. In this sense we commonly talk of these virtual objects as having an existence in cyberspace.

- Virtual means 'potentially present'. This sub-concept of virtual is often used to describe resource pools. The resource pool is basically a repository of resources; as soon as the need for a certain resource configuration is allocated, an operating unit will be formed. This simply means that the resource pool has the potential to be real when it is needed. The 'virtual Web' is a good example of this sub-concept.

- Virtual means 'existing, but changing'. This sub-concept describes the fluid and dynamic network approach. This kind of organization reconfigures itself permanently; it is dynamic, progressive and only temporary. 'Virtual corporations' and 'virtual teams' are good examples of this sub-concept. While it is accepted that business conglomerates may buy and sell subsidiaries, thus changing their components over time, we do not think of them as virtual because of this. However, the very speed with which an organization may reconfigure itself and its components using modern information and communication technologies (ICTs) does tempt us to see this as a new organizational form, not simply a faster-moving old form.

1.7.1 A taxonomy of the virtual

Figure 1.4 is introduced as a handy way of seeing how various ideas of virtual can be related.

Figure 1.4 shows how we may think of virtual organization from both an intraorganizational and interorganizational perspective. The interorganizational perspective is divided into virtual markets and virtual corporations. Virtual markets means e-commerce, market transactions between companies using sophisticated ICT, i.e. the Internet. In contrast, virtual corporations are basically partnership networks of dispersed organizational units or independent companies.

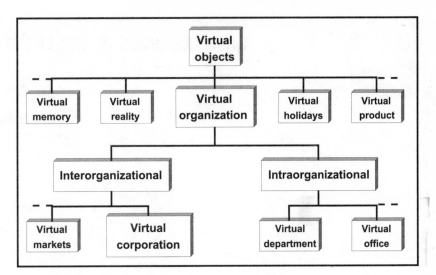

Figure 1.4
Virtual objects, Scholz
(1997)

1.8 Summary

In this first chapter we have introduced the notions of e-business and the Internet economy together with that of the virtual organization. To help us navigate through a complex area, we have set out the elements which go to make up the environment for e-business (or the new economy?) as a table. This table has shown us the relationship between the technical infrastructure, the services, and the products and structures of our economy.

The impact of e-business has been introduced together with a preliminary discussion of the meaning(s) of virtual as it is used in the discussion of virtual organizations. These ideas will be developed more fully in later chapters: in particular we shall examine the notion of the possible form of a virtual organization in Chapter 2, and at emerging forms of enterprise structure that incorporate some parts of this concept to yield different models for success in Chapter 3.

2 Characteristics of the virtual organization

Ce sont les lapins qui ont été étonnes!
(A. Daudet, Lettres de mon moulin)

2.1 Introduction

We think of ourselves as living in an age of change; change unprecedented; change of a complexity that enfolds and drives us in a way and at a rate unknown just a generation ago – or so it seems to us. Perhaps each generation marvels afresh at change and its burdens.

Whether or not change and its rate are new on this scale we are certainly seeing an overwhelming abundance of new technologies, with concomitant newness of usage and procedures by which we achieve goals and complete tasks. In dealing with change and complexity, our need for information typically increases, while our ability to find all the requisite knowledge and skills within one individual decreases. We become increasingly reliant on working with teams of people, on the more effective dissemination and exchange of information amongst group members, and on the more effective coordination and management of disparate activities and individuals with multiple and often conflicting perspectives and objectives.

The more recent developments such as the Internet, intranets and extranets, which facilitate networks both within and between organizations, mean that in certain circumstances, the former requirement for collocation of people, tasks, resources all at much the same time has to some extent disappeared. This results in fundamental changes and rethinks to potential and satisfactory organizational structures, and also to the way in which organizations position themselves within their environ-ment to compete and/or cooperate with other organizations. Hence we see the emergence of the notion of virtuality, of the virtual organization, which has been defined as 'an amorphous entity which is a combination of different companies or individuals that have combined to complete specific projects or business propositions and development' (Lawrence *et al.* 1998). In the face of change and uncertainty in business, virtual organiza-tions offer a low cost, highly responsive and adaptable way to organize and compete. This chapter deals with the essential reasons why virtual organizations are an effective way to organize. In presenting this argument we will examine the essential features of virtual organizations, then go on to examine some essential business processes that characterize the operation of virtual organizations, and then finally deal with the issues involved in successfully managing virtual organizations.

2.2 Characterizing the essence of the virtual organization

When reading the literature on the virtual organization, we find the online concept and the collaborating parties concept, and the hybrid that combines these two concepts.

2.2.1 The online VO

For some, a virtual organization is essentially an electronic one, an online organization. Proponents of this position offer Amazon.com and Ebay.com as examples of organizations that have been created primarily to exist in and exploit the opportunities offered by the WWW and cyberspace. This so-called virtual, or electronic, organization is discussed in contra-distinction to the traditional 'bricks and mortar' retail outlet.

2.2.2 The collaborative VO

An alternative to this first definition is to present the virtual organization as an organizational structure based primarily on the notion of collaborating entities, coming together to share competencies, skills, knowledge and other resources for the purpose of producing a particular service or good, or of taking advantage of a particular opportunity. While there is the clear expectation that IT and telecommunications would play an important role in coordinating and controlling the activities of disparate components of the virtual organization, IT becomes a key component, rather than the distinguishing characteristic.

The position adopted in this chapter corresponds to the second approach discussed, and as a precursor to more detailed discussion, a virtual organization can be defined as 'composed of several business partners sharing costs and resources for the purpose of producing a product or service . . . can be temporary . . . or it can be permanent. Each partner contributes complementary resources that reflect its strengths, and determines its role in the virtual corporation' (Turban *et al.* 1999: 142). This stance suggests a need to discuss more fully the essential and fundamental attributes of the virtual organization.

2.2.3 The hybrid VO

The third approach with respect to the virtual organization is perhaps the most confusing. This approach represents an amalgam of the previous two approaches, where authors move almost interchangeably between the virtual organization as an electronic or online organization, and the virtual organization as a somewhat transient network of people, ideas, competencies and resources which come together for a particular purpose.

2.3 The collaborative VO as the agile contender

A key characteristic of the virtual organization is its adaptability and flexibility in the face of turbulent business environments, a condition sometimes described as 'agility'. Virtual organizations are capable of rapid and adaptable response to changing markets whether these arise as a result of globalization, changing cost structures, changing customer needs and wants, or other similar reasons. Virtual organizations use existing organizational structures from one or more existing organizations, combining these in creative ways to forge new organizational capabilities and competencies, thus averting the need to recruit, train, and forge new work teams, buy new equipment and buildings, and work through a period of organizational learning. Thus, allied with its agility, an important attribute of the virtual organization is argued to be its more effective utilization of existing resources, thus creating an important source of competitive advantage.

2.3.1 Essential partnership practice

The formation of business partnerships and alliances is thus pivotal to the concept of the virtual organization (Grenier and Metes 1995, Henning 1998). Acquiring and/or developing all the required resources and competencies in order to avail itself of windows of opportunity can be both too time consuming and too costly to be an appropriate response for organizations acting on their own. In other words, in the brief period of time available to exploit business opportunities, a single organization may not have the time or the financial resources available to obtain and/or develop the needed skills, infrastructure, resources, or to develop efficient business processes. However, access to the required knowledge, skills, resources and infrastructure may be available through entering into alliances or partnerships with all, or a part only, of other organizations. This notion is captured pictorially in Figure 2.1.

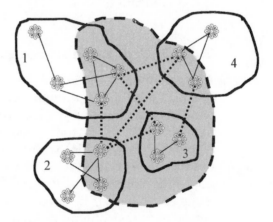

Figure 2.1
Formation of business alliances

Thus organization 1 on its own may not have the capability to take advantage of a particular perceived business opportunity. But by working cooperatively and synergistically with others, a virtual organization (depicted by the shaded area) may be formed to exploit that opportunity. By each contributing different knowledge, skills, and resources, the virtual organization formed by the cooperative leveraging of assets and resources in organizations 1, 2, 3 and 4 may be highly successful in availing itself for a time of the original business opportunity.

Implicit in this description of the formation of business alliances is the notion that various components of the virtual organization may well be geographically dispersed, giving rise to the

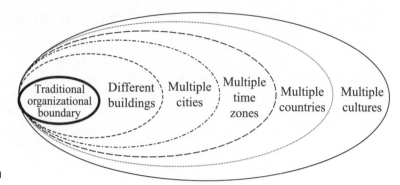

Figure 2.2
Characteristic dispersion
of the virtual organization

challenge of communication and coordination across different time zones, different locations, different cultures and different languages (IMPACT Programme 1998). This is illustrated in Figure 2.2, and typically implies a need for excellent IT to support communication and coordination throughout the virtual organization.

2.3.2 The human resources component

A key component of the agility ascribed to and required of virtual organizations is its human resources (and the management practices associated with those human resources). The needs and requirements of virtual organizations demand that each employee has the skills to contribute directly to the value chain of product and service design, production, marketing and distribution, thus contributing directly to the 'bottom line'. As each member of the virtual organization contributes its core competencies, the resultant team of human resources would be anticipated to be excellent, geared appropriately and directly towards exploiting a particular opportunity, and thus better collectively than any of the contributing organizations would be expected to accomplish on its own. Employees must also be capable of learning new skills, be positive towards the need for constant change and tolerant towards ambiguity and uncertainty in their working lives as well as sensitive to the possibly changing needs and wants of the organization's customers. For this to be achieved, virtual organizations are characterized by the empowerment of their employees, where decision making, responsibility and accountability is devolved to appropriate component parts of the structure, and is readily accepted as such.

The need for responsiveness and competitiveness in global markets implies a need for constancy and excellence in the development of appropriate skills and skill levels. It also requires of employees that they accommodate their work procedures, skills and skill levels, work times and even working lives to the demands of the organization's customers. However, the virtual organization also rewards skilled and psychologically tough employees highly. This is done both financially and in terms of giving employees as much freedom as possible to structure their workplaces and working hours to fit their own needs and personalities. Outputs and results are required and measured carefully, but human inputs are left as much to the individual as possible. However, what is clearly implied is the need for the virtual organization to be rigorous and effective in its management and exploitation of its intellectual capital (its knowledge) while providing a satisfying work experience for its employees.

2.3.3 The flight from central control

Agility and responsiveness also imply a need for cost effective administration, and an absence of heavy, clumsy bureaucratic practices which would appear to be the very antithesis of the agile virtual organization. To serve an agile organization with responsibilities devolved downward as far as practical, the inertia, heaviness and clumsiness associated with the bureaucratic hierarchical organization of the late 20th century should be avoided at all costs. Any unnecessary administrative activities should be minimized or abolished altogether. Administrative work is done as efficiently as possible by as few staff as possible. Where administrative overheads can be carried by those staff directly involved in the value creating activities of the virtual organization, this may be preferable since they will do only what administration is directly useful and needed by them and their team, and when it is necessary for them to cease a certain activity because it is no longer viable, the administrative activity winds down naturally and without the difficulties of reducing or reassigning central administrative staffs. It is essential that the organization retain its ability to respond and adapt to changing conditions and high administrative overheads and/or slow and bureaucratic procedures can always threaten this essential characteristic.

Acknowledging the transient nature of business opportunity in contemporary business environments, virtual organizations are opportunistic and avail themselves of profitable business circumstances even if they are apparently temporary. There is an acceptance of, even an enthusiasm for change and uncertainty with respect to its products and services, its customer base, its structure and scope, and in its very approach to doing business. This characteristic means that virtual organizations are at ease with the idea of porous and changing organizational boundaries, changing their skills and skill levels through outsourcing and alliances. In these ways virtual organizations incorporate the competencies of other organizations' employees so as to quickly adapt and change their skills base and thus take advantage of emerging business opportunities.

Underpinning and enabling the opportunistic behaviour of virtual organizations, and coordinating and managing disparate resources and activities in the virtual organization supply chain going right through to the customer, is a heavy reliance on IT and communications technologies. IT supports some of the new organizational alliances and forms necessary to design and produce new goods and services quickly, and provides a fast and convenient channel through which to promote and inform potential customers of organizational product and service developments, and to accept and process sales to customers. These new technologies provide the information and communication framework necessary for the anywhere anytime work that takes place in virtual organizations. In addition, it must be noted that virtual organizations are information intensive and hence may well be expected to be heavily reliant on information technology. However, it must be acknowledged that the virtual organization can exist without heavy reliance on IT, although it is generally acknowledged that in most contemporary cases, IT will occupy an important position.

2.4 Summary of characteristics of the agile VO

The virtual organization is put forward as a low-cost, highly responsive and adaptable way to organize and compete in the face of extreme turbulence and uncertainty in the business environment. The essential characteristics of the virtual organization have been argued to be:

- adaptability, flexibility and responsiveness to changing requirements and conditions;
- effectiveness in utilization of resources;
- formation of business alliances of varying degrees of permanence;
- dispersion of component parts;

- empowerment of staff;
- stewardship of expertise, know-how, and knowledge (intellectual capital);
- low levels of bureaucracy;
- opportunistic behaviours, embracing change and uncertainty;
- high infusion of IT to support business processes and knowledge workers.

The practical implications for managers adopting the virtual organization structure and the strategy of virtual organizing in their organizations need to be considered further. It may be noted that as soon as one mentions managing in a virtual organization, or of adopting virtual organizing as a deliberate strategy, then there is a sense in which one is almost inevitably talking about interorganizational management, and thus about the coordinated and cooperative behaviours and endeavours of actors/managers who originate in different organizations and who, after a period of time, may again actually be in different organizations.

2.5 Essential organizational processes and activities

Having outlined the essential characteristics of virtual organizations it is now appropriate to look at the *essential organizational processes and activities* by which virtual organizations are created and sustained. These processes include but are not exhausted by the utilization of outsourcing, the formation of short- and long-term *alliances*, and the use of interorganizational systems.

2.5.1 Outsourcing

Outsourcing is a fundamental organizational design strategy for increasing organizational skill levels and expanding the organizational skills profile. It is an important strategy for coping with increased as well as variable demands for certain skills, such as the skills needed to develop new information systems or the skills needed to design certain types of new products. If these skills are in high demand in an organization, particularly if this need is short term, then outsourcing is a way of providing those skills quickly without recruiting permanent workers and thus increasing the need for infrastructure and administrative support services (Oates 1998). In using outsourcing, the organization can not only gain fully working and skilled teams of workers already supplied with offices and equipment, but if the need for these skills is very temporary, then it is less of a problem to dispense with the outsourcing arrangement than to make permanent workers redundant. The expectations of outworkers or contract employees differ from that of permanent employees. Furthermore, persons in such arrangements can organize their lives in a manner appropriate to the arrangement.

2.5.2 The art of alliances

Another organizational design strategy that is fundamental to the creation and maintenance of virtual organizations is the formation of alliances. The objective here is similar to out-sourcing. It is to enhance and augment the skill and competency profile of the virtual organization both quickly and effectively. Suppose that organizations 1 and 2 collaborate on a certain range of products that they manufacture and sell, and need a new set of skills plus some new capital equipment in order to design and produce a new product that changing market demand has shown could be profitably manufactured and sold (see Figure 2.3).

Organization 3 has a department with a number of employees with the required design skills and who are not fully occupied at present. Organization 4 has capital equipment that is essential to the manufacture and testing of the new product line, and that equipment has spare capacity in the evenings and at the weekends. Organization 5 has the computer software that is needed to design the product range. It also has spare computer

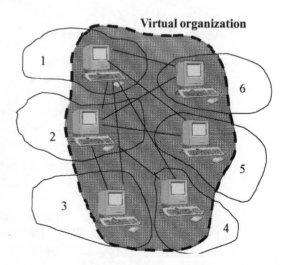

Figure 2.3
Virtual organizational
structure

capacity as well as some persons familiar with the software and some knowledge of designing similar products. Negotiations could take place between organizations 1 and 2 and the other organizations to form a virtual organization to design and manufacture the new product line. It is expected that this can be done more quickly than any of the organizations separately could do it by the traditional means of getting a new product team together by recruitment and by purchasing the necessary equipment. Suppose that the new product launch is successful, but a new set of product testing skills becomes necessary. Further assume that the product design skills are no longer needed. The virtual organization could form an alliance with organization 6 for its product testing equipment and its skilled employees who operate and use the equipment. It could also reduce costs by ceasing to utilize the design employees from organization 3.

2.5.3 Interorganizational systems

The establishment of appropriate interorganizational systems (IOSs) to facilitate organizational effective work between groups in various organizations and different locations is another accepted design strategy for virtual organizations. The coordination of groups from different organizations and different locations is a necessity for the virtual organization, and this coordination may be made possible by information systems implemented via modern computer and communications technologies. Such systems may include electronic mail facilities, shared databases, as well as the capability to carry out business processes and transactions across organizations and organizational groups. Such IOSs may enable the coordination of work across regions, nations or continents, and across the same or different time zones. Although virtual organizations may exist without such systems, the establishment of such systems enables virtual organizations to be created and maintained more easily.

2.6 What makes the VO different?

Partnerships and alliances are nothing new. Menelaus called on all the partnerships and alliances he could when he set sail for Troy nearly 3000 years ago. So what is it we have in mind when we assert that the VO of today is different in nature from traditional business alliances. Table 2.1 sets out accepted thinking in this regard for us.

Table 2.1

Familiar interorganizational partnership models	How they differ from virtual organizations
Strategic alliance	• a less closed relationship; • hardly any virtual added value processes; • mainly formed by large corporations; • existence beside the core business
Conglomerate	• dependency agreement
Cartel	• aims to limit competition
Consortium	• existence of formal agreements
Franchise	• long lasting dependency agreement
Joint Venture	• establishment of a new business
Keiretsu	• stable membership of partners

2.6.1 Transient nature

The VO is a temporary partnership. It is neither set up for an agreed period of time, nor is it an open-ended cooperation, i.e. joint venture. The partnerships last as long as it is in the interests of all parties. The partners may also be involved in several virtual corporations at any one time. However, the VO model provides independent companies with the option to continue their original business in addition to their involvement in partnerships.

The ideal VO is fluid and flexible, the cooperating partners contributing only their core competencies to the partnership. Once a specific market opportunity is allocated, the partners quickly unite and pool their resources according to customer needs. If the market changes, it might be necessary to change the virtual corporation configuration, if it is to remain competitive. The relationship between the partnering companies has to be flexible and grounded in mutual trust in order to enable rapid market response. A crucial competitive advantage of virtual corporation is that they can come and go rapidly.

2.6.2 Chance for the smaller company

A feature of the virtual corporation concept is that it should provide a means for smaller companies to compete against larger players, even multinationals, in their field. Therefore, the virtual corporation model is particularly attractive for small and medium-sized enterprises (which includes outsourced functions). It provides them with the opportunity to keep their independence while at the same time improve their competitiveness.

2.6.3 Communications as lifeblood

The exchange of information is vital for VOs. A VO might be feasible without information technology (IT), but recent IT developments in volume, speed and quality have made it possible to synchronize activities which were previously considered hardly possible due to the high costs involved. High speed communication facilitates the coordination of activities between partner companies and generates knowledge, which leads to innovative products and services.

2.7 Managing in the virtual organization: success factors

Many of the defining characteristics of the virtual organization on paper sound delightfully and seductively simple, indeed obvious. Yet, it would seem that there are a number of important managerial tasks that must be accomplished if the virtual organization is to function effectively. People in the virtual organization are drawn from different sources, but perhaps working in teams, need to find a shared purpose or vision in order to arrive at successful outcomes and results. The shared purpose or vision serves as a 'glue' of the virtual organization and also determines the life cycle of the virtual organization, as it only exists for a reason – when the desired purpose has been accomplished, then the virtual organization ceases, as there is no longer glue to hold the structure together. A key function for management and organizational members, therefore, would seem to be to quickly identify and seize ownership of this shared purpose and vision.

However, in order that purpose may be genuinely shared and for linkages to operate unimpeded, there must exist extraordinary levels of trust. Indeed, it is generally put forward that in the virtual organization, trust must function to replace the usual rules, procedures and policies that dictate the behaviour of the more traditional hierarchical and bureaucratic organizations.

With a trusting relationship in place amongst virtual organization members, there is also a requirement for the risk(s) associated with the joint initiative (i.e. inherent in the purpose of the virtual organization) to be shared. In traditional organizational structures, risk is typically totally the preserve of a single organization, which alone tends to implement measures to manage its exposure to risk. The more interdependent the nature of the activities of the virtual organization, the more risk must be seen to be and accepted as shared. If risk is to be shared, and high levels of trust maintained, then clearly the purpose of the virtual organization must be such that all members benefit in more ways than they would from remaining outside the virtual organization relationship. Thus, the successful virtual organization relies on the ability of the alliance to offer benefits to individual members in terms of increased productivity, increased revenues, increased profitability, increased market share, and the like.

Fundamental critical success factors for the virtual organization can therefore be posited as being a shared purpose, a trusting relationship, a willingness to share risk, and a mutual benefit being derived from the virtual organization's existence. This is illustrated in Figure 2.4.

Thus it is argued that a successful virtual organization is very much based on the notion that mutual benefit for the parties involved is derived through the timely and appropriate initiation and formation of alliances to take advantage of possibly short-lived business opportunities. But for the alliances to operate in an efficacious manner providing benefits to all concerned, then there is the very important assumption made that management activity has achieved the requisite level of shared vision and purpose, a high degree of trust amongst

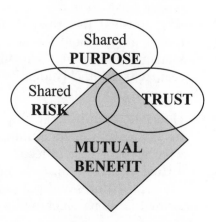

Figure 2.4
Critical success factors for the virtual organization

virtual organization members, and an acceptance and understanding that risk is to be shared amongst those standing to benefit.

Some caution needs to be exercised at this point, for the virtual organization and virtual organizing should not be presented as *the* way of the future, almost akin to a business imperative for the successful enterprise in this internetworked era. Many of the characteristics, strategies and claims for the virtual organization are conceptually appealing. Yet there seems to be a range of challenges for managers to nurture a successful business within the conceptual framework of virtual organizing, and we shall return to this issue in Chapter 11 below. It would seem, prima facie, that many of the strengths and powerful characteristics of the virtual organization also tend to render it vulnerable, and hence can be a source of weakness. Table 2.2 displays some of these tensions that would support this thinking.

The type of innovation involved and the associated information flows and knowledge management strategies can also enhance or moderate the likely success of the virtual organization. Autonomous innovations (basically stand-alone, independent of

Table 2.2 Inherent tensions in behaviours of the virtual organization

Strengths	How strengths become weaknesses
Opportunistic, entrepreneurial, risk taking	Personal incentives and rewards for risk taking increase, leading to self-interest in behaviours, etc., making coordination and cooperation amongst parties more difficult.
Mutual trust, shared risk, opportunistic	When conflicts or misunderstandings do arise, or unforeseen opportunities work to favour some of the parties more than others, there exist few established procedures for negotiation and conflict resolution.
Opportunistic	The spirit that drives parties to collaborate may also cause virtual organizations to fragment if one or more of the parties deliberately act to exploit more benefits for themselves than for the other parties.

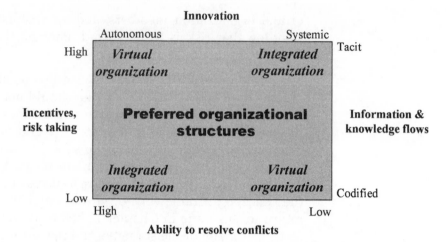

Figure 2.5
A framework for
success in virtual
organizing

other innovations) are argued to be more suitable for the virtual organization than the highly interconnected systemic type of innovations because of the information flows essential for innovation. Codified information (that which can be easily captured in industry standards and rules, for example), is argued to be as easy to transfer from one party to another in the virtual organization form as it is to transfer within a single organization. Tacit knowledge (such as know-how, or ingrained perspectives), however, is not easily transferred or diffused, and is also subject to opportunism by individual parties who can control how much of the tacit knowledge they share. Thus, autonomous innovation involving codified information and knowledge transfer may be more suitable for exploitation along virtual organizing principles than systemic innovation involving tacit information and knowledge. These notions are captured in the framework below which itself can become important in predicting likely success for the virtual organization.

2.8 Summary

In this chapter we have taken an extended look at the virtual organization viewed as an emergent construct from the collaboration, generally enabled by ICT, of **pre-existing** companies.

We have noted that this newly emergent organizational form is characterized by an ability to respond to changing circumstances in an agile manner; a marked degree of decentralized control and devolved authority, reliance on interorganizational systems and trust networks.

We have also remarked that this organizational form is not merely technology plastered onto an existing model, but differs intrinsically from such familiar forms as alliances, consortia and conglomerates.

In Chapter 3 we shall extend our range of organizational forms that use some or all of the features we have introduced here to encompass a wide range of organizational responses to circumstances and opportunities.

3   e-business models for virtual organizations

The mystery of Tao:
'That which cannot be seen is formless'.
(The sayings of Lao Zi)

3.1 Introduction

Virtual organizations obviously have a need for business models, which are different from the traditional, but there is no one single business model that is appropriate to all forms of virtual enterprise. Different organizations will require different business models and these will reflect the extent and strength of their interorganizational links within their networked alliances. In the most basic sense, a business model is the method of doing business by which an organization can best sustain itself – which in most cases means generating revenue. The selected business model will therefore be that which spells out how the organization positions itself within the value chain in order to make financial return.

e-business has given rise to many new kinds of business model but has also allowed organizations to reinvent some. One of the most obvious cases is that of the auction model. eBay did not invent this model but merely reapplied one of the oldest business models in existence. Popularization of this model has broadened its application on the Web to a wide array of goods and services. A number of other forms of model exist and these typically reflect the e-business strategy, i.e. how the organization intends to create an online community. However, there are also models which reflect the strategic structure of the virtual organization. These models relate to the virtual culture adopted by the organization and the communication linkages within the network of alliances. While there are many different classifications of these models within the literature there is no single, comprehensive taxonomy and so here we offer our own view of some of the generic forms of virtual organization models. These include virtual face, coalliance, star alliance, value alliance, market alliance, virtual broker and virtual space.

Selecting the structural and strategic forms of business model will effectively set the strategic agenda for the virtual organization and define the relationships, roles, business processes and partnerships which should be exploited.

3.2 The contemporary context for organizational change

Virtual organizations are best understood as electronically networked organizations transcending conventional boundaries with linkages both within and/or between organizations. In its simplest form, however, virtuality exists where IT is used to enhance organizational activities while reducing the need for physical or formalized structure. Degrees of virtuality then exist which will reflect:

- the virtual organizational *culture* (strategic positioning);
- the internal and external *networks* (the intensity and nature of links between stakeholders);
- the *market* (IT dependency and resource infrastructure, products, customers).

3.2.1 Culture

We define *culture* as shared values and beliefs (Schein 1990). Organizational cultures that are accepting of technology, highly decentralized, and change oriented are more likely to embrace virtuality and actively seek these opportunities both inside and outside the organization. Virtual culture results from a perception of the entire organization and its operations held by its stakeholder community.

This is operationalized in choices and actions which result in a feeling of unity with respect to value sharing (i.e. each client's expectations are satisfied in the product accessed), and time–space arrangement (i.e. each stakeholder shares the feeling of a continuous access to the organization and its products). The embodiment of this culture comes through the virtual strategic perspective (VSP) which the organization adopts. Its value derives from the ability to operate with diminished constraints of space and time, yielding opportunities for expansion of reach with marked reduction of transaction costs.

3.2.2 Networks

Networks are groups within and between organizations where communicative relationships are integral to the existence of a virtual entity. However, the simultaneous need to establish alliances and retain a particular identity creates a tension between autonomy and interdependence, competition and cooperation. These relationships are often described as value added partnerships based on horizontal, vertical or symbiotic relationships. These in turn relate to competitors, value chain collaborators and complementary providers of goods and services all of whom combine to achieve advantage over outsiders. The nature, strength and substitutability of links define the inherent advantageous structure.

3.2.3 Markets

Markets differ from networks in that pricing mechanisms coordinate them. In this respect, the electronic market is one where any buyer or seller can interconnect with a network to offer wares or shop for goods and services. Hence, ubiquity is by definition a prerequisite.

Different risks arise from being a market maker and a market player, and different products also carry different risks. Criteria for successful electronic market development include products with low asset specificity, ease of description and a consumer willing to effect transactions by means of networks. Necessarily,

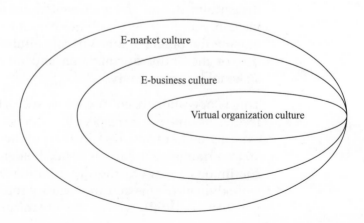

Figure 3.1
Virtual organizations and
virtual cultures

the defining characteristic of an electronic market is the availability of pervasive information and communication technology (ICT) infrastructures available to a critical mass of customers. An organization is both constrained and supported by the ICT adopted within the business ICT environment. Figure 3.1 shows this set of relationships.

Despite the growth of online activity, many firms fear a deterioration of profit margins coupled with lack of control as a consequence of market transparency and new forms of intermediation. Nevertheless, as markets are challenged by new entrants using direct channels to undercut prices and increase market share, traditional businesses need new forms to adapt to new marketspaces and channels. The first step is to develop a strategy for creating a widespread presence in the marketplace.

3.3 Strategies for widespread presence

3.3.1 Are you going to develop an online market?

The more ordinary and unexciting the commodity, it seems, the better the potential for an online market. With more than 20 industry exchanges now publicly traded at a combined value of more than US$100 billion, high-tech analysts are falling over one another to learn about seafood-spoilage rates, gas-valve supply chains and similar specialized matters. Everyone is on the lookout for the next VerticalNet or Chemdex.

Chemdex claims to be the only comprehensive B2B e-commerce solution for the life sciences industry with rapid acceptance among pharmaceutical and biotechnology companies. In March 2000 over 90 major enterprises had signed up with Chemdex for life science product procurement. This list includes customers such as Genentech, Rhône-Poulenc Rorer, and SmithKline Beecham. But finding e-business opportunities is easy compared with your task of judging their prospects. In their brief history, Internet exchanges have gone through three phases, and the accepted successful business model has not been found.

- The first phase introduced firms, such as General Electric and Wal-Mart, moving much, if not most, of their buying and selling online to cut costs and speed supplies. At that time (barely five years ago) this looked revolutionary. Today, their original aims of taking transactions online and cutting paperwork and time seem pedestrian, even though they have clearly led to big savings in procurement time and cost.

- Next came third-party exchanges, independent firms that bring together many buyers and sellers to create a genuine market. The potential is bigger, but gaining critical mass is harder. There are still plenty of companies who fail to see why they should go out of their way to cut their profits by taking part in an open trading system.

- Now comes the third phase: when the giants of an industry get together in a consortium. On 25 February 2000 General Motors, Ford and Daimler Chrysler abandoned their stand-alone efforts and joined forces to create the world's largest virtual market, which will buy $240 billion worth of parts from tens of thousands of suppliers. Within days Toyota, Renault and its Japanese affiliate, Nissan, had all expressed interest in joining; others will follow. On 28 February 2000 America's Sears, Roebuck and France's Carrefour announced a retail consortium, called GlobalNetXchange, that will handle US$80 billion worth of purchases annually. And on 1 March Cargill, DuPont and Cenex Harvest, an American farm cooperative, set up Rooster.com, which will both supply farmers and sell their crops. These consortia are an improvement on previous independent online efforts.

How will other markets evolve? The answer depends on the structure of their industries. Compare the following two extremes. Pyramid-shaped industries are exemplified in car manufacturing, the PC industry and chemical markets. These are ones in which there are few big buyers and an enormous and fragmented mass of small suppliers. In PCs, Ingram Micro aggregates big manufacturers and sells to thousands of small resellers. FOB.com aggregates small chemical suppliers for DuPont, Dow and a few other big buyers. Because of the asymmetry in these industries, such exchanges tend to be 'biased markets': they naturally favour one side of the deal flow.

Exchanges have several advantages. Because of the power they consolidate, they easily reach critical mass and so avoid the Catch-22 of having to persuade sellers to join when buyers are scarce. They can also be financed, or owned, by market participants (as in the car and retail exchanges) without compromising themselves, since small firms are used to the idea of working with big ones.

Other markets are 'butterfly shaped': highly fragmented on both sides. These are 'neutral' markets that lend themselves to independent, third-party exchanges. They have the advantage of being closer to true markets, such as stock exchanges, and thus better at lowering prices and improving liquidity by matching buyers and sellers. Most B2B exchanges today fit into this category, and for good reason. Car makers and big retailers already had tremendous power to drive down prices and to extract value from supply chains. But in markets such as food, print and paper, few have such clout. When there is market fragmentation with enormous numbers of participants, the costs of processing transactions are high for all concerned.

3.3.2 Do you need an online community?

The Web is rapidly changing. Just a few years ago it was mainly an information source and an e-mail tool. Today it is also a place to shop, to contact customer services, and to interact with others. Recognizing the opportunities afforded by this last activity, many companies are choosing to build interactive communities on their websites. Some start by providing for staff, some for customers, and others for specialized sections of the community such as the press, government bodies, and the like. What's emerging in common to these is essentially a virtual network that allows two-way communication between interested parties.

The marketing benefits of an interactive community were discovered almost by accident by an early pioneer, TuneUp.com. The TuneUp website was originally designed as a site where users could go to get computer problems diagnosed. As an afterthought, the site owners provided a message board and chat facility. Before long, customers started using the message and chat functions to swap advice and support to each other, bypassing the provider. The provider had unwittingly created value where there was none before. Use of the service boomed, and attention was drawn to the phenomenon.

Noting the success of this type of operation, Frank Cohen, chief technology officer for Inclusion Inc., surveyed over 200 organizations to find out what kinds of community-building functions or services they considered valuable. Forty-four per cent of the replies rated the ability to download files as the most sought-after or valued function for building a community. But that service was followed closely by the ability to create smaller special interest groups that are subsets of the Internet community at large. This latter finding, and the public perceptions of the value of such communication, is driving the development of community groups on the Internet today.

Online communities are groups of businesses, customers, or employees with common interests interacting via the Internet. They take many forms, but generally fall into three classifications: business-to-business, B2B, business-to-customer, B2C and employee-to-employee, E2E. These will have different business objectives and member compositions and may include some or all of the four types of programmes identified below:

- member-generated content – profiles, home pages, product ratings and reviews;
- member-to-member interaction – discussion forums, technical forums, FAQs and Q&A forums;
- events – guest events, expert seminars, virtual meetings/trade shows;
- outreach – newsletters, volunteer/leader programmes, polls/surveys.

In almost every case, the more participation that occurs the greater the value for both the community members and creators and this frequently results in economic results for the community creator.

In creating an online community, the first priority is to ask 'Who will use it?' Some users are strictly on the hunt for facts. They have no particular problem to present to a group and may not take an active part in discussions. Others are interested problem solvers who want to offer help based on their expertise or findings. Some users are team players who find it enjoyable to assume a leadership role and work toward building the community. Others simply enjoy taking part in a discussion. A successful community meets the needs of those it attracts.

Williams and Cothrel (2000) identify three kinds of activities which appear critical to a community's continued viability:

- member development;
- asset management; and
- community relations.

Keeping track of a community is very important: if discussion threads lose their appeal, if visitors fall away, it is important to recognize this early on and to take steps to remedy it. Nothing is as so dispiriting as an empty chat room, or a discussion topic which has generated no response. Further discussion on the creation and maintenance of online communities is found in Chapter 10.

3.3.3 What commercial face will you adopt?

A useful distinction between two types of commercial websites was proposed by Hoffman *et al.* 1995: destination sites and traffic control sites. Table 3.1 identifies the sub-categories and two further models for discussion.

Table 3.1 Website categories

Types of websites	Sub-categories
Destination sites	Online storefronts Internet presence sites Content sites
Traffic control sites	Malls Incentive sites Search agents
Business models	
Auction models	

Destination sites

Destination sites are those which a web user wants to get to, and which compete for the consumers' share of web time. This group further divides into online storefronts; internet presence sites; and content sites.

- The online storefront is conceived as a website that offers the possibility of a sales transaction, whether this is completely effected by electronic interaction or relies on a phone call, fax or other means to complete it. Sites of this nature range from utility companies allowing users to pay bills, through to virtual grocers like Webvan, florists such as Fleurop, and even bankers such as First Direct. The online shopfront combines the attractions of direct mail shopping with in-store shopping and has possibilities for customizing product presentation and delivery far in advance of anything yet seen. Unfortunately for its devotees, this model will rely on fast and cheap bandwidth to deliver satisfactorily. This is not yet a widespread reality.

- Internet presence sites are advertising or 'brochure' sites with a distinction between image presence and information presence. Using this model requires the user to formulate more clearly in advance just what purpose the site is intended to achieve. Image sites that entertain and engender a feel-good response are particularly suited to products such as clothing and lifestyle objects. The information presence model suits businesses whose success (or so it may appear to them) is predicated upon the provision of timely and accurate customer information; airlines being an obvious example. Others might include travel packages, financial investment opportunities and car makers.

- Content sites are divisible into fee-based, sponsored and searchable database systems, with the emphasis on value added content available to the consumer. These are either paid for directly by the client, paid for through advertising or where merchants or providers pay an information provider for placement in an organized listing such as a catalogue mart. These offer significant opportunities for fast searching and maximum hit rates in an information overloaded market.

Traffic control sites

Although each of these sub-groupings has evolved since the original proposal, the categories of malls, incentive sites, and search agents are still useful to work with.

- The mall typically constitutes a collection of online presences. These may be individually created and specified, or made by the mall provider to a common format for ease of navigation and sharing common technology for customer tracking, electronic payments, mailing lists, shopping cart technology and the like. You may like to see these in action at http://www.worldshopping.com/ and http://www.internetmall-.com/. It is interesting to effect a search for malls relevant to your business and to compare the costs. Obviously taken from the idea of a physical shopping centre or street in which businesses cluster to gain mutual advantage from the presence of shoppers looking to spend, it takes more care and thought to justify association in the virtual world in which physical proximity counts for nothing. When another site is only a link away, what advantage is there in being on the same server? There are advantages of sharing the costs of supply and service of common technology and services, but the effective implementation of these calls for different strategies than those operative in the physical world. The virtual mall model may be most effective when combined with a generalized portal such as Yahoo!Stores.

- The incentive site is the next type of traffic control site. This site, intended to attract surfers and searchers, aims to pull traffic to the commercial sites it promotes, functioning in much the same way as malls but not offering the support services. The incentive to visit these sites is that seen at the front end, not the underlying sponsor – free web-based e-mail services may be viewed in this way as pure or hybrid incentive sites. Another, UK-based incentive site is http://www.barclaysquare.com. This site is ostensibly a portal in that it directs traffic to other businesses, but is an incentive site in that it has been established to promote awareness and use of the sponsor Barclay's banking tools and facilities.

- Making their appearance now, as they recognize the importance of traffic control, are free Internet service providers (ISPs). The old model of paying a service for access to the Web is being replaced in many countries by the model of companies offering connection for nothing. These companies aim to benefit from the advertising space on the viewers' screens, and to promote their own businesses in December 2000 a single simple web search for free ISPs in the UK produced a list of 20 from which to choose in under a second. Many companies clearly believe in this model for a successful virtual enterprise.

Also springing up are portals concentrating on core businesses or trades and related services. While there are many of these available for inspection, an outline of one will serve as a paradigm for this type.

Business portals

TravelHero.com is a full-service Internet travel agency, offering accommodation, airline, and rental car reservations worldwide. It claims the largest database of hotels, motels, bed and breakfasts, inns and other lodging properties on the Internet today. With over 100,000 properties in 18,000 cities throughout the world, this site offers the user a powerful tool to find a bed for the night or the week in any popular destination. The company also wants to get you to that destination, by offering airline reservations on all of the world's major airlines, along with discounted prices. Supplementing this service is the rental car reservations service for a large number of worldwide destinations offering a choice between providers such as Hertz, Avis, Discount, Alamo, and Enterprise.

The company's website, in addition to seeking retail customers, urges suppliers to join the network of providers linked by this portal. A common graphical interface and uniformity of display help the user to quickly master the site instead of dealing with and querying a multiplicity of sites to arrange a trip. If the company can live up to, and retain, its claim to be the largest and most comprehensive supplier of travel, car hire and accommodation on the Web, it is difficult to see how others will long resist joining the operation.

Auction models

While auctions have traditionally been conducted face to face, there is nothing particularly new in allowing agents to bid at a distance from an interested principal, or more recently, accepting bids from pre-qualified buyers at a distance using telephone lines.

The Internet, and in particular the Web, has brought the potential for efficient and more widespread auctions into the forefront of business once again, however. The celebrated case of the Dutch Flower Auction is an early example of web technology being applied to create a more efficient local market, emulated by livestock marketspaces, while start-ups such as eBay, AuctionNet and Onsale have popularized the notion among individual buyers and sellers whose goods and finance do not justify larger and more expensive auctions.

Auctions can be of many different kinds: Dutch auctions, regular open cry auctions, sealed bid auctions, etc. Each type of auction can further have many variations such as reserve prices, information available to the bidders, tie breaking rules, etc. We shall consider an overview of the types available for implementation. Each of these types is currently found in operation where they have been chosen to optimize different business objectives such as best price, guaranteed sale, minimize collusion possibility, and so on.

Once the strategy for widespread presence has been identified virtual organizations need to address the specific structural models of effective response which align with this business strategy.

3.4 Models of efficient response

Based on work by Burn, Marshall and Wild (1999) we propose a taxonomy of seven models of virtual organizations as efficient responses to identifiable circumstances. These we term virtual faces, coalliances, star alliances, value alliances, market alliances, virtual brokers and virtual space. The value of each model lies in its being an appropriate response to a given nexus of market forces and opportunities.

3.4.1 Virtual face model

A virtual face is the cyberspace incarnation of an existing non-virtual often described as a 'place' as opposed to 'space' organization. It commends itself by creating additional value such as empowering users to effect transactions efficiently with ICT in place of spatio-temporal contact. Common examples include Dell, Fleurop, and Travelocity. The interactive communications may additionally provide an impetus for a shift in focus of activity, extending rather than simply mirroring them, as seen in the web-based versions of television channels and newspapers with constant news updates and archival searches.

Jane Brook Winery, a small family-operated vineyard in Western Australia, provides an example of such a model (a more detailed version of this case study is provided at the end of the book to illustrate the evolution of virtual culture, networks and markets in the organization). The company is a family-run winery business established in 1972 and owned by two members of the management. The company harvests from its 12.5 acres and contract growers. Jane Brook produces 10 000–15 000 cases of Australian wines annually for markets in Australia and SE Asia. It established an online site in June 1995 focusing on marketing products and also providing corporate and industry information to its clients. The site also provided information about its key agents and sales outlets. A major emphasis in the site was to attract customers to visit the winery and to encourage cellar sales and enjoyment of dining and catering facilities. There are a total of five permanent staff of the company including three members of the Atkinson family. The company also employs approximately 15–20 part-time staff to support café and cellar door activity. With a slight investment in a website and no additional staff, Jane Brook has boosted its cellar door sales (with a greater profit margin than wholesale trade) by almost a third while extending its reputation and reach among distant buyers.

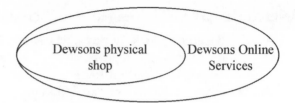

Figure 3.2
The virtual face

There is a tight link between the virtual face and the parent organization: a fresh communications channel has been forged between the existing corporate structure and the customer. This model is used by the majority of companies who offer web pages to complement existing channels to market.

3.4.2 Coalliance model

In a coalliance each partner brings approximately equal amounts of commitment to the consortium whose composition may change to reflect market opportunities or the core competencies of each member. Focus can be on specific functions such as collaborative design or engineering or in providing virtual management. Links are either contractual for enduring alliances or by mutual convenience on a project basis. There is not normally a high degree of substitutability within the life of that virtual creation. This organizational form is not unique to cyberspace, but its attractiveness as a virtual model is a consequence of the benefits flowing from low friction communications in real time and the ease with which such structures can be assembled and restructured. Its novelty lies in the speed and efficiency with which alliances can usefully form, perform their tasks, and reform owing to efficient communications, and hence the ease with which others can treat the partners as a virtual (single) entity existing for a specified time. Examples include real estate vendors who form an alliance to cater for interstate relocations such as LAA.com – an Australian-based consortium of estate agents with independent operators (such as Acton operating in Western Australia) in each state but a coalliance to facilitate interstate transfers where two of the consortium will ally with each other under the LAA alliance.

Figure 3.3
Coalliance model

Communications are direct between the specific state partnerships and may involve no other partner. These may choose to evolve into more complex structures with links of varying intensity forming along a value.

3.4.3 Star alliance model

The star alliance is a core surrounded by satellite organizations. The core is typically a dominant player in the market on whom members rely for competency, expertise, or leads to customers. Such an alliance is commonly based around similar industries or company types. While this form is a true network, typically the star or leader is identified with the virtual face (perhaps by brand ownership) and so is difficult to replace, whereas the satellites may have a far greater level of substitutability. Well-documented examples of this configuration are given by the Swiss watch industry and the Italian shoe industry.

Where the core controls communication channels a hierarchical communication structure may emerge, as evidenced by Recreational Equipment Inc. (REI). REI is an established outdoor gear and clothing cooperative mail-order business with 49 bricks-and-mortar retail outlets across the USA. REI first considered the Internet as a channel for product information, in response to customer requests, in 1995. Now the biggest outdoor store on the Internet, REI.com is the company's virtual face which features more than 10 000 products displayed in a 100-page catalogue. REI recently moved a step further by creating an online store offering special deals that have no store counterpart. This online resource has been a benefit not just for the online

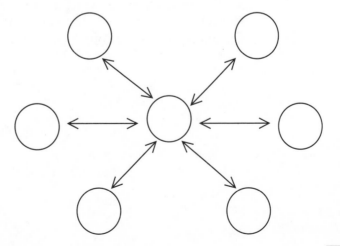

Figure 3.4
Star alliance model

store, but for REI's physical stores as well. It has achieved this by creating virtual alliances, first by establishing firm and fast relationships with the printing company that continues to provide the paper brochures used by the physical stores, then by forming similar alliances by extranet technology between the online store and its suppliers. This vendor extranet will result in tighter integration for better supply chain management and stock planning – moving toward a star alliance model, or perhaps a value alliance. Business pressures will determine the outcome and future extent of cooperation.

3.4.4 Value alliance model

Value alliance models bring together a range of products, services and facilities based on the value or supply chain (value and supply chains are discussed in greater depth in Chapter 5). Unlike the star model with its single core, the alliance model may take any one or a combination of steps in the value chain as the face or linking node of this chain to other parties. Normally companies will identify the highly information-dependent processes and form the value alliance along these lines. Participants may come together on a project-by-project basis but generally the general contractor provides coordination. Where longer-term relationships have developed the value alliance often adopts the form of value constellations where firms supply each of the companies in the value chain, and a complex and enduring communications structure is embedded within the alliance. Substitutability has traditionally been a function of efficiency and transaction costs: creating partnerships has been a costly and slow business procedure, relying as it does on information transfer, the establishment of trust and business rules across time zones, culture, currency and legal frameworks. These have determined the relative positioning of partners on the chain and the reciprocity of the relationship. This model is

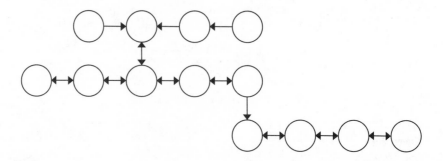

Figure 3.5
Value alliance model

particularly suited to taking advantage of new communications efficiencies and therefore changing components extremely rapidly in response to shifting market forces and opportunities.

3.4.5 Market alliance model

Market alliances are organizations that exist primarily in cyberspace, depend on their member organizations for the provision of actual products and services and operate in an electronic market. Normally they combine a range of products, services and facilities in one package, each of which may be offered separately by individual organizations. In some cases the market is open and in others serves as an intermediary. These can also be described as virtual communities but a virtual community can be an add-on such as exists in an e-mall rather

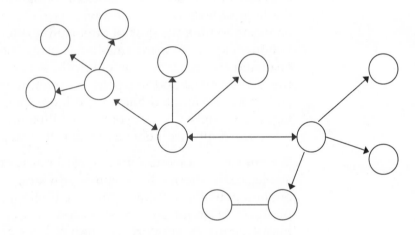

Figure 3.6
Market alliance model

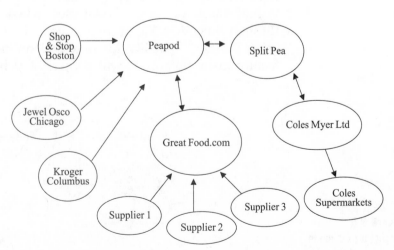

Figure 3.7
Market alliance model
(example)

than a cyberspace organization perceived as a virtual organization. Amazon.com is a prime example of a market alliance model where substitutability of links is very high. Fast and responsive communication channels are essential to preserve such alliances, which could only have formed occasionally, and relied on duration to be cost effective hitherto.

An example of a market alliance model using Peapod – an online retail grocery – is presented in Figure 3.7 and is later referred to in section 3.4.7.

3.4.6 Virtual broker model

Virtual brokers are designers of dynamic networks. These provide additional opportunities either as third party value added suppliers such as in the case of common web marketing events (e-Xmas) or as information brokers providing a virtual structure around specific business information services. This has the highest level of flexibility with purpose-built organizations enduring to fill a window of opportunity and dissolving as that window closes. New intermediaries using the Internet (such as eBay and the many auction enterprises) epitomize the growing trend to take fast and inexpensive communications across time and space for granted and to configure themselves for advantage accordingly. The case of Sofcom illustrates how a firm may move to adopt this model as an effective response.

Sofcom (www.sofcom.com) is a Melbourne company acting as an electronic intermediary, which provides, in addition to other online content publishing, an online shopping mall for 4835 products in about 60 stores. Sofcom has an extensive online infrastructure to support its product lines and to manage the virtual faces of other businesses whose transactions pass through Sofcom's SSL secure server. The site offers an online Store Builder™ facility for potential online storeowners. The facility takes potential store owners step by step through the

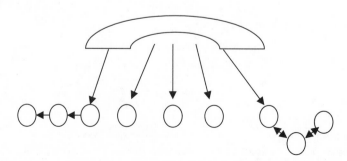

Figure 3.8
Virtual broker model

process of setting up a storefront at Sofcom and doing business online. There is a flat charge of AU$40 per month for stores available to the public and selling. Potential storeowners may develop and test run a store for free. Sofcom act as virtual brokers (see below) and businesses using the facilities of the mall are embedded in a market alliance model. The market may be described as an example of a virtual community given this company's extensive linkages and the diversity of online firms involved with its business.

3.4.7 Virtual space

The seventh category proposed is that of the virtual space. In interactive home shopping systems (IAHS) this is instantiated by companies such as Webvan, Streamline and to some extent Peapod: three companies with the avowed aim of becoming large networks of IAHS for groceries in North America.

The virtual space is characterized by being wholly dependent upon virtual contact with the client. There is no other channel to market, nor need they be dependent upon any particular existing intermediaries between themselves and the makers/ suppliers of goods and services. Unlike companies such as Peapod who form alliances and act as the virtual face for small chains of retail shops with walk-in retail outlets and existing brand image, these companies hide their warehousing and distribution chain from the customer. They may elect to choose goods and services from companies with a retail face, but they may equally elect to operate (or subcontract) warehousing and delivery service specifically designed for this channel to market. Different forms are currently emerging using this basic form, although there is evidence that the temptation to focus on 'core competencies' and form market alliances with others still operates, as shown by Streamline below.

Webvan has been operating from June 1999 in the San Francisco bay area of the USA with plans to extend across the United States in 26 cities within two years. Webvan offers major branded grocery and drugstore items with more than 300 fresh vegetables, 300 cheeses and 700 wines. In addition it operates its own kitchens for prepared meals, all from a 330 000 square foot dedicated warehouse with no public walk-in facilities. The company does not rely solely on a single supply chain and sources from major fish, vegetable and meat markets in addition to manufacturers and wholesalers, opening new channels to market for local growers and suppliers.

Figure 3.9
Virtual space model

While Webvan expects to deliver to a person in place, at office or home within a 30-minute window, Streamline offers to install shelving and refrigeration units at the customer's premises, secured by combination locked access control. This removes the need to accept physical delivery. While the grocery supply chain comes through the company's own warehouse and distribution service, the company also has alliances with other Internet-enabled suppliers for goods and services (www.webvan.com). Within the Streamline order branded services from, among others, Starbucks (coffee), Kodak (film and processing) and UPS (package collection). In addition their website offers links to alliance partners Barnes and Noble for books, CDNow for music, eToys for games and Outpost.com for small office and home office equipment supplies.

Peapod, once a coordinator and market alliance leader, is now creating and operating purpose-built centralized distribution centres to replace picking from existing stores owned by others. It predicts that the new warehouses will improve service, improve gross margins and allow for the charging of lower fees. Success of the initial ventures may impel the company to move to this model entirely.

3.5 Virtual alliance framework

As discussed, each of the seven models embodies a set of tensions related to autonomy and interdependence. Virtual culture is the strategic hub around which virtual relationships are formed and virtual links implemented. In order to be flexible, links must be substitutable to allow the creation of new competencies, but links must be established and maintained if the organization is going to fully leverage community expertise. This presents a dichotomy.

The degree to which virtuality can be implemented effectively relates to the strength of existing organizational links (virtual and real) and advantages they bring to the virtual structure. However, as essentially networked organizations they will be constrained by the extent to which they are able to redefine or extend their linkages. Where existing linkages are strong, e.g. co-located, shared culture, synchronicity of work and shared risk (reciprocity), these will reduce the perceived benefits from substitutable linkages and inhibit the development of further virtual linkages. Figure 3.10 provides a diagrammatic representation of these trade-offs within the virtual alliance framework (VAF). An organization must identify the virtual culture it wishes to adopt to develop the virtual strategic perspective (VSP), identify the value alliance partnerships and the strengths of such linkages and align these within the electronic market.

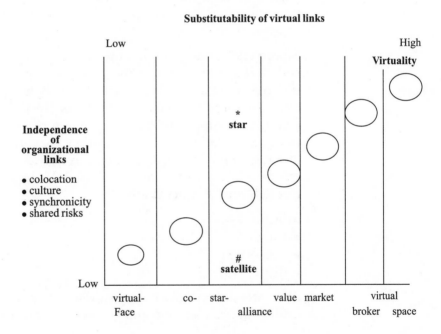

Figure 3.10
Virtual alliance framework (VAF)

These seven models clarify the forms an electronic business model may assume. Some are an electronic reimplementation of traditional forms of doing business; their attractiveness increases as ICT enables their cost-effective implementation. Others are add-ons for added value, or extend through value chain integration or cyber communities. Their commonality is that they add value through information and change management and a rich functionality. Managing the creation of value through embracing the opportunities of virtuality is only feasible if the processes supporting such transformations are clearly understood.

3.6 Virtual organizational change

3.6.1 e-market ecosystem

As observed, virtual organizations operate within a dynamic environment where ability to change determines survival. Organizational theorists point out that the ability to change is a function of many factors. Primarily these include the organization's technology; structure and strategy; tasks and management processes; individual skills; roles and culture; and the business in which the organization operates, together with and the degree of uncertainty in the environment. These factors also determine optimal organizational form for the virtual organization.

Moore (1997) suggests that businesses are not just members of certain industries but parts of an ecology that incorporates different industries. The driving force is not pure competition but coevolution. The ecosystem is seen as 'an economic community supported by a foundation of interacting organizations and individuals. Over time they coevolve their capabilities and roles, and tend to align themselves with the direction set by one or more central companies' (p. 26). The ecosystems evolve through four distinct stages:

- birth
- expansion
- authority
- death

And at each of these stages the ecosystem faces different leadership, cooperative and competitive challenges.

This ecosystem can be viewed as the all-embracing electronic market culture within which the e-business maintains equilibrium. This ecosystem concept is further developed in Chapters 5 and 10.

3.6.2 Virtual organization change model

The virtual culture of the organization is the result of interplay between the virtual strategy, virtual structure and the use of ICT. However, in order to align these processes and manage change,

Table 3.2 e-market ecosystem (after Moore 1997)

Ecosystem stage	Leadership challenges	Cooperative challenges	Competitive challenges
Birth	Maximize customer delivered value	Find and create new value in an efficient way	Protect your ideas
Expansion	Attract critical mass of buyers	Work with suppliers and partners	Ensure market standard approach
Authority	Lead coevolution	Provide compelling vision for the future	Maintain strong bargaining power
Renewal or death	Innovate or perish	Work with innovators	Develop and maintain high barriers

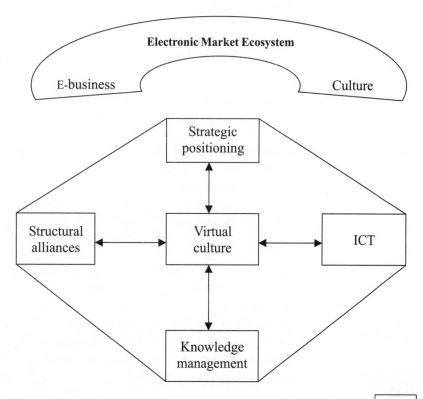

Figure 3.11
Virtual organizational change model (VOCM)

the virtual organization will also encompass knowledge of the overall electronic marketplace. These relationships are depicted in a dynamic virtual organizational change model (VOCM) as shown in Figure 3.11. We will return to this model in Chapter 7 and expand on these concepts.

The degree to which virtuality can be applied in the organization will relate to the extent to which the VOCM factors are in alignment. When these are not aligned then the organization will find itself dysfunctional in its exploitation of the virtual marketspace and so be unable to derive the maximum value benefits from its strategic position in the virtual alliance framework.

3.7 Summary

The virtual organization is recognized as a dynamic system and hence one where traditional hierarchical forms of management and control may not apply. Little, however, is known about the new forms which might replace them. In an organization in constant change there has to be a system that can capture the organizational core competencies and leverage these to provide strategic advantage. This may be a competitive advantage or a strategic advantage in collaboration with competitors. This implies that the virtual organization will have a far greater need than a traditional organization to manage communication channels and rethink interorganizational systems.

The seven models introduced are not exclusive but serve to classify the diversity of emerging electronic business models. Some are essentially an electronic reimplementation of traditional forms of doing business; others are add-ons for added value possibly through collaboration; and others extend through value chain integration or cyber communities. What these share are innovative ways to harness efficient low-cost communications, change management and a rich functionality. Creating strategic advantage through virtuality is only feasible if the appropriate form is identified and the communications needs and opportunities are identified and accepted. Further, these structures exist in a state of dynamic change and may evolve rapidly from one form to another. Consequently communication channels will change, necessitating revised forms of communications. The successful organization will be that which regards the storage and communication of knowledge as the core asset. Communicating for advantage will become the primary mission in the virtual marketspace.

References

Burn, J.M., Marshall, P. and Wild, M. (1999) When Does Virtual Have Value? In: C.T. Romm and F. Sudaweeks (eds), *Doing Business on the Internet: Opportunities and Pitfalls*, London: Springer Verlag.

Hoffman, L., Novak, T. and Chatterjee, P. (1995) Commercial Scenarios for the Web: Opportunities and Challenges, *Journal of Computer Mediated Communication*, Vol. 1(3).

Moore, J.F. (1997) *The Death of Competition: Leadership and Strategy in the Age of Business Ecosystems*, New York: Harper Business.

Schein, E. (1990) Organizational Culture, *American Psychologist*, **45**, 2, 109–119.

Williams, R.L. and Cothrel, J. (2000) Four Smart Ways to Run Online Communities, *Sloan Management Review*, **41**, 4, 81–91.

IS planning strategies for emerging business models

4.1 Introduction

With the advent of the Internet and e-commerce and the increasing transformation of business through the expanding use of ever more reliable and powerful IT, business is becoming increasingly interconnected and interdependent. This interconnectedness, arguably, helps business face challenging contemporary environments increasingly characterized by a global span of business operations, turbulence, change and uncertainty, innovation, hypercompetitiveness and the like. In this chapter we shall discuss how the interconnected world of business spawns new organizational forms. Important among these is a virtual corporation of collaborating partners, linked and communicating with the help of modern IT. We generalize the virtual organizational form and talk about an interconnected strategic business network of a business, its business partners, its suppliers and potentially its customers. In this context we introduce the new term, if not entirely new construct, of 'coopetition' to describe the information and resource-sharing strategies that are replacing naked aggression and competition in many business contexts.

Most effective modern corporations, we believe, are embedded in strategic business networks to a greater or lesser extent. In this chapter we look at approaches to strategy formulation for virtual organizations or strategic business networks, commenting on the need for some changes in emphasis in strategy formulation, given the realities of contemporary business environment.

4.2 Background to planning theory

As the use of computers and telecommunications has changed over time, so too have the approaches to planning the utilization of an organization's information, information systems (IS), and information technology (IT).

The established approaches to information systems suitable to an era of inward-focused automation of basic activities are unlikely to be suited to an age which focuses on information to support executive decision making, or to an age where a major role of IS is to connect the organization to other organizations in the business environment. We saw that the business and IS/IT planning approaches that were appropriate in the era of hierarchical integrated organizations of the 1960s were found wanting in the emerging, interconnected business environments of the 1990s. How much more so this will be in the coming environment: highly interdependent firms each focusing on core competencies, and increasingly dependent on IS/IT to support and manage core business activities.

There are a number of factors in contemporary business environments that indicate a need for new forms of business and IS/IT planning. One of these factors is the growth in the number and complexity of interorganizational systems (IOS) which, as their name implies, stretch between two or more organizations with distinct and probably different structures, strategies, business processes, IT infrastructures and organizational cultures. Another factor centres on the business realities and philosophies concerning virtual organizations or extended enterprises with important alliances and linkages to suppliers and business partners. These factors, together with the significant changes involving globalization, electronic commerce, new technological developments, and the like, mean that new approaches to planning and envisioning the future of organizations that are appropriate to and effective in contemporary business environments are critically needed.

New approaches to planning, both business and IS/IT, seem to be lagging both contemporary business practice and thinking. While it may have almost become fashionable in some quarters to suggest that businesses should not indulge in planning at all, the argument could be made that the extreme volatility and uncertainty that characterize modern business environments imply an even greater need for some form of strategic thinking and planning.

Claims may be made that the whole notion of planning is an anathema in contemporary business environments, suggesting that the need for responsiveness, flexibility, and agility, so often touted as the hallmarks of success in the new 'e-environment' of business, are the antithesis of formal planning. Such planning is typically dismissed as being too ponderous and bureaucratic, and too much based on an unchanging, forecastable future to be of much help.

However, there is little empirical evidence offered to support such claims, and indeed arguments could be raised to suggest that unplanned, whimsical, capricious decision making with respect to future directions is just as damaging as more traditional, bureaucratic modes of planning.

We hold the view that strategic information systems planning (SISP) today need concern itself for planning strategies on behalf of enterprises with increasingly blurred boundaries and increasingly important connections and interconnections among an ecology of interdependent organizations.

4.3 How IS planning has evolved

4.3.1 Introduction

The evolution of IS planning is somewhat linked to the spread and development of computer-based IS in organizations. Most IS professionals identify three eras or stages of computing in organizations to date. The first was the data processing (DP) era, followed by the development of management information systems, and thirdly the growing importance of strategic information systems (SIS) thinking.

4.3.2 The data processing age

The data processing (DP) era is generally identified as beginning in the 1960s, when the emphasis was primarily on applying the newfound technologies of computing to the automation of basic business transactions and so achieving efficiency gains for the organization.

Typically, this process of automation took place function by function, and the planning horizons were primarily constrained by a project-by-project outlook and system implementation. At this time systems were being developed according to simple economic criteria (can we automate this process to do it more cheaply?) with little regard to other, related systems. The deployment of IT was generally in the category of localized exploitation, and so fragmented islands of automation developed within organizations. This in turn led to subsequent planning efforts directed towards developing interfaces between these disparate systems.

4.3.3 The rise of management information systems (MIS) thinking

As more data became stored across the organization and with the advent of more flexible and user-friendly tools, managers were encouraged and increasingly enabled to access data from more than one of the 'islands of automation' that created, manipulated and stored records for the organization. They were provided with new tools for the job through what were called management information systems (MIS).

As well as continuing the task of the business process automation characteristic of the DP era, the new MIS thinking took a broader view of organizational activity. Within MIS systems the effectiveness of managerial performance and decision making was highlighted, with IS planning focusing more on developing a portfolio of information systems that supported and facilitated management decision making and the effective monitoring and control of employee activities.

In addition, IS planning came to involve the development of organizational policies to prioritize organizational information requirements and to coordinate the roles of empowered end users and the IT department in an increasingly complex IT environment. IS planning was thus concerned with an explicit attempt to integrate at both a technical and informational level, and thus changes envisaged for the organization would involve elements of internal integration.

It is important to note that planning during both the DP and MIS eras was primarily internally orientated.

4.3.4 On to strategic information systems (SIS)

Extending the scope and range of existing DP and MIS-type systems, the 1980s and 1990s saw the advent of strategic IS (SIS) systems geared to improving an organization's competitive position, to changing the way business is conducted, and/or to establishing close links to business partners and customers. SIS are viewed as flexible, externally focused, and driven by business initiatives and requirements. The emphasis in planning thus shifts to understanding customer requirements and the business environment, with efforts directed to aligning IT efforts with the articulated business strategy. Thus there was a shift in ISP from essentially planning basic support services using IT, to recognizing the potential of IT to offer competitive advantage and relying on ISP as a key enabling factor in the achievement of business strategy. Another important shift involved the recognition that process design considerations would often be an essential aspect of the business strategy–IS strategy nexus, with the transformatory impacts of IT becoming more evident.

4.3.5 Planning for the new SIS

Not surprisingly, given the emerging tools, unprecedented scope of systems thinking, and intense management interest, planning thinking changed significantly during the SIS era. Although still primarily internally focused, for the first time, planners were encouraged to look outwards from their organization into the external business and IT environments. The external environments were believed to offer insights into appropriate developments to protect, defend and reposition the organization, and also to take advantage of particular opportunities that may be available. External forces could sometimes even have the effect of initiating an investment decision. ISP was now underpinned by the recognition that business success in the modern business environment might now be contingent upon strategic and appropriate IS/IT investments, with particular consideration given to the role of IT in effecting transformation of existing business processes. This evolutionary process of SISP is illustrated in Figure 4.1. It is worth noting in passing that although SISP planners thus made gestures of concern regarding the external environment, they did not usually or routinely engage with the external environment in the planning of interorganizational systems.

In the section which follows, some of the basic frameworks for SISP that emerged during the late 1980s and early 1990s will be reviewed, and their contribution to planning considered. In particular, some of the assumptions underpinning these frameworks will be considered, particularly in the light of modern business environments.

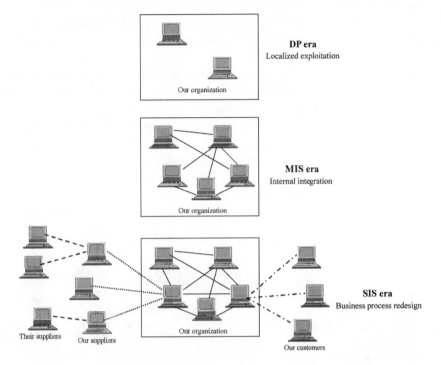

Figure 4.1
The evolution of IS/IT planning

4.3.6 Information systems planning at the end of the 20th century

By the mid-1990s, it was reasonably well established that some sort of formalized SISP was an appropriate undertaking for most organizations. SISP was to be closely allied to the organization's business planning activity, the accepted wisdom at that time suggesting that SISP should only be attempted once a business strategy has been developed and articulated, and hence an understanding reached of the direction the organization was planning to follow for the next few years, its goals, objectives, core business processes and its change agenda, for example.

With this business strategy established and a shared understanding reached amongst executives, an IS plan could be developed, determining the information and information systems needed to support the business strategy, and thus guiding investment decisions into the future. Once an IS plan was defined, an organization's technology requirements could be articulated, such that the technological infrastructure and hardware would be made available to support and enable the provision of relevant information and information systems. An iterative and generative process was envisaged, recognizing a general trend of establishing a business strategy, then an IS strategy, and finally an IT strategy, but acknowledging the constraints and pressures in the real world which may act to limit the strategies somewhat. Given the rate of technological change, and the potential and impact that modern IT could have directly on business strategy, at the outset of this process it was important to be aware of technological advances that may impact or alter the chosen or desired course for an organization (Peppard 1993, Liedtka 1998). Issues of strategic alignment between the business and IS/IT came under increased scrutiny, with frameworks developed to help alignment or 'fit'. Figure 4.2 is a typical example.

Figure 4.2
Achieving strategic alignment (adapted from Henderson and Venkatraman 1994)

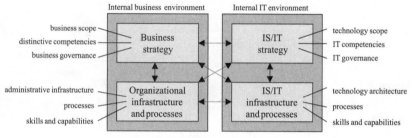

For parsimony in subsequent discussions, the business components will jointly be described as the internal business environment, and similarly, the IT components as the internal IT environment.

In Figure 4.3, there is an example of one of the frameworks that was developed for SISP during the 1990s. Essentially, this framework underpins directly an approach to SISP articulated by Ward and Griffiths (1996). However, it is asserted that its general nature suggests that most modern SISP methods would employ a variety of (albeit different) tools and techniques to accomplish exactly what this framework encapsulates. In simple and succinct terms, this SISP framework suggests the following assumptions:

- That a business plan, setting the general future direction for an enterprise, is an important source of input to the SISP effort (or is, at least, concurrently developed with the IS plan).
- That the SISP should consider the external business environment of the organization. The external business environment provides an assessment of a range of forces (competitive, economic, social and political, for example) impacting on the organization, thus encouraging debate on specifically how IS/

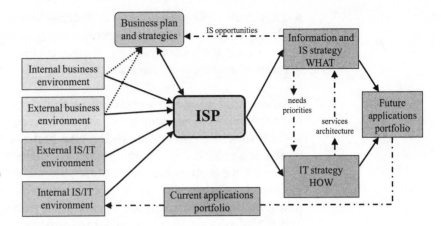

Figure 4.3
A framework for SISP
(Ward and Griffiths
1996)

IT can be deployed to act as a buffer, neutralize, or indeed in some cases, capitalize on the effects of these forces, depending on the competitive situation of the organization involved. A consideration of how IS/IT may reduce or minimize threats to the organization and how IS/IT may help the organization avail itself of opportunities are thus important components of SISP.

- That the SISP should consider the internal business environment of the organization, to understand the strengths and weaknesses, skills and competencies, and so on, with emphasis on understanding if, and how, IS/IT can build on and support the strengths while reducing or eliminating the weaknesses.

- That an understanding of the external IS/IT environment regarding technological advances, the use (and the degree of success of that use) of IS/IT by relevant outsiders, and so on, is also a vital ingredient in the SISP process

- That an understanding of the internal IS/IT environment, including issues such as how well existing IS/IT currently serve the institution, existing skills and competencies, and inventory and evaluation of existing IS/IT assets and resources, areas of weakness and limitation, known future needs, and so on, is also an essential component of SISP.

- That out of the SISP process would be derived both an IS strategy (articulating needs and requirements for information and information systems now and into the future to best support the achievement of organizational goals and objectives), and an IT strategy (the technological and infrastructure requirements to provide the required information and information systems).

- That the SISP articulates a future applications portfolio, closely aligned to the business strategy, and designed so as to maximize the potential and impact of IS/IT on the achievement of business goals and objectives.

Fundamental to this framework is the iterative and ongoing nature of SISP. Thus over time, the future applications portfolio will become the current portfolio, and hence scrutinized as part of the internal IS/IT environment in subsequent SISP efforts. Furthermore there is a distinct sense in which SISP should not be regarded as a one-off (or a once a year) activity, but should manifest itself as much in everyday thinking and reflection about the use of IS/IT in the business as in any formalized planning process (Masifern and Vila 1998). This point is important, and is assumed in much of the subsequent discussion about SISP.

Having described the framework, let us examine the assumptions that this framework makes about the world. The framework basically suggests that organizational members (members of the SISP team) should look out into their external business and IS/IT environments, take note of trends, threats, opportunities, and so on, and then basically plan internally their own information, IS and IT requirements. The plan should be devised such that perceived opportunities could be exploited and perceived threats averted or destroyed through an appropriate investment in and use of IS/IT. But the SISP activity (and the resultant IS and IT strategies and priorities for IS/IT investments) is largely an internal one. To suggest that Ward and Griffiths (1996), in developing this framework, did not envisage linking the organization to suppliers and buyers in the external environment would be unfair, but this framework does primarily present the organization as an 'island', operating independently within its business environment, while acknowledging the impacts of the external business and IS/IT environments. While outside views and information may be sought and used as input to the SISP process, SISP is seen as being primarily an internal, and somewhat independent, activity. The external business and technology environments are acknowledged, but there is no actual engagement with those environments.

In the section which follows, it will be considered whether these assumptions are still appropriate given the changes in contemporary business environments.

4.4 Planning for new and forthcoming business environments

In section 4.3, the type of business and IT environments assumed in the SISP framework presented were described. We move now to consider the changing realities of the business environments in which many organizations now operate. From this we question the appropriateness of the SISP framework to support and inform IS planning activities in emerging business forms which are the theme of this book. Specifically, we address next issues raised by the trend to globalization and virtual organizations or alliances – sometimes called strategic business networks (SBNs).

4.4.1 Globalization

Globalization, the breaking down and dissolution of barriers between countries, organizations and individuals, seems an important trend. Driven by a number of important political, economic and technological trends and factors such as the demise of communism, the removal of trade tariffs and free trade agreements, the rapid advance in telecommunications technologies and the Internet, and so on, operating on a global stage offers organizations a much larger marketplace, and hence opportunities to specialize, to further develop and enhance excellence in their core competencies. However, it also creates much more competition, as traditionally local markets become the playing ground of global operators, who, in encroaching, experience fewer barriers. These factors, coupled with an increasing rate of change, and sudden, unpredictable changes or turbulence, mean that most organizations face a beguiling mix of increasing opportunities coupled with increasing challenges, increasing complexity and increasing uncertainty in their business environments.

4.4.2 Alliances and strategic networks

One response to the increasing pace of change and the concomitant need to reposition organizations in an increasingly interconnected and dynamic business environment is to move from a formal and methodologically based strategic and IS/IT planning to a more flexible, lighter and less bureaucratic mode of strategic thinking. This move also includes a move from rigour and analysis in strategic planning towards a softer, more creative, intelligently opportunistic and more collaborative strategic thinking mode that emphasizes values and culture along with business goals, objectives and directions. The need to make such a move has been a common theme in the strategy/ strategic planning literature since the mid-1990s. For example, Kanter (1994) writes that:

Alliances between companies, whether they are from different parts of the world or different ends of the supply chain, are a fact of life in business today . . . In the global economy, a well-developed ability to create and sustain fruitful collaborations gives companies a significant competitive leg up. (p. 96)

Thus, it is asserted that the formation of a variety of business alliances, partnerships and collaborations is both an important and increasing trend for many organizations, and it is also a strategic device for catering with an increasing rate of change, increasing complexity, increasing competition, while retaining flexibility and adaptability. Furthermore, an overt purpose in entering into such collaborative relationships may be to ultimately create added value for customers by each of the partners contributing a unique, but complementary set of skills, resources and competencies not available to the other partners on their own, but which are jointly valued by the end consumer.

While the mutual benefit of improved customer satisfaction may be an important facet of the formation of the business relationship, additional value to the collaborators stems from the potential for a stream of opportunities to be realized together over a period of time. Interorganizational collaborations can thus provide opportunities for greater stability in business relationships and can build switching costs for all parties concerned, perhaps an attractive proposition in turbulent times. However, we need to be aware that increased stability may find itself at odds with the need and desire for flexibility and adaptability.

Most managers today agree that IT plays an important role in supporting, facilitating and indeed enabling these strategic alliances. Telecommunications technologies and interorganizational systems (IOS) thus become an important component of the virtual organization or strategic business network. Such systems are argued to offer the positive impacts of reducing costs and improving the efficiency of transactions, of facilitating communication, information quality and information provision, and of improving the competitive positioning of the collaborating partners. To an extent, therefore, it must be concluded that skill, foresight and excellence in exploiting the capabilities of IT must be an ingredient in successfully forging strategic business networks.

So we conclude that the business environment that is rapidly developing (if it is not already a pervasive reality in your area) is one in which distinct boundaries between organizations diminish and dissolve as organizations enter into a variety of possible relationships of varying degrees of strength and commitment with their suppliers, their business customers, their business partners, their end consumers, and even their business competitors. The respective fates of collaborating enterprises become increasingly intermingled; these interdependent business environments being described as an 'interconnected ecology of firms', or 'symbiotic networks'. This is offered in contradistinction to the organization as an 'island' notion that was argued to be assumed by the SISP framework previously described. This notion is captured in Figure 4.4.

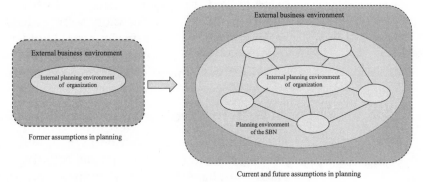

Figure 4.4
Planning adopts a
business network focus

The question that can thus fairly be posed at this stage is whether the ISP framework of the mid-1990s offers an appropriate model for the strategic business networks of the next century.

4.5 Developing planning strategies for the networked organization

While the IS planning literature written during the 1980s and early 1990s did emphasis the external focus of SIS, there was a definite sense in which SISP remained primarily an *internal* activity of organizations acting largely in isolation. (A legacy from the original 'islands of computing' background from within which most practitioners still drew their paradigms.)

Various methods, tools and techniques used to guide SISP processes involved members of an organization scanning their external business environment (for opportunities and threats), in developing an understanding of their customers' needs and values (with the view to developing systems to provide real benefits to customers), to considering their business strategies (with a view to using IT to help achieve desired objectives and goals), and so on. Thus, SISP activity acknowledged the external business and IT environment and hence became more outward looking, without too much consideration of the potential of various characteristics of the virtual organization (flexible, temporary structures, heavy reliance on outsourcing of various functions and activities, and interorganizational business processes, for example) to make fundamental changes to the IS requirements of a network of associated organizations.

In practice, some consultants sought involvement of external stakeholders in the SISP process, but again this seems to have been geared to ensure that the business strategy and IT initiatives of the organization were indeed targeted towards value adding for these various stakeholder groups. To understand why this is a significant shortcoming, we turn now to an introduction to interorganizational systems.

4.5.1 Interorganizational activity

There has been no real sense in which SISP has been viewed or presented as an *interorganizational* activity, where SISP is taking place simultaneously in a number of organizations whose operations have become highly interdependent and interconnected. There seems to be a distinct sense in which SISP cannot sensibly be undertaken in one part of the 'organism' or 'ecosystem' (Moore 1996) without also being conducted in other parts of the organism at much the same time. Admittedly some 'big' players still use market dominance to stretch their systems outwards into other, smaller players in an industry, simply through enforcing their adoption and compliance, but electronic commerce networks and marketplaces of interconnected small and medium enterprises imply that these might be the exception rather than the norm. Figure 4.5 is an attempt to represent this notion.

If the model of the virtual organization, the agile organization, or the strategic business network becomes more prevalent, then there are important ramifications for SISP. Notions of organizational boundaries blur, implying that notions of corporate

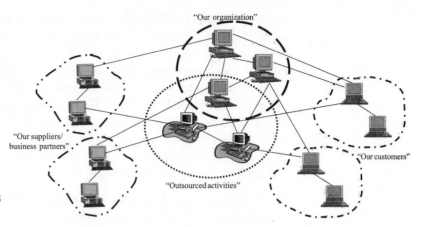

"Our organization"

"Our suppliers/
business partners"

"Outsourced activities"

"Our customers"

Figure 4.5
Interconnected ecologies
of firms

ownership of particular databases may need to be reconsidered, as must the concept of corporate data as an important resource. So too must concepts of business processes change. If organizational boundaries become more 'rubbery' and porous than previously was the case, concepts of internal and external processes, and hence ownership of and responsibility for business processes change. If simultaneously both loose and tight linkages are sought to suppliers and business partners, to satellite entities to whom former activities have been outsourced, and to customers, and if there is heavy reliance on IT to communicate, coordinate and control activities in this organic structure, then it seems totally inappropriate to continue to regard SISP as something done within a single organization for reasons of efficiency, effectiveness and competitive advantage, even if this is accomplished through peeping outwards into the external environment.

4.5.2 A sample case

Let us take three enterprises with strong motivation to collaborate. They have recognized the mutual benefits of working together, acknowledging the contribution that each can make, and have formally entered into some sort of deal or contractual arrangement. They are now in the process of making the collaboration work and of realizing the benefits of that partnership. A real life example of this type of scenario can be provided by considering the relationship that developed between three government departments, with complementary interests in issues surrounding family welfare.

The three agencies can be called Police (A), Justice (B) and Family Welfare (C). The benefits from collaborating exist at a number of levels. With pressures across government generally to maintain or enhance services to the public while decreasing costs, any prospect of efficiency gains through collaboration is attractive. Important also is the recognition of potential improvements to service performance in all three agencies if all three worked collaboratively. The actions and responsibilities of all three departments are somewhat mandated by law, and prior to the decision to work more closely on aspects of their responsibilities, contacts between the departments had been minimal in terms of the issues of interest.

A, B, and C each bring to the relationship not only a set of complementary skills, assets and competencies, but also three discrete internal business environments, including notions such as visions, goals and objectives, decision-making styles and processes, patterns of communication and interaction, business processes and approaches to 'doing business', corporate cultures, learning styles, attitudes to risk and planning, and so on. As A, B, and C strive to work together at some level for some purpose, as they strive to reconcile different objectives and approaches, they individually bring internal business environments to their collaboration from which over time evolves a network business environment.

Participating in the collaboration, however, and hence becoming part of the network business environment, is likely to cause changes to the individual internal business environments. Each individual organization's interaction with the external business environment is thus now mediated through the network business environment, at least as far as the extent of their collaboration is concerned.

Take, for example, the issue of domestic violence. A, B, and C individually have a set of strategies, competencies, structures, processes, procedures and infrastructure by which they individually address their responsibilities in terms of domestic violence. As they collaborate and start to share and explore one another's perspectives on the issue, realizations of new possibilities occur, and the recognition of joint initiatives, shared resources, new cooperative procedures, etc. emerge. So too does the recognition that changes to individual internal business environments to 'give' to the network business environment will take place.

Each individual member of the alliance experiences the creation of network business environment, and changes to the internal business environment. This process repeats and evolves over

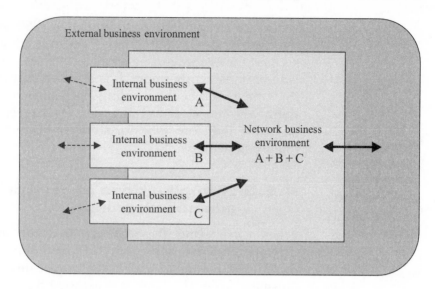

External business environment

Internal business environment A

Internal business environment B

Internal business environment C

Network business environment A + B + C

Figure 4.6
The interrelationships between internal and network business environments

time. A, B, and C individually may in other circumstances interact directly with the external business environment, but at least in terms of the strategic business network formed through their collaboration, this is tempered by the emergent network business environment. Figure 4.6 illustrates this point.

As the strategic business network develops and matures, collaboration will arguably develop on at least three levels. At a strategic level, arguably an important task will be to articulate a shared vision and purpose for the collaboration, and to develop shared goals and objectives. This is argued to be an ongoing activity throughout the life of the strategic business network. At a more tactical level, collaboration and planning for specific projects or ventures needs to occur, and strategies for knowledge management and transfer put in place to appropriately service the life of the project. And at a much more operational level, mechanisms need to be in place to ensure that people have the information resources and support required to accomplish these tasks.

If this collection of activities was going on within the confines of a single organization, or business unit, they would typically nowadays be well supported by information, IS and IT, and would thus come under consideration during an SISP exercise, during which an inventory and evaluation of existing IS/IT assets as well as a prioritized statement of future information, IS and IT needs would be articulated. If the strategic business network created through organizational collaboration were to be anything more than transient and totally opportunistic, then it would seem reasonable to assert that an SISP activity (including the notion of everyday thinking and reflection about IS/IT) to support the ever-maturing strategic business network over time is important. Furthermore, it is asserted that in current climes, IS/IT may itself be the enabling mechanism by which collaboration at a strategic, tactical and operational level is made possible. Arguably therefore, SISP for strategic business networks is an important activity.

4.5.3 IT implications of network and alliance planning

When considering the SISP required for strategic business networks, internal and external IT environments must also be considered. Figure 4.6 could thus be repeated, simply replacing 'business' with 'IT'. Thus, it is asserted that organizations A, B, and C each individually possess an IS/IT maturity and legacy which they bring to the strategic business network. As a network business strategy emerged, so too did a network IT strategy, requiring additional IT investments for all parties, and all requiring changes to the individual internal IT environments. These changes were not simply technological: in all three agencies the most significant changes that emerged had to do with rethinking the use, exchange and management of information with a view to improving service to parties caught up in domestic violence affairs. Issues to do with the compatibility of the respective IT technical infrastructures, compatibility of management attitudes to IS/IT, and stages of maturity with respect to IT needed to be addressed here. So too did the use of and reliance on consultants, as individually the organizations had had very different histories and experiences in this regard.

4.6 Coopetition: the new (name of the) game in town

In this book we talk of an emerging nexus of business ideas as alliances, strategic business network, strategic partnerships and so on. But one area of new business thinking stresses a type of cooperation called coopetition, the notion of deliberately dealing with and supporting a business rival. This works in many forms, from strong to weakly competing parties joined, and for varying time frames. Let us think in terms of this construct.

In much of modern business theory, emphasis is laid on the value of aggressive competition as one of the key forces that keep firms lean and drive innovation. That emphasis has been challenged across the board today as the notion of coopetition gains currency. Cooperation with suppliers, customers and firms producing complementary or related products can lead to expansion of the market and the formation of new business relationships, perhaps even the creation of new forms of enterprise.

In place of seeking to compete within the market, taking as much customer base and profit as possible, regardless of the interests of other companies, and seeking to drive competitors out of business, coopetition seems a gentler, if more difficult, game. Some people see business entirely as competition. They think doing business is waging war and assume they can't win unless somebody else loses. Other people see business entirely as cooperative teams and partnerships. But business is both cooperation and competition. It's coopetition.

Coopetition often involves companies agreeing not to battle in one market even as they fight like dogs in others: witness the current 'grand alliance' of Sun, IBM, Apple, and Netscape, which is supporting the open programming language Java to undermine Microsoft's market power. More commonly, companies will compete on actual products even as they cooperate on technical standards, sacrificing a degree of independence to increase the odds of success for the technology as a whole. Look at the huge success of American Airlines in opening its Sabre reservation system to competing carriers.

The concept, and the word, seem to have been taken up most enthusiastically in the computer industry, where strategic alliances have long been common in order to develop new products and markets, particularly between software and hardware firms. Another motivator for the computer industry is that its consumers want to know in advance that a broad range of companies will support a given technology. Companies cooperating helps such markets grow faster, without waiting a long time to dump competing technologies. It also helps focus scarce resources – though not necessarily on what is ultimately the best technology.

Needless to say, coopetition makes regulatory authorities nervous. There is an old-fashioned word for competitors who agree not to compete – cartel, with its overtones of price fixing. Today's regulators say that they appreciate the theoretical advantages of coopetition, but in practice they still want to be sure that they can distinguish it from old-fashioned collusion. And as Microsoft's on-again, off-again antitrust investigation shows, separating new ways of doing things right from old ways of doing things wrong is far from easy.

We can expect the trend of 'working with the enemy', as some describe it, to continue. And its deployment is not restricted to computing or high tech examples. Industry by industry, corporate giants and newcomers alike are finding ways to work with their rivals on Internet projects. Competitors such as Compaq and Hewlett Packard, Goodyear and Michelin, and Kmart and Target are cooperating on the development of e-hubs (see Chapter 11). When Ford and General Motors decided to merge their separate procurement plans into a single e-marketplace, both the scale and the cooperative nature of the new beast stunned the business world.

4.7 Proposed new SIS planning model

From the argument developed above, we see that a revised framework for SISP is needed, and we offer such a revised framework in Figure 4.7. This, we argue, takes into account the particular nature and requirements of strategic business networks in an age of cross-boundary systems and the need for business alliances to integrate systems for rapid response.

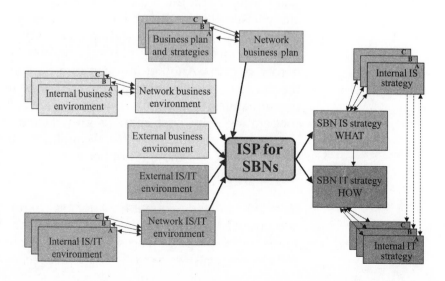

Figure 4.7
A revised framework for SISP in strategic business networks (SBNs)

Note that there are parallel changes to the outputs of the SISP. Arguably an emergent strategy for the strategic business network will be articulated, detailing the information, IS, and information management required to support and enable the activities of the strategic business network into the future (whatever that is perceived to be).

Also considered in the SBN IS strategy are concerns regarding IT human resource requirements and change management strategies. This strategic business network IS strategy will likewise impact the respective internal IS strategies of A, B, and C, and will be shaped and limited by those internal IS strategies. An IT strategy for the strategic business network will also likewise be derived.

4.8 Conclusion

The framework articulated above stems from concerns that existing frameworks to support SISP in modern businesses are inadequate given the changing nature of contemporary business environments and the emergence of strategic networks and the like. SISP in its broadest sense – encompassing not only formalized planning processes but also including everyday thinking and reflection on the role and deployment of IS/IT in an organization's business activities – is still argued to be an important organizational activity. The conceptual perspective spelt out here is an early attempt to start moving existing frameworks for SISP forward to embrace new organizational realities.

However this framework may be tempered by a number of different factors. For example, the relative size and power of the collaborating partners may be significant. Also, this framework has not been designed for a star-alliance model (see Chapter 3) of collaboration, in which one central player has the power, size and dominance to dictate courses of action and requirements to other collaborating partners. The strategic business network referred to here is much closer to the notion of a market alliance or value chain alliance (see Chapter 3) or where no player is in the position, or has the predisposition, to dominate the others.

Thus considerations of the leadership of the SISP for the strategic business network must be given. Is leadership required that is external to the network (perhaps in the form of an independent consultancy), or can a team drawn from the senior ranks across collaborating enterprises be created that provides sufficient drive and vision to sustain the ISP activity? Furthermore it is envisaged that vital to the success of the SISP activity would be boundary spanning activity. Individuals from each organization must operate to articulate their organization's issues, concerns and needs to the team, while serving to communicate ongoing progress and decisions of the team to their respective organizations.

The history of the collaborators with respect to establishing routine, transaction-based interorganizational systems may be important in facilitating their migration to more strategic-type IOS, and hence it could be argued, to SISP for alliances or networks. We suggest also that the learning involved in establishing operational level IOS is an important precursor to a willingness to establish more strategic level connections. Thus it might be expected that a successful history amongst the collaborators in the planning and development of a specific system may be necessary before there is a willingness to engage in any interorganizational SISP.

New techniques that emphasize strategic thinking and positioning as distinct from formal bureaucratic planning and that focus on the nature and richness of partnerships and alliances with suppliers, customers and business partners would also enhance SISP for SBNs. While such techniques as value chain analysis and critical success factors identification can be focused on the external business network, they do not focus naturally on the issue of the number and nature of synergistic partnerships that are best for the organization.

However, techniques that focus on the positioning of the organization in a network of relationships which include customers as well as business partners and suppliers are a valuable addition to the strategy process for the extended enterprise. We shall be examining this in greater detail in Chapter 11.

Arguably behavioural models of SISP need to change as well. Too often it seems that SISP is regarded as a formal, finite activity, done to produce a specific document (the IS plan), and then is no longer done for some time. This view is completely at odds with the view of the authors who see planning in turbulent and uncertain times as a vital and increasing activity, such that it permeates everyday thinking about IS/IT. Along with this idea there is clearly a need for new thinking that emphasizes strategy and positioning as distinct from formal bureaucratic planning. This new thinking must focus on the nature and richness of partnerships and alliances with suppliers, customers and business partners as input for the next generation of SISP for networks and alliances.

References

Henderson, J.C. and Venkatraman, N. (1994) Strategic alignment: a model for organizational transformation via information technology, in: T.J. Allen and M.S. Scott (eds), *Information Technology and the Corporation of the 1990s: Research Studies*.

Kanter, R.M. (1994) Collaborative advantage, *Harvard Business Review*, pp. 96–108, July–August.

Metes, G., Gundry, J. and Bradish, P. (1998) *Agile Networking: Competing through the Internet and Intranets*, Upper Saddle River NJ: Prentice Hall.

Moore, J.F. (1996) *The Death of Competition: Leadership and Strategy in the Age of Business Ecosystems*, New York: Harper Business.

Venkatraman, N. (1998) IT-enabled business transformation: from automation to business scope redefinition, in: V. Sethi and W.R. King (eds), *Organizational Transformation through Business Process Reengineering: Applying the Lessons Learned*, Upper Saddle River, NJ: Prentice Hall.

Ward, J. and Griffiths, P. (1996) *Strategic Planning for Information Systems*, 2nd edn, Chichester: Wiley.

Moving from e-business to i-business strategies in virtual markets

. . . where we knock down the walls that separate us
from each other on the inside, and from our key
constituencies on the outside.

(Jack Welch, CEO, GE)

5.1 Introduction

Driven by such phenomena as the World Wide Web, mass customization, compressed product life cycles, new distribution channels and new forms of integrated organizations, the most fundamental elements of doing business are changing and a totally new business environment is emerging. This environment variously described as the electronic business community (EBC), electronic economy, electronic market, electronic marketplace or marketspace and the virtual market is characterized by rapid exchange of information within a virtual network of customers and suppliers working together to create value added processes. The virtual market (Figure 5.1) brings with it new forms of IT-enabled intermediation, virtual supply chains, increasing knowledge intensity and information-based business architecture strategies. This new business paradigm goes beyond e-business and can be described more effectively as i-business where core business processes may need to be rethought and redesigned, new organizational forms and interorganizational forms may need to be developed and where the emphasis will be on collaboration rather than competition within the virtual market.

i-business is defined as a business with the following core elements:

- internetworked market;
- internet-enabled supply chain;
- interorganizational systems;

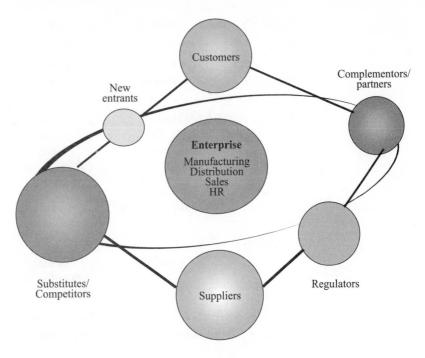

Figure 5.1
Virtual market

- integrated organizational systems;
- intelligent knowledge-based decision systems;
- information-based business architecture strategy.

The first three of these concepts are explored in depth and we return to the other three components later in Chapters 7, 8 and 9.

5.2 Internetworked markets

5.2.1 Virtual markets ecosystems

As noted in Chapter 3, Moore (1997) suggests that businesses are not just members of certain industries but parts of an ecology that incorporates different industries. The driving force is not pure competition but coevolution. The term 'coevolution' originated in biology. It refers to successive changes among two or more ecologically interdependent but unique species such that their evolutionary trajectories become intertwined over time. As these species adapt to their environment, they also adapt to one another. The result is an ecosystem of partially interdependent species that adapt together. This interdependence is often symbiotic (each species helps the other), but it can also be commensalist (one species uses the other). Competitive interdependence can emerge as well: one species may drive out

Table 5.1 e-market ecosystem (Moore 1997)

Ecosystem stage	Leadership challenges	Cooperative challenges	Competitive challenges
Birth	Maximize customer delivered value*	Find and create new value in an efficient way	Protect your ideas
Expansion	Attract critical mass of buyers	Work with* suppliers and partners	Ensure market standard approach
Authority	Lead coevolution*	Provide compelling vision for the future	Maintain strong bargaining power
Renewal or death	Innovate or perish	Work with* innovators	Develop and maintain high barriers

the other, or both species may evolve into distinct, non-competitive niches. Interdependence can change, too, such as when external factors like the climate or geology shift.

This ecosystem can be viewed as the all-embracing electronic market culture within which the i-business maintains equilibrium. In Table 5.1 a possible evolution path is shown for an i-business as*. The i-business initially focuses on gaining new customers. As the business expands they realize that they need to extend alliances with suppliers and so set up a number of different alliances throughout their value chain. This requires more rigorous management of different communication channels reflecting different degrees of dependency and reciprocity. At this stage the i-business may decide to impose more control over the alliance in order to lead a coevolution to a market alliance. Simultaneously other i-businesses have been formed as the market has matured and at stage 4 the i-business faces a choice which may result in a completely new virtual form with the same or different players in the virtual market and the recommencement of the evolutionary cycle.

This view is supported by Eisenhardt and Galunic (2000) who point out that the new roles of collaboration in i-business are

Table 5.2 Traditional collaboration versus coevolution (after Eisenhardt and Galunic 2000)

	Traditional collaboration	Coevolution
Form of collaboration	Frozen links among static businesses	Shifting webs among evolving businesses
Objectives	Efficiency and economies of scale	Growth, agility, and economies of scope
Internal dynamics	Collaborate	Collaborate and compete
Focus	Content of collaboration	Content and number of collaborative links
Corporate role	Drive collaboration	Set collaborative content
Business role	Execute collaboration	Drive/execute collaboration
Incentive	Varied	Self-interest, based on individual business unit performance
Business metrics	Performance against budget, preceding year, or sister-business performance	Performance against competitors in growth, share and profits

actually counterintuitive and that collaboration does not naturally lead to synergy.

Where synergies are achieved the managers have mastered the corporate strategic process of coevolving. These managers routinely change the web of collaborative links – everything from information exchanges to shared assets to multibusiness strategies – among businesses. The result is a shifting web of relationships that exploits fresh opportunities for synergies and drops deteriorating ones.

5.2.2 Models of virtual markets

This ecosystems approach can be applied to different market models such as the four models of virtual market environments identified by Ticoll *et al.* (1998) in their examination of e-business

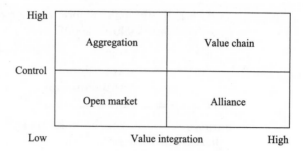

Figure 5.2
Four models of virtual market

communities. They suggest that such markets differentiate along two primary dimensions: economic control and value integration (Figure 5.2).

The open market model is basically a business-to-consumer model without any single player in overall control although different players and market alliances can drive events at different times. The aggregation model normally has one business in control positioning itself between suppliers and producers. Value chains have a similarly hierarchical model but maximize value integration through operational effectiveness and alliances retain that high value integration but rely on shared visions, standards and business practices to provide a full solution environment without any single company exercising overall control. Another classification can relate the control variable to the emphasis on efficiency or flexibility and innovation, and that this will imply a stable or dynamic market. In many virtual market environments this can be seen as a staged growth evolution of i-business maturity. Each of these stages of maturity demands different approaches to strategy and different approaches to process management.

5.3 Strategies for i-markets

Berryman *et al.* (1998) suggest there are three types of marketplace: those controlled by sellers, those controlled by buyers, and those controlled by neutral third parties. Marketplaces controlled by sellers are usually set up by a single vendor seeking many buyers. Its aim is to create or retain value and market power in any transaction. Buyer-controlled marketplaces are set up by or for one or more buyers with the aim of shifting power and value in the marketplace to the buyer's side. Many involve an intermediary, but some particularly strong buyers have developed marketplaces for themselves.

Table 5.3 Types of electronic markets

Seller controlled	Information-only vendor Web Vendor websites with online ordering	Cisco Systems
Buyer controlled	Website procurement Planning purchasing agents Purchasing aggregators	Japan Airlines Freemarkets Online TPN Register
Neutral	Industry/product specific search engines Information marts Business malls Auction spaces	FastParts

Companies wanting to evaluate which model suits them best should answer the following four questions to help them determine an appropriate strategy.

- Are there transaction savings or benefits to be realized?
  - cost reduction through greater process efficiency;
  - improved reach;
  - reduction in prices to buyers.
- Is an electronic market for our product developing quickly?
  - do we have transaction inefficiencies?
  - how sophisticated is the buyer?
  - is the product e-friendly?
- Would a neutral intermediary be beneficial?
  - advantage of scale in transaction processing;
  - value of the information acquired during buying and selling;
  - anonymity.
- Do we have substantial market share or buying power?

For buyers, the strategic imperative is clear. They have little to lose and much to gain, and should therefore organize a buyer-controlled marketplace as quickly as possible. The dynamics of electronic marketplaces also create clear opportunities for third-party intermediaries, which can create value by virtue of their neutrality. Sellers are the most vulnerable participants, because they will increasingly have to compete with other vendors in a transparent environment. The dynamics and rapid growth of electronic marketplaces are forcing businesses to choose their strategies now. Electronic business-to-business commerce is not simply a question of automating existing channels and processes. It is a whole new way of doing business. Aligning these approaches with the i-business model and stage of maturity of the virtual market requires the i-business to explore its supply chain management and to exploit its business value chain beyond the enterprise level to include interorganizational relationships.

5.4 The chain gang

Supply chain analysis involves working across multiple enterprises or companies (inter-enterprise) to shorten the supply chain time in the delivery of goods and services to the consumer or customer. The demand uncertainty in supply chains can be addressed by faster response times. A basic product supply chain can afford longer lead times and batch manufacturing of large lot sizes to meet the demand. A supply chain that produces fashion, electronic, or mass customization products must respond quickly and be more agile. Most supply chains are moving in the direction to support a more rapid changing of demand by the consumer or customer.

Value chain analysis is used to identify a variety of potential sources of economic advantage. The analysis divides a firm into its major activities, considered as steps which each add value to the goods as they are transformed at that stage. This may take the form of complex operation upon the goods, or simply moving them from one place to another. This is done in order to understand the behaviour of costs and the existing and potential sources of differentiation from others in the market. It determines how the firm's own value chain interacts with the value chains of suppliers, customers and competitors. Companies seek to gain competitive advantage from such analysis by finding out how to do some or all of these activities at lower cost, or with greater differentiation, than competitors.

What these two terms have in common is that each business activity – upstream to exterior suppliers, internal to the company, and downstream to the end customer – is examined in the context of an overall value chain to reduce costs and improve responsiveness to the customer. Customer focus – the delivery end of the value chain – is the correct starting point for both supply chain and value chain analysis.

5.5 Supply chain management (SCM)

Supply chain management (SCM), also known as supplier–retailer collaboration (SRC) or efficient consumer response (ECR), is an idea that has gained considerable attention. In the US, supply chain management projects are often allied with efforts to create 'virtual corporations', i.e. a more opportunistic approach to collaboration. Ford and General Motors web portals demonstrate the changes that have been wrought in this area by the integration of web-based systems with EDISCM.

SCM is a well accepted concept in logistics and operations management theory and aims to improve coordination and competitiveness beyond the enterprise level to include inter-organizational relationships. Supply chains exist in virtually every industry and generally involve the procurement processes, transformation of raw materials into finished products and delivery of the product to customers through a distribution system. The supply chain of a packaged consumer goods manufacturer, for instance, comprises manufacturing, packaging, distribution, warehousing and retailing. Managing this involves the coordination of the materials inventory and production capacity availability across several organizations to produce products that can satisfy forecasted demand in an environment with a high level of uncertainty. While often regarded as a manufacturing concept (IT systems for bill of materials processing (BOMP) have been around in the manufacturing sector since the late 1960s) it can equally well apply in a university or any other service industry and may specifically relate to the management of information rather than materials.

Suddenly, however, SCM has become a 'hot' topic for a number of different reasons. These include the trend towards multi-site operations with several independent entities involved in the production and delivery process, new and increasingly cut-throat marketing channels and the electronic marketplace. Traditional supply chains and trading partner relationships are exploding into intricate and dynamic virtual networks of trading partners and service providers. The emphasis in these relationships is to derive significant value through increased revenues and decreased costs as shown in Table 5.4. Achieving this in any organization directly depends on the performance of all the others in the network and their willingness and ability to coordinate. The question facing organizations today is not if they should join these new electronic networks, but how.

Table 5.4 Value from networked processes along the supply chain (adapted from Benchmarking Partners, Inc. 1999)

Networked processes	Value
Design and product management	• Competitive advantage through faster time-to-market • Reduced R and D expenses • Lower unit costs
Order management, planning, forecasting and replenishment	• Competitive advantage and higher revenues from reduced stock-outs • Lower costs through reduced inventory • Lower costs through reduced return rates
Distribution	• Lower costs through optimized shipping and fulfilment
Sourcing	• Competitive advantage and increased revenue through faster product introductions • Decreased costs through and increased revenue from higher quality
Customer relationship management	• Increased revenue through improved customer segmenting and targeting • Increased revenue through improved customer service • Decreased costs from efficient salesforce automation
Merchandizing/ category management	• Competitive advantage and increased revenue through the proper product assortment, pricing and promotional strategies, and shelf placement

5.5.1 The logistics paths

When considering supply chain management from a logistics perspective, we will find two areas that have a considerable impact on the efficiency and effectiveness of the operations being performed – product logistics and information logistics. While product logistics is concerned with the flow of physical goods along the supply chain, information logistics reflect the need for handling the information flow and administrative tasks around the products. Within each of these dimensions, we can identify the following areas for improvement: operating standards and replenishment.

By applying common operating standards the retailer's regional distribution centres or stores can be optimized. When a regional distribution concept is used, this strategy normally does not include the exchange of information regarding the flow from the retailer's regional distribution centres to the stores, nor analytical EPoS (electronic point of sales) data. However, there is still a significant potential for improvement, e.g. delivery planning, advanced shipping notes, cross-docking, and the use of bar codes on pallets.

Efficient replenishment strategies build on EPoS data being transferred to the supplier, who takes responsibility for deliveries within agreed stock levels. If a direct-store-delivery system is in operation, EpoS sales data is regularly included in the data transfer from customer to supplier, otherwise the data flow is normally restricted to contain the aggregate levels from the customer's regional warehouses. This concept contains a potential risk for increasing the supplier's costs, when the underlying supply chain management strategies are not reconsidered. Since retailers generally aim at minimizing their warehouse costs, they tend to increase the frequency of orders, while reducing their volume, thus striving for a 'just-in-time' delivery concept. This will result in costs being transferred to the supplier, and most likely an increased total cost volume within the supply chain. A way of reducing the negative impact on the supplier is to provide him with sales data and forecasts on either PoS or RDC level, thus allowing a more accurate production and logistics planning.

Beyond the improvement of physical logistics, the flow of information between the parts being involved in collaboration and the handling of administrative issues play an important role for succeeding with SRC efforts. Reducing non value added activities by using information technology will result in cost reduction, improved data accuracy, and less paperwork.

5.5.2 Driving supply chain management

In its current state, most of the impetus for supply chain economics is coming from the retail side, based on achievable cost reduction. While there may be a difference between economies which focus primarily on increased gross margins and those which target cost reductions, the strategy of supply chain management that results is similar.

Another reason, beside the directly financial, is awareness of the changing demands of final consumers and the ability to harness them. The emerging concentrations of power in a small group of retail organizations, for example in the retail grocery trade across Europe, allows the retailers to exert pressure on the suppliers and along the entire chain of supply.

5.5.3 Knowledge exchange and enabling technology

The exchange of knowledge and information between the partners participating in the improvement of a supply chain is a precondition for success. Depending on the chosen collaborative level, this may include the free access to analytical sales data, sales forecasts and internal logistics figures, but even more qualitative information regarding purchasing behaviour, consumer requirements and changing demands. This information flow improves the planning ability throughout the entire supply chain, and allows fast responses to changes in environmental dynamics and variations in demand. Information technology in various forms is the enabling factor for the successful implementation of improved supply chains in operations, since it makes possible the inexpensive, frequent and extensive exchange of information between the parties involved. It is for this reason that proprietary EDI first justified its cost. Among large corporations this is one of the most common tools employed to allow information exchange at the required pace and intensity. Several studies, conducted in many different industries, have shown that the electronic exchange of primarily quantitative data, but even quantitative information, works very effectively if the necessary preconditions are satisfied. The ability of retailers and suppliers to integrate effectively within improved supply chains requires two basic elements – electronic point of sales (EPoS) data and (EDI). We discuss briefly how these integrate.

The data scanned at the retailer's points of sale can be used for managing the physical flow from the retailer's regional distribution centres to the stores, and to improve the retailer's warehousing at regional and store level. In this case, the data need not necessarily be transferred to the supplier, but can be used to develop sales forecasts that enable the supplier to better plan its own operations. When a direct-store-delivery system is in place, the data can even be used to improve the planning of deliveries to the retailer's stores. Used in conjunction with point of sale data, the electronic transferral of orders can significantly reduce the time, work, and costs required for order handling. This benefit can be accessed by both parts, thus resulting in reduced individual and total chain costs, and lead time improvements.

It appears that the employment of various replenishment strategies have a higher potential benefit for the retailer than for the supplier. In order to leverage the obtainable benefits among the SRC partners, the implementation of replenishment strategies has to be aligned with other strategies. The simultaneous implementation of joint operating standards and efficient administration strategies, where the benefits are more leveraged, can significantly increase the suppliers' will to join an efficient replenishment initiative. This problem is clearly depicted in the following table, which describes the main reasons for firms to undertake efficient replenishment efforts. While suppliers expect primarily cost reduction, retailers conceive better service from suppliers as their most important expectation. However, without being embedded in an overall collaboration, these two expectations are mutually exclusive of each other.

Table 5.5 Expected benefits from supply chain efficiency

Suppliers	Retailers
1. Cost reduction	1. Better service from suppliers
2. Better service to retailers	2. Cost reduction
3. Better information flow	3. Better information flow

Another strategy for balancing the benefits throughout the entire supply chain would be to further integrate the supplier's value chain with its own suppliers, thus ultimately considering the entire industry value system as a single value added chain.

5.5.4 Some examples of change

The importance of supply chain management is such that many companies today are adding to the already extensive capabilities of their enterprise resource planning systems with collaborative applications that let them share data over the Internet. And a handful of companies in the automotive, electronics, and biotechnology industries have undertaken an even more ambitious project: to build private portals that link buyers and suppliers, providing a platform to exchange information about products, inventory, capacity, shipment, and payment.

IBM Microelectronics, a division of IBM, began to reshape its supply chain management system in 1995. The division wanted to move from supplying semiconductors and packaged goods exclusively to divisions of IBM, to supplying parts to outside buyers such as Advanced Micro Devices, Cisco Systems, Dell Computer, and Qualcomm.

The company replaced the system it had built itself with SAP's manufacturing resource planning software to gather and store data, capture and store orders, and track current inventory. The IBM division also began to transmit information to customers over the Internet, including purchase orders, ship dates, logistics, and payment information. The idea was to extend and improve communications along the supply chain by making use of the Internet as a means of communicating requirements and sending status information back out. This created immediate benefits in reduced transaction processing, enhanced reliability, and improved customer responsiveness.

The demand trend for improvements such as this has generated new software that can help companies defray the costs associated with finding and buying products and services. Chemical company DuPont & Co. is deploying web procurement software to give its 95 000 employees a single interface and consistent business rules to buy products such as office supplies, test tubes, and service contracts. The use of a common system is intended to simplify purchasing while leveraging buying power for better deals.

Similarly, catalogue software from Commerce One Inc. helps companies source the raw materials and finished products used in the production of their goods more efficiently; the software archives and searches large databases of product information from multiple vendors, significantly reducing search times.

The Internet is promising to change how companies manage their supply chains in other ways as well. Using their foundations in web-based software from Ariba, Commerce One, i2, and Manugistics, companies are beginning to explore using trading hubs – online marketplaces such as Altra Energy Systems, Chemdex, and e-Steel that let businesses buy commodity goods such as bulk chemicals, metals, and power more efficiently.

Daimler, Chrysler, Ford, and General Motors are looking to portals to help connect them to suppliers, original equipment manufacturers, and resellers on the Web. The companies have joined forces to build an automotive marketplace that will use open Internet protocols and the Extensible Markup Language (XML) to help the participants exchange information on orders, inventory, demand, and payment with tens of thousands of trading partners. The potential benefits include more accurate planning, easier data exchange – especially with small suppliers not equipped with electronic data interchange – and faster response times to customer needs.

Genome Therapeutics Corp. is experimenting with a number of services from online marketplaces. It's using chemicals exchange site Chemdex to source and buy about 10% of its indirect goods – the reagents, enzymes, plasticware, test tubes, and other finished products used in the research it conducts into human and pathogen genetics. The online marketplace also lets all lab personnel view and search the same product data via a web browser – something Genome Therapeutics' four-year-old requisition software could not accomplish.

When it comes to how companies find, buy, make, and move goods and products, the world is changing. Analysts predict the way companies manage their supply chains will continue to morph with each technological advancement and new Internet business model, and according to rules unique to each industry. What won't change is the fact that supply chain management is an increasingly critical element of running a successful online business.

5.6 Value chains

A value chain partnership is a strong and close alliance in which a company forms a long-term arrangement with one or several key suppliers or distributors for mutual advantage. In the past the introduction of computing into organizations had largely been on the justification and acquisition of individual information systems. The degree of attention paid to systems introduced was justified by the expected dollar value of each particular acquisition with little attention to the cumulative affect of these acquisitions on the overall business capability. The result of this has been the painful lesson that a focus on individual information activities, within individual business units, will not necessarily result in an advantageous position. To improve competitiveness, many companies have adopted a 'value chain' viewpoint. Porter

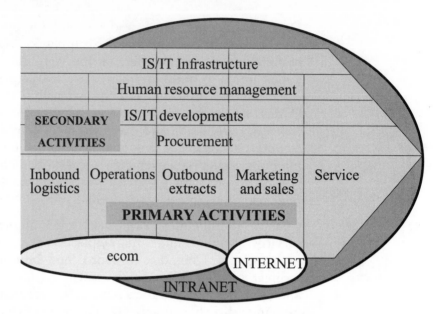

Figure 5.3
Internet-enabled
commerce and the
value chain

(1985) considered these concepts when he derived his classic internal value chain showing primary activities which a business must do to exist and the secondary activities required to control and develop the business and which are common across the primary activities. An organization today must consider the effect of Internet-enabled commerce on their distribution channels and the value chain. Figure 5.3 illustrates the interconnections.

Value chain analysis is used to identify potential sources of economic advantage. The analysis disaggregates a firm into its major activities in order to understand the behaviour of costs and the existing and potential sources of differentiation. It determines how the firm's own value chain interacts with the value chains of suppliers, customers and competitors. Companies gain competitive advantage by performing some or all of these activities at lower cost or with greater differentiation than competitors.

This approach requires an understanding of the linkages between activities and the way the performance of one activity impacts the cost and performance of others. To perform value chain analysis:

- divide a firm into its key activities and assign costs to those activities;

- for each activity, understand the cost drivers, the linkages between activities and the company's cost position relative to competitors;
- identify linkages to the buyer's value chain and assess potential sources of differentiation; and
- develop a differentiation strategy that maximizes value to the buyer and minimizes increases in cost.

5.7 The basic concept

The focus of Porter's argument is that winning by charging less or by having distinctive features should be understood and planned for as a result of the total activities that a company performs. By splitting these activities into 'strategically relevant' groups, managers should be able to understand the behaviour of costs as well as work out potential sources of differentiation.

5.7.1 What is a value chain?

In this analysis 'value' is defined as 'the amount buyers are willing to pay'. The value chain is therefore designed to display total value and consists of the firm's value activities and its margin ('the difference between total value and the collective costs of performing the value activities'). This allows us to describe the generic value chain for any single firm in terms of three main elements: its primary activities, its support activities and the margin.

5.7.2 Primary activities

Primary activities create the product, its sale and transfer to the buyer as well as after-sales service. These are:

- Inbound logistics – warehousing, materials handling, inventory control, etc.
- Operations – the activities that change inputs into finished products (e.g. machining, testing, packaging, equipment maintenance, etc.).
- Outbound logistics – the activities that store and distribute products to buyers (e.g. warehousing, delivery fleet operations, order processing, etc.).
- Marketing and sales – the activities that provide the means for the buyer to purchase (e.g. advertising, sales force operations, selection and management of distribution channels, etc.).
- Service – activities that enhance or maintain the value such as installation, upgrade, repair, spare parts, etc.

5.7.3 Support activities

Support activities are those which support primary activities and each other. Three of these – procurement, technology development and human resource management – can be associated with specific primary activities while the fourth, business infrastructure, supports the entire chain. Support activities comprise:

- Procurement – while raw materials procurement is usually concentrated in a purchasing department, other purchasing is often dispersed throughout a firm.
- Technology development – includes engineering and process development and, while usually associated with an engineering or development function, may also be dispersed (office automation, telecommunications, etc.).
- Human resource management – recruitment, hiring, training, development and compensation of all personnel. Partly centralized but increasingly dispersed, Porter points out that the skills and motivation of employees and the costs involved may be critical to competitive advantage.
- Firm infrastructure – broadly encompasses general management activities, as well as finance, accounting, legal, corporate affairs and quality management. Often viewed as an overhead, these can be a considerable source of advantage (e.g. skilful negotiations with regulatory bodies).

5.7.4 Defining a value chain

Starting with the generic value chain, individual value activities are identified for the particular firm within its particular industry. Each of the main categories in the overall model can be subdivided into separate activities. In this way, sales and marketing might be subdivided into marketing management, advertising, sales force administration, salesforce operations, technical literature, promotion, etc. This process of subdivision can continue down to increasingly narrow activities provided that they are bounded from each other.

Determining which activity lies within which category requires judgement. In particular it depends on the nature of the firm, its industry and where it derives the competitive edge which keeps it in business. Thus, we can regard order processing within outbound logistics or, if it is an important element of the way a firm interacts with its buyers, it could be defined within marketing. One way or another, however, everything a firm does should be captured and identified.

5.7.5 Linkages within the chain

Although definition needs this process of disaggregation, the value chain is not a series of independent activities – it is a system of interdependent ones. Linkages exist because of the relationship between how one activity is performed and its impact on the cost or performance of another. Porter argues that competitive advantage frequently emerges from such linkages – for instance, how buying high quality, well-prepared raw material can simplify manufacturing and reduce scrap, or how the timing of promotional campaigns can help production and capacity scheduling in a fast food chain. Linkages are not always obvious: the same function can be performed in different ways. Thus, keeping parts within specification can be achieved by buying in high quality parts, by specifying tight manufacturing tolerances or by imposing 100% inspection of finished goods – different firms will choose different routes and achieve different potential advantages. Another under-recognized factor is that the cost or performance of direct activities is improved by greater efforts in indirect activities. For example, better scheduling (indirect) can reduce time spent by either the sales force (customer complaints) or the cost of delivery vehicles (by making fewer runs).

5.8 The value system

Porter extends the value chain concept to what he defines as a 'value system'. This takes account of the fact that an individual firm's value chain is inevitably 'embedded' in a larger stream of activities. This suggests that there are at least three additional value chains of which account must be taken:

- *supplier value chains* – these create and deliver the essential inputs to the firm's own chain;
- *channel value chains* – these are the delivery mechanism(s) for the firm's products on their way to the end buyer, customer or consumer; and
- *buyer's value chains* – these are the ultimate source of differentiation because it is the product's role in this chain that determines buyer needs.

For this reason managers need to understand not only their own firm's value chain, but also how it fits into the industry's overall value system. The underlying point being that the value chains of separate firms in an industry will differ according to each organization's history, its strategies and its skills at implementation. For instance, one or more firms may have restricted their competitive scope. This decision to serve a focused industry segment may enable a firm to tailor its particular value chain to that segment and thus gain advantage either through lower costs or greater differentiation.

Since Porter introduced the notion, it has become ever clearer, particularly when the explosive growth in, and reduced costs of, ICT is studied, competitive advantage does not just arise within the firm. It may be derived from looking at the entire system and recognizing that different firms can adjust and improve their own value system. For instance, it is often the case that supplier linkages mean that the relationship with suppliers is not a zero sum game in which one gains only at the expense of the other, but a relationship in which both can gain. Similarly, coordination and joint optimization with different distribution channels can be important – especially in those industries where the channel may represent as much as 50% of the ultimate selling price to customers (e.g. consumer goods, wine, newspapers, etc.).

5.9 Implementing the value chain analysis

The following summarizes the process of using value chain analysis to gain a competitive edge through either lower costs or differentiation.

5.9.1 Six steps in strategic cost analysis

1 Identify the individual firm's value chain and then assign costs and assets to it.
2 Diagnose the key elements that drive the costs of each value activity (cost drivers).
3 Identify competitors' value chains and determine both their relative costs and the sources of differences in cost.
4 Develop a strategy to lower relative costs by controlling cost drivers or by reconfiguring the value chain itself.
5 Ensure that any cost reduction does not erode differentiation or, if it does, make sure that this is a conscious choice.
6 Test the cost reductions to ensure that they are sustainable.

5.9.2 Eight steps for determining the basis for differentiation

1 Determine who the real buyer is – the one or more specific individuals, within the buying entity, who set the purchase criteria.
2 Identify the buyer's value chain – the value the firm provides to the buyer is determined by the way, directly or indirectly, it impacts upon the buyer's value chain, either by lowering costs or improving performance.
3 Determine and put in rank order the buyer's reasons for purchase – analysis of the buyer's value chain will identify such criteria which should then be ranked according to the value the buyer attaches to each.
4 Assess the current and potential sources of differentiation – by determining which of its value activities impact each of the purchase criteria, a firm can identify its current or potential sources of uniqueness.
5 Identify the cost of these sources of differentiation – the cost of differentiation is a function of the cost drivers for those activities that – distinguish a firm from its rivals.
6 Design the value chain to maximize value relative to cost – the aim is to create the widest gap between what the buyer will pay and the cost of providing it.
7 Test for sustainability – identify both stable sources of buyer value and erecting barriers to competition.
8 Reduce costs in activities that do not affect the chosen forms of differentiation.

Porter's advance of this analysis foresaw the globalization of businesses and industries and with it a shift from straightforward growth as the main corporate objective to an era when companies would need to identify and strengthen their competitive position if they were to survive.

Porter's identification of five competitive forces and his arguments for positioning companies so as to reduce their impact has become known as the 'strategy as position' school of thought. As we have seen, understanding an enterprise in terms of the value chains involved brings home to us the centrality of communication systems in implementing any business activity. It is the restructuring of value chains and the reduction of costs of communicating between these activities that keeps value chain analysis very much to the forefront of enterprises today.

5.10 Demand chains

Traditionally, suppliers reengineered only their end of the supply chain by reducing obsolete inventory and cutting down cost and time of goods to market. However, a much more powerful concept lies in the demand chain where, for example, a retailer's demand chain would consist of assortment planning (deciding what to stock), inventory management (deciding the quantity of supplies needed), and the actual purchase. Together with SCM we have the demand–supply chain and these are linked and managed in two places – the order penetration point (OPP) and the value offering point (VOP).

The OPP is the place in the supply chain where the supplier allocates the goods ordered by the customer. Goods might be produced after orders come in (make to order) or allocated from a warehouse once the orders have been received (package to order) or from distribution (ship to order). Each order penetration point has different costs and benefits for the supplier and its customer – for example, rapid delivery (a benefit for the customer) depends on holding a large inventory (a cost for the supplier).

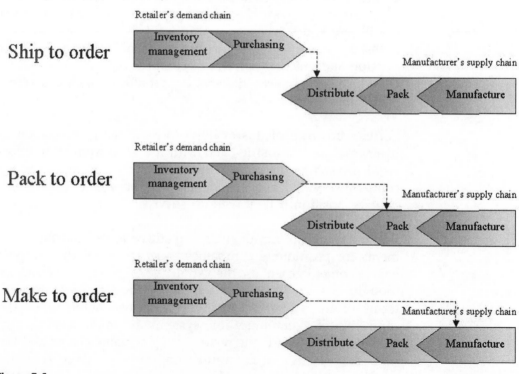

Figure 5.4
The OPPs (adapted from Holstrom *et al.* 2000)

The further back in the supply chain the supplier moves the OPP, the more steps there are to complete without disruption and the more difficult it becomes to fulfil orders promptly. The advantage to the supplier of this approach depends on the amount of cost savings effected by lower inventory, on the one hand, compared with the reduction in sales that may be brought about by longer delivery times and higher total costs for customers, on the other. Customers and suppliers never benefit equally.

The value offering point (VOP) – the second place where the demand and supply chains meet – is where the supplier fulfils demand in the customer's demand chain. Moving the VOP back in the demand chain largely benefits the customer, requiring more work from the supplier. There are three principal VOPs. In the conventional buyer–seller relationship, the VOP is the purchasing department, which accepts an 'offer to purchasing' by choosing the supplier and deciding when goods are needed. An 'offer to inventory management' moves the VOP further back in the demand chain: by carefully monitoring the customer's inventory levels, a supplier can cut down on stock that is unlikely to sell and ensure that the customer never runs out of

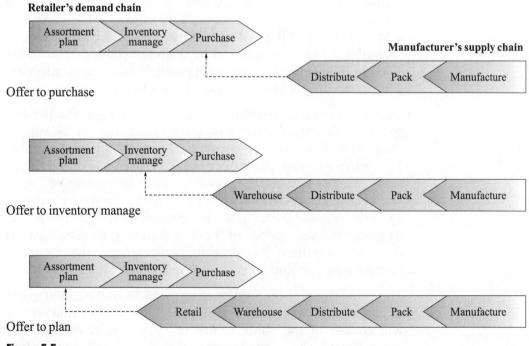

Figure 5.5
The VOPs (after Holstrom *et al.* 2000)

fast moving goods. An 'offer to planning' moves the VOP back to merchandising or production. As the VOP is moved back so this means more work for suppliers and greater benefits for retailers or even end users. The fourth VOP is the 'offer to end user', such as Dell Computer's direct-sales model for business clients. Rather than fulfil orders from wholesalers (an offer to purchasing), Dell went all the way back in the demand chain to the end consumer by fulfilling orders for customized PCs – complete with software and network configuration.

By coordinating changes in both the supply and demand chains a supplier can raise its customers' efficiency, as well as its own, i.e. simultaneous movements of the OPP and VOP will be of mutual benefit to customer and supplier. Effectively, this can result in the development of a virtual value chain.

5.11 Virtual value chains

An e-business must then consider the following two questions:

- Can we increase the number of electronic connections, simplify interorganizational processes and at the same time discover ways to shrink, speed up, or virtualize the value chain?
- What is likely to happen with our wholesalers, distributors, or retailers? Are they going to be disintermediated or are they likely to survive by transforming their businesses into new types of intermediaries operating in a neutral market?

One obvious scenario is that the old value chain gets smaller and so more efficient as you bypass some of the steps in the supply chain (for example, as currently happens with the online delivery of software and other products that can be digitized). In some cases as one cuts out previous links in the supply chain, new intermediaries will arise (for example, selling may move to an industry-wide portal or vortal to reach a larger market). This dynamic reconstruction of intermediaries can also lead to dynamic allocation of intermediaries where the channels become invisible and so creating the virtual value chain.

The value chain of the firm does not exist in isolation but exists as part of an industry value system and the whole value system will consist of the value chains of suppliers, customers and competitors. This can become the model for the virtual organization as it links electronically into value networks.

Buyer	▯ ▯ ▯ ▯ ▯	Seller

Old value chain

Buyer	▯ ▯ ▯	Seller

Shrunk value chain

Buyer	⬭	Seller

New intermediaries

Figure 5.6
The evolving virtual value chain

Buyer	— · — · — · — · —	Seller

Virtual value chain

5.12 Strategies for value networks

Value network alliances were described in detail in Chapter 3 and are shown again in Figure 5.7.

This model is particularly suited to taking advantage of communications efficiencies not previously available and therefore changing components extremely rapidly in response to evanescent market forces and opportunities. Different models present themselves to retailers and manufacturers as shown in Figures 5.8 and 5.9.

Figure 5.8 summarizes the current and potential supply chain structures for electronic channels in retailing. Models 1 and 2 represent the current structures for e-tailers and models 3 and 4 represent potential structures for interactive home shopping systems (IAHS).

Figure 5.9 summarizes how manufacturers in models 3 and 4 have applied the supply–demand chain to cut out retailers and

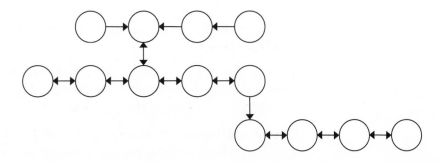

Figure 5.7
Value alliance

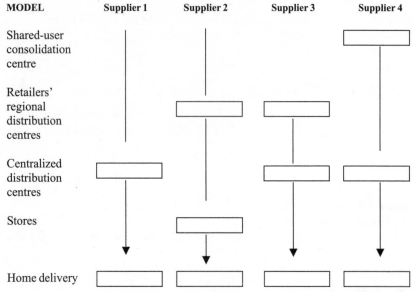

Figure 5.8
Supply chain structures for retailers (adapted from Younger 1999)

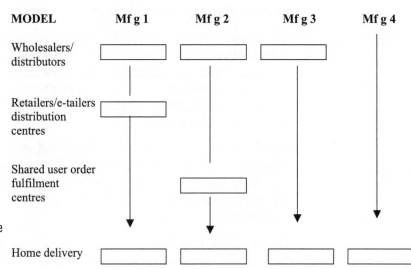

Figure 5.9
Supplier chain structure for non-FMCG (Younger 1999)

sell direct to the consumer in the fast moving consumer goods (FMCG) market.

The savings for consumers are clearly significant and from a manufacturing perspective the increased profit margins will undoubtedly accelerate the process.

One of the most interesting aspects of these networks is the speed at which companies are focusing on core competencies and outsourcing non-core functions to other service providers in the value network. With virtual relationships, companies can more easily outsource but still integrate these outsourced functions into their virtual organization. A manufacturing company with superior strengths in branding and selling could transform their organization to focus on these and outsource the manufacturing into its virtual value chain. Many organizations have moved towards this model (particularly the new dot-com companies) and are becoming virtually integrated rather than vertically integrated. These companies can now focus specifically on their customer communities who act as information gathering and information dissemination conduits. This will involve increased personalization and customization of product offerings and the aggregation and disaggregation of information-based product components to match customer needs and to support new pricing strategies. This requires the organization to develop effective virtual encounter strategies (discussed in detail in Chapter 7) but also to identify the framework for market mediation and the management implications involved in such interorganizational systems (IOS).

5.13 Market mediation

As organizations form and reform these value network alliances they also have to develop capabilities to cope with strategic, technical, cultural and operational change. Logistics, manufacturing and customer interfacing functions will become prime areas for outsourcing or incorporation into the virtual value chain and the ability to form and manage these is of critical importance. As the virtual value chain is formed facilitating direct exchange between the producer and consumer so we see the role of intermediaries being threatened but at the same time opportunities for new intermediaries arise.

5.13.1 Intermediaries

In traditional consumer markets, intermediaries (such as a traditional retail store) provide a variety of explicit and implicit services for their customers. These include assistance in searching and evaluation, needs assessment and product matching, risk reduction and product distribution and delivery. They also benefit producers by creating and disseminating product information and creating product awareness, influencing customer purchasing, providing customer information, reducing exposure to risk and reducing costs of distribution through economies of scale. A large supermarket chain can provide market opportunities that a small producer would find impossible to generate on its own. The mediation roles for customers and producers are normally juxtaposed and so part of the role of intermediaries is to balance this situation. While the truly virtual organization with a virtual value chain may be able to fully disintermediate, the fact remains that most organizations will still rely on an intermediary to integrate producer and consumer services and present the consumer market with a large-scale community front end and one that can take advantages of economy of scale. Interestingly, some of the biggest Internet businesses act as major intermediaries between other players. Amazon, CDNow, Egghead.com and E*Trade can all be thought of as middlemen! Portals and vortals are both some form of electronic intermediary. This suggests that rather than disintermediation becoming the norm, a new form of intermediary, cybermediaries, may evolve.

5.13.2 Cybermediaries

We suggest the following list of cybermediaries:

- Gateways
- Directories
- Search services
- Malls
- Publishers
- Virtual resellers
- Website evaluators
- Auditors
- Forums, fan clubs and user groups
- Financial intermediaries
- Spot market makers and barter networks
- Intelligent agents

These intermediaries will continue to be necessary where customers demand choice, require quality assurance and want additional social and entertainment value. Producers may be unable to impose producer-centric structures on the market and may also be threatened by the power of retaliation from the existing intermediaries. They may also choose to operate along known trust relationships in certain cultures and, indeed, using this system may be actually reducing the costs implied by legal contractual arrangements in place between producer and consumer. In many cases, electronic sites will continue to complement existing physical infrastructures but certainly restructuring of the processes is likely and the networked organization needs to be fully aware of the impact of such changing relationships.

5.14 Strategies for i-business

i-business involves collaborations among multiple organizations with several complex economic, strategic, social and conflict management issues as well as major organizational and technological factors. Planning and managing such systems requires an integrated multi-dimensional approach across the IOS.

As a first step the following questions need answering:

- What do consumers ideally want to buy?
- What business should I be in?
- What are my current core competencies?
- What are the opportunities for new products or service lines?
- What are the opportunities for new business channels?
- What is the most effective value proposition in the short, medium and long run?
- What roles should I play – make, sell or service – and who are my customers?
- Who are my competitors, and how do I need to be positioned?
- What is my operating model?
- With whom should I partner/network?

Your answers, if they are guided by a deep understanding of the economic implications and opportunity of the e-economy, will produce a very different picture of your company from the one you see today. Bring that picture to life with a compelling, enterprise-wide vision for your future in the e-economy; you'll need this vision to bring everyone on board who will help you get there. For many companies, achieving that vision will require building greater expertise in the strategic and operational application of technology – which, for better or for worse, is driving the rapid evolution of e-commerce. But you'll certainly need to temper that technology focus by applying cross-disciplinary, cross-functional and cross-industry perspectives and expertise – because industry boundaries will be shaped by customer needs rather than by core competencies.

5.15 Managing i-business

In the end, of course, strategy is only as good as its execution. New economic strategies will need to be translated into changes related not only to technology but also to processes and people. This will mean executing a complex, global change programme – on a large scale.

Management of such systems is significantly more complex than managing IT within individual organizations. In order to put in place an IOS, the cost of communications and the cost of the technology needed must be justifiable to all parties, while any implementation must first deal with congruence with long-range strategic planning. While this may already be in place within an organization, the formation of alliances or partnerships may serve to require a radical rethink in terms of the revised landscape of opportunities and strengths.

Against this background, a shared approach to conflict management may need to be formalized, as existing implicit procedures may not suffice. It can be readily appreciated that the means of resolving a conflict in a company founded, owned and run by a single dynamic individual will be far distant from those employed by a publicly owned multinational with partially independent subsidiaries. Within a single language group or country, many business models may exist: with increased interest in forming transnational or global alliances, such issues assume high importance and call for considered investigation and resolution lest unstated different assumptions wreck collaboration unnecessarily.

Against this, organizational issues need to be plotted: partners may not have the same resources to throw at a project, they may have widely different views on the appropriate levels of responsibility within their forms and unstated beliefs in the business and social value of technology will affect implementation. Added on to these issues are those relating to the technology to be deployed within any IOS. Any discussion of standards, equipment, networks and the like will quickly throw up the fact that technology is not neutral. What is taken for granted in one company – a perceived value of a networking technology, or adherence to proprietary standards – may be dismissed out of hand in another. The choice between proprietary EDI and Internet-enabled EDI alone is one calling for careful consideration and mutual understanding at the outset of any IOS project. The value of the resulting choice is unlikely to be symmetrical across partners, with a concomitant need for conflict resolution – and so it goes on.

Key criteria to be used in the selection of appropriate technology should include:

- Scalability
- Open platforms
- Knowledge management
- Internet based
- Support and leverage for back-end systems such as ERP
- Support for mobile users
- Workflow
- Robust security
- Integration

Table 5.6 Staged strategies

Model	Strategy	Stage	Website
Virtual face	Customer service, personalization and marketing	Presentation	Static or mail order website – brochureware and advertising, online orders
Coalliance/star	Cost reduction and speed of processing	Communication	Tailored to trading partner – view inventory/orders in hand
Star/Virtual broker	Efficient pricing and expanded product lines	Interaction	Customer/Supplier order placement/mall/auction bids
Value alliance	Core business concentration	Fulfilment	Links to back-end fulfilment systems
Market alliance/ Virtual broker	Expansion of products/ services/business	Collaboration	Dynamic interaction
Virtual space	Diffusion of niche markets	Collaboration and competition	Virtual decision making and diffused control

5.16 Summary

The implications of virtual markets, virtual value chains and IOS have been discussed in the context of drivers and strategies for i-business but also have to be related to the execution of i-business strategies. This implies the development of:

- information-based business architecture strategy;
- integrated organizational systems;
- intelligent knowledge-based decision systems.

This will require an evolutionary approach to overall i-strategy typically encompassing a number of stages of website development. These should not be viewed as a stage growth model but rather embody the particular strategy of virtual culture as described in Chapter 3. Possible examples of these stages of development are shown in Table 5.6. It is essential to understand and incorporate the processes and business requirements of customers and suppliers and to build a foundation of trust. It is also essential to apply 'outside-the-box' thinking to capture information from sources of innovation and create the opportunity to share information in non-competitive situations.

The i-business that excels will learn from others.

References

Benchmarking Partners Inc. (1999) Driving Business Value Through E-Collaboration Sep. http://www.benchmarking.com

Berryman, K., Harrington, L., Layton-Rodin, D. and Rerolle, V. (1998) Electronic Commerce: Three Emerging Strategies, *The McKinsey Quarterly*, No. 1.

Burn, J.M. and Hackney, R. (2000) Strategies for I-Business Change in Virtual Markets: a co-evolutionary approach, *International Journal of e-Business Strategy Management*, Vol. 2, No. 2, 123–133.

Eisenhardt, K.E. and Galunic, D.C. (2000) Coevolving. At last, a Way to Make Synergies Work, *Harvard Business Review*, Jan–Feb, 91–101.

Holmstrom, J., Hoover Jr., W.E., Louhiluoto, P. and Vasara, A. (2000) The Other End of the Supply Chain, *The McKinsey Quarterly*, No. 1, 62–71.

Moore, J.F. (1997) *The Death of Competition: Leadership and Strategy in the Age of Business Ecosystems*, New York: Harper Business.

Mougayar, W. (1998) *Opening Digital Markets*, McGraw Hill.

Porter, M.E. (1985) Competitive Advantage: Creating and Sustaining Superior Performance, New York: Free Press.

Ticoll, D., Lowry, A. and Kalakota, R. (1998) Joined at the Bit, in: Don Tapscott, Alex Lowy and David Ticoll (eds) *Blueprint to the Digital Economy Creating Wealth in the Era of E-business*, McGraw-Hill.

Younger, R. (1999) *Supply Chain Challenges for Electronic Shopping*, FT Business.

6   Globalization and e-business strategies for SMEs

Utopia: 'The ideal state is small and the inhabitants few'

(Lao Zi)

6.1 Introduction

SMEs (sometimes referred to in this chapter as *small firms*) are defined in this chapter as firms with fewer than 500 employees. In the literature, SMEs are variously classified based on a wide range of criteria including number of employees, sales turnover, size of capital assets, etc. The most popular criterion is the number of employees (NOE) on a company's payroll. Most national accounting systems would define SMEs as those with NOE within the range of 1–500. These may be further sub-classified as micro with NOE < 5; small-sized $5 \leqslant$ NOE < 20; and medium-sized $20 \leqslant$ NOE < 500. The sub-classification may be further modified on the basis of industry sector. For example, in the manufacturing sector the NOE of a small-size firm may be in the order of 200 as compared with about 20 for a similar category in the services sector.

The SME sector is generally recognized as a window of opportunity for rejuvenating mature industries, creating new and innovative markets, and achieving rapid economic growth through employment generation and wealth creation in all economies. The availability of the Internet and web technologies provides unique advantages for SMEs to build effective global infrastructures in at least three ways:

- Internet-based infrastructures are relatively cheap; requiring significantly reduced capital investments over proprietary ones.

- They provide an ever converging and rich environment for effective business networking and interorganizational process management.
- They provide SMEs with access to a huge mass of consumers through e-business.

This means that e-business is an extremely attractive option for most SMEs, especially given the huge publicity and support provided by governments to push growth in the sector. Also, the unique features of small firms, namely flexibility of operations, relatively simple organizational structures, entrepreneurial culture and high propensity to engage in business networks, can be advantageous in the electronic marketplace.

However, along with these opportunities come threats. Most SMEs have little experience of operating in a global marketplace and rarely have formal procedures for strategic planning and management. This coupled with limited exposure to online markets and a slow take-up of IT makes e-business a daunting option for the majority of SMEs. e-business implies that SMEs can extend their environments without acquiring the traditional measures of large size, namely large employee base, vast capital resources, and extensive investment in proprietary networking technology. They do need, however, to understand how to exploit the virtual values associated with online information infrastructures in the most effective and appropriate manner for their business.

While there appears to be a lot of enthusiasm about the Internet and electronic business, current studies show that it is the minority of SMEs (OECD 2000) who are reaping significant benefits from the Internet. The majority of SMEs employ the Internet as a basic communications facility using it as a cost-effective alternative to the more traditional means (e.g. fax and telephone) of communication with partners or customers. The reasons for the relative low level of use include: uncertainty about benefits, low level of technological expertise, low commitment of owner/manager, poor understanding of the dynamics of the electronic marketplace and their inability to devise strategies to leverage online infrastructure for profit.

These challenges are not helped by the general lack of clearly defined frameworks for analysis of the entire process of strategy building, implementation and management with respect to this emerging global information economy. This chapter attempts to address the problem by providing a holistic framework for the study and design of global information infrastructure within the organizational context of SMEs. With such analytical tools and specific e-business strategies SMEs could and should capitalize on the opportunities offered in the electronic marketplace. The framework is supported by a number of international case studies centred on successful online SMEs.

6.2. Developing infrastructures for global e-business

6.2.1. Internet-based infrastructures

An Internet-based information infrastructure may be described as a three-tier model of technologies, systems and business applications (Tapscott *et al.* 1998), namely:

- *Level 1: Base technologies* – these include the underlying open-systems network platforms and devices supporting multi-environment integration and interoperability of systems across groups, organizations, industries, and regions. Examples are Internet-based network equipment and connections, network printers and scanners, and domain server computers.
- *Level 2: Network systems, server technologies, and applications development utilities* – these are the building blocks for electronic business applications and facilities. Generally, components at this level deal with network and process management, digital imaging and security management aspects of the infrastructure. Process management tools at this level form the basis of developing collaborative features into supply chain manage applications for e-business.
- *Level 3: e-business applications and solutions* – These include routine enterprise system management and web authoring programs (e.g. Microsoft FrontPage); client interactive communication and information management applications (e.g. Netscape Communicator and Microsoft Explorer Browsers); applications for online shopping and ordering (e.g. CART 32); secured payment facilities (e.g. Digicash) product delivery tracking programs. There is a growing market for complete e-business solutions, which provide a flexible and scalable environment for developing an Internet-based infrastructure to support e-business. Examples of these are Inte-Pay and IBM Net.commerce.

Competitive advantage is associated with the third level of infrastructure deployment. This is because as the underlying technologies and systems mature, relatively cheap and effective resources in the first two levels become affordable to most businesses. Indeed in the near future, real competitive perform-ance will be linked more and more to strategies employed by firms to manage the third level systems rather than to the mere ownership of them.

For a global-orientated SME, these strategies must be targeted at the transformation of the firm's environment through the functionalities associated with the Internet environment. These may be understood from two interrelated views of the Internet, namely:

- as an interorganizational system (IOS) platform;
- as the marketspace.

Each of these perspectives reveals potential benefits and contributions to the global strategy of the online SME. It is important to appreciate how these functionalities can be brought together to create a winning strategy for any particular business.

6.2.2 Internet – an inter-organizational system (IOS) platform

The Internet provides a platform for building flexible, adaptive and innovative organizational formats. The Internet's open systems architecture allows the SME to achieve a high level of integration of its enterprise-wide infrastructure by building on the installed bases of PCs, digital assets and competencies of clients, suppliers, partners and others on a global scale. Indeed, designing an infrastructure on the Net, allows the SME to focus on only a core set of ICT equipment, tools and personnel to support its operations. This can lead to huge savings in IT investment and management costs. The core assets and resour-ces may be distributed across wide geographical regions. Thus the cost of transactions with clients and partners can be significantly reduced leading to improved profit margins. Also, the increasing simplicity and familiarity of the user interfaces and online applications mean that employees, clients and other stakeholders can learn quickly and participate in knowledge creation and development of end products.

6.2.3 Internet – the marketspace

The Internet effectively simulates an electronic marketspace through its ability to intermediate among market players and to integrate diverse markets. As a *marketspace* it can reduce search costs and thereby enhance the efficiency of interorganizational transactions. Specifically, it has the capacity to lower the marginal costs of electronic business processes, reduce the criticality of many intermediaries and enable the efficient handling of large volumes of transactions leading to superior cost/performance for the business. However, these functionalities are not equally available to all businesses across all industries. The extent of disintermediation (i.e. the process of removing the role of middlemen) will depend on product and service characteristics. Information intensive businesses, especially the services sector, may witness a reduction in layers of intermediaries as compared with those in the manufacturing industries. There is also increasing recognition of the emergence of new forms of intermediaries which seek to exploit the emerging niches in the electronic marketspace. Thus it is critical for the global-orientated SME to articulate its current and future business directions and to analyse how these relate to developments in the electronic marketspace. This will allow it to choose the appropriate business model, infrastructure configuration and an effective management strategy.

In the next section we present a broad framework for managing an Internet-based information infrastructure that facilitates the achievement of extended market access and competitive performance of a global-orientated SME. A number of case examples will demonstrate how this online infrastructure can facilitate the extension of the scope of operations of the SME, especially in:

- managing core organizational activities which may now be dispersed over multiple geographical sites;
- mediation of the cooperative efforts between business partners and other stakeholders;
- management of the client community;
- development of a consistent global image of business and products.

The cases also reveal that to be successful, an online enterprise needs a strategy that aligns its business logic/model with its infrastructure configuration on a continuous basis.

6.3 Strategic framework for managing a global SME business

Figure 6.1 describes the broad framework for managing a global e-business strategy within an SME context. Readers will note that this builds upon the conceptual framework introduced in

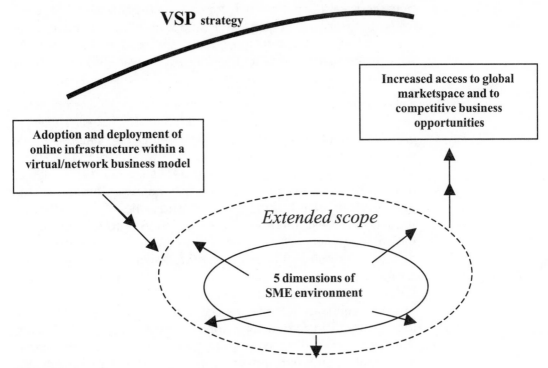

Figure 6.1
Internet-enabled transformation of business scope

Chapter 3. For the online SME a useful perspective to adopt in managing its global orientation is the virtual strategic perspective (VSP) which emphasizes the management of values associated with the electronic market environment through the innovative use of its online infrastructure. The core elements of the strategy are:

- Organizational system redefinition, which involves the choice of a business model to align the strategic objectives with its business activities as well as the electronic market environment.
- Transformation of the scope of business of an SME.
- Virtual infrastructure management.

In the following sections brief descriptions of each of the elements are provided.

6.4 The virtual strategic perspective

Virtual organizations are those which employ extensive networked information infrastructures to attract resources and manage a value chain which transcends organizational boundaries, geographical regions and time zones. Such firms deal in products which lend themselves to a virtual market, namely mass-customized goods and services produced and deliverable anywhere, anytime and in any variety.

The concept of organizational virtuality is a characteristic of the firm's entire environment. It defines *the perception of globalness* held by its stakeholders about the business scope with respect to its presence, processes, products and relationships. It is associated with features such as flexibility of operations, responsiveness to market changes, agility in the management of interfirm relations and other linkages within industry. The exploitation of these features through the strategic management of a global infrastructure platform can enhance the perception of an extended scope of business even though in reality the enterprise may be operating with a limited physical scope. In other words, the firm may be able to project itself and its products as being available at multiple locations and in varied time zones. Venkatraman and Henderson (1998) refer to the concept of managing a virtual enterprise as virtual organizing and we here apply the term VSP to this overall e-business strategy.

6.5 Choice of online business model

An online business model is a generic organizational format adapted to the electronic market environment and emphasizing the use of Internet-based information infrastructure to do business. While there exists a wide spectrum of online formats for e-businesses (as described in Chapter 3) those relevant to SMEs may be broadly categorized under three generic online business models (Table 6.1).

Each category may have sub-classifications, which can only represent generalized descriptions with significant overlap. For example, portals and electronic malls may both be described as virtual communities since both represent a collection of a wide variety of services and service providers working as a community. The unique feature of virtual communities is that they provide a sense of a uniform marketspace to all players including manufacturer, service providers, suppliers, and customers.

Table 6.1 Online business models

Online business model	Features	Examples
Virtual face e-Shop	• Providing an extra space for presenting organization and products to a wider market • Usually involves a single enterprise • Limited commitment to common business goals in relationships with others	• Harris Technology • Boots Online • Hawaiian Greenhouse
Virtual alliance	• Involve a number of firms sharing resources and competencies to develop some product offering • Site may represent the common interface for the group or may place varied degrees of emphasis on a focal firm while providing visibility to the alliance • Significant use of online infrastructure and e-commerce technologies • Cross-reference to sites of participating firms	• SCB Co-op • LAA
Virtual Community e-Mall portals	• Represents an electronic marketspace involving a large number of firms and grouping of other online models	• Best of Italy • Sofcom

6.5.1 Virtual face

This model is similar to that discussed in section 3.4.1. In its basic format, the enterprise usually exists as a single business entity with some online presence primarily to advertise itself and its products. The business may also be organized around the virtual face model as the primary point of access to their entire business and products. Harris Technology, Sydney, and Boots Online, Melbourne, are typical examples of online SMEs employing the virtual face business model to enhance their competitive performance. While Harris Technology targets the Australian national market in computer related products, Boots Online is a global-orientated SME selling to worldwide markets. Both businesses have witnessed substantial growth in sales and profit margins within two years of going online. In an elaborate form of the virtual face model, as in the case of Harris Technology, the SME may undertake extensive business activities online, including sourcing of resources and services, communication and collaboration with other firms, and the management of its customer base. This will usually require a significant redefinition of business processes to enhance the information processing aspects and to ensure a high level of integration and interoperability with the stakeholder environment. Another requirement will be the development of enhanced online information management skills in employees.

6.5.2 Virtual alliance

An SME employing this model participates in a cluster or group of autonomous businesses both online and offline, and organizes its core operations and offerings around the shared resources, competencies and markets that the group creates. An example of this type is SCB Co-op, Scotland. The strategic advantage of the online infrastructure is to provide a cost-effective collaborative medium for pooling critical resources to achieve the objectives of individual participants. In the case of SCB Co-op the online infrastructure has enabled very small traditional Scottish breweries to market their products under a common label across the UK and globally. Leading Agents in Australia (LAA) is another example of a virtual face business model. Even though each member of the alliance maintains an elaborate website, their alliance is not uniformly represented online as a single site. The main gains of the online infrastructure for the group is fast access to information that they share about regional opportunities. Also extensive referrals to each other provide potential clients and visitors to their sites an assurance of dealing with a well-connected group of professionals in the Australian real estate market. This increases trust in their services and can be a source of competitive advantage.

6.5.3 Virtual community

The third generic category of online business model is the *virtual community*, which is a large collection of firms in the online market, including other stakeholders such as customers and government agencies. In that environment the focal SME is highly integrated with those of others and its separate existence is hardly discernible to stakeholders of the community. Examples of a virtual community are portal services such as BOI (Best of Italy) Srl. and Sofcom.com.au. In both examples, the virtual community owner supplies and manages the online infrastructure on behalf of participating SMEs. This reduces the need for substantial investments in technology and infrastructure management. Participant enterprises can concentrate on selling their products. On the other hand, clients are offered a one-stop access to a wide range of goods and services and at reduced prices due to the relatively low cost associated with marketing and distribution channel management for the vendors.

6.6 Transforming the SME environment

Tetteh and Burn (2001) suggest that central to the global strategy of the online SME is the virtual transformation of five key dimensions (or attributes) of the SME environment. These attributes, which capture the scope of business operations of the SME, are:

- *Size/value of assets and resources;*
- *Market coverage and product mix;*
- *Activities and processes;*
- *Linkages and relationships within environment;* and
- *Locational diversity/scope.*

Together they form the **S-M-A-L-L** framework.

The attributes focus on those aspects of the SME that impact on its ability to reach wider markets; access extensive resources; enhance, diversify and integrate its activities; manage collaborative engagements with others; and deal with temporal and locational diversity issues. By gaining a wider market the SME is placed in a favourable position to enhance its competitive performance estimated as a composite measure of a number of performance variables including value of sales, profits, enhanced global image, increased market access and broader customer base. Leveraging the online infrastructure can lead to an extension of the dimensions of the SME to varying degrees. The extent of transformation depends on the fit between the firm's business model, its strategic direction and the appropriate infrastructure management strategy. Table 6.2 provides detailed descriptions of each attribute and the associated organizational variables. For any SME, relative values can be assigned to each of the attributes using a set of discrete values low, medium high on a Likert-type quantitative estimation.

6.7 Virtual infrastructure management

The extent of contribution from the infrastructure will depend on the information intensity of the business value chain. The information intensity of the value chain derives from four

Table 6.2 S-M-A-L-L – key attributes of SME environment

Size (S)

(i)   Number of employees
(ii) Number of branch offices
(iii) Value of assets
(iv) Annual turnover of business
(v)   Investments in IT

This attribute may be defined in terms of number of employees, sales turnover, and assets, etc. It may also include the size or investment in infrastructure. The adoption and management of a successful online infrastructure strategy may result in an increase or decrease in size.

Market (M)

(i)   Share of market (value of sales)
(ii) Product mix (variety and novelty)
(iii) Number of states/regions covered

This attribute describes the firm's share of the market and the number and variety of products. By developing an online presence it is possible to extend its markets and reach out to a wider customer base. It is also possible to develop new products and offerings based on exposure to opportunities made available to the firm going online.

Activities and processes (A)

(i)   Nature of activities
(ii) Information intensity of activities and products
(iii) Level of electronic mediation
(iv) Changes in products/processes

Application of online infrastructure can lead to increased integration and enhanced efficiency of processes. The infrastructure can also support reengineering of business processes and to enhance the value added. New opportunities can emerge. Innovative products may be developed through the application of the infrastructures.

Linkages (L_1)

(i)   Number of strategic partners
(ii) Nature of partnerships/networking (regularity, permanence)
(iii) Type of contractual arrangements

This attribute refers to relationships and cooperative arrangements, which span the firm's internal and external environment. Also implied here is the frequency of forming and breaking links with others.

Locational Diversity (L_2)

(i)   Spread of regional/international branches

This describes the geographical spread of sites from which the firm's core operations are conducted. It also involves the diversity of time zones that the enterprise can effectively manage. With an online infrastructure individual or small groups of employees may work from wider geographical locations and/or diverse time zones without establishing branch offices. On the other hand, the online infrastructure may allow concentration of total workspace.

related factors: nature of partnerships' internal arrangements, nature of market or industry, and the product offerings. The analysis of the information processes in each of these factors would reveal the aspects of the business that may be transformed by leveraging the online infrastructure. These factors also provide the basis of virtual infrastructure management by seeking continuously to enhance the alignment between these factors while increasing the firm's ability to work with them across multiple sites and time zones.

Employing an adaptation of Henderson and Venkatraman's (1993) strategic alignment model, Figure 6.2 shows the interaction of the SME's strategic objectives, information infrastructure and its relevant business environment. The firm seeking to leverage

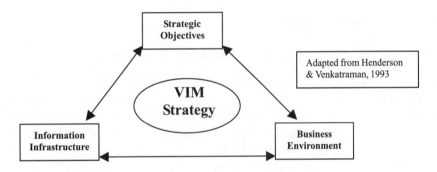

Figure 6.2
VIM strategy

its information technology infrastructure must work out a close fit between these three aspects. In general, the strategic objectives of an online SME will relate to seeking increased access to wider markets and resources through extension of its environment. The firm's infrastructure (based on Internet technologies) and its industry environment (i.e. electronic business) present a virtual market environment. Thus it becomes critical to identify and exploit those features of the infrastructure that facilitate and optimize virtual values in the business chain. The strategy for alignment and exploitation of the online infrastructure to achieve increased virtuality may be described as a virtual infrastructure management (VIM) strategy.

Based on the above discussions on virtual organizing, an effective virtual infrastructure management strategy would include among others the following aspects:

• Develop components of the infrastructure that add value to the business chain.

- Install networking features – e.g. to facilitate collaborative effort and linkages among stakeholders.
- Use of infrastructure to develop virtual values of process, products and image – e.g. through customer interaction with website content including product information, use of graphics for retention and encouragement to revisit, cultivate value for virtual products.
- Cultivate information skills and virtual culture in customers – e.g. through the website tutorial, development of virtual communities (e.g. newsgroups, chatlists, forums).

The following cases illustrate various aspects of the infrastructure management to extend the business environment of online SMEs and how this leads to enhanced market performance.

6.8 Case studies

6.8.1 Boots Online

Boots Online is an example of a global SME employing the virtual face model. The company is the online shopfront of Stitching Horse Bootery, a small business established in 1977 as an authorized retailer of R.M. William brand of boots, leatherwear and travel accessories. The Melbourne-based company established the online shopfront in 1995 with a total investment of AU$3000. The company's strategic goal in going online was to market the best of Australian boots and leatherwear to a worldwide market. With a staff of only four people this company has transformed itself from a local agent of a renowned product to a global business with over 15% of total sales from online customers. Over 95% of its online customers are located overseas. Boots Online has reaped significant benefits from its online strategy. Within a year of establishing an online presence the company achieved huge increase in sales (15%) with six additional sales per week. It makes about AU$1500 worth of online sales per week and total company sales of AU$75 000 are projected to double in one year. Profit margins on online sales have increased due to reduced inventory costs. Also the company has seen an increase in customer satisfaction over the period – www.bootsonline.com.au

6.8.2 Hawaiian Greenhouse, Inc.

Hawaiian Greenhouse, Inc. is a family owned business located in Pahoa on the island of Hawaii. The installation of an online infrastructure has resulted in a remarkable transformation of the business scope and led to increased profitability. The company, established since 1965, has been growing anthuriums and other tropical flowers and foliage and shipping them worldwide. Traditionally it has thrived on growing large crops and selling to a small group of wholesale customers who in turn market them worldwide. The effects of globalization and intensifying competition from many other growers in the region have prompted the company to rethink its business logic. Focusing on retailing as a more lucrative sales channel, the company set out in 1997 to exploit the capabilities of the Internet to increase its sales volume and expand its customer base, while keeping its operational costs to a minimum. It started by automating its order fulfilment, accounting and customer-tracking functions with an IBM e-business solution based on Lotus Notes and Lotus Domino application environments. Since then, the company has developed a fully functional web-enabled shopfront based on the Lotus Domino.Merchant. There has been a complete transformation of core business processes. As recalled by the manager of the company: 'When we first started, we were manually doing all the work orders, message cards, labels and so on ... At present, the online infrastructure supports a simplified and fully automated sales and distribution process.' In less than a year of building the virtual shopfront, Hawaiian Greenhouse's e-business had grown tremendously. Currently, over 1400 customers visit its site each month, generating 10–15% of the company's new orders. The company now makes three times as much from its retail business compared to the operating value as a wholesale business. Also it expects to double retail sales within another year. Other performance improvements include: 100% annual growth in retail sales, 100% ROI in 18 months, 10–15% revenue from online orders, 50% reduction in processing time, and improved customer services. The business plans to add new products to its portfolio including the possibility of marketing products of their competitors on its site – www.hawaiian-greenhouse.com

6.8.3 Harris Technology (HT)

Harris Technology is another Australian SME, which has transformed its scope of operations from a metropolitan base in Sydney to cover the entire Australian market through its online business. HT is a computer technology reseller established over 11 years ago and listed as one of Australia's top 100 fastest growing private companies for five consecutive years. The company online shopfront has yielded significant benefits and increased sales and its share of the computer equipment retail market. In its first year of going online the company made AU$1 million in e-business and another AU$3 million in its second year. HT currently employs about 80 staff all of whom are actively involved in the use of the online infrastructure. The online site was designed, built and managed by an in-house team. The company considers its website to be a great success: 'Our Web-presence has been so successful for us that we believe almost any business would benefit from a well presented Website.'

The website is designed around the QUIDS (Quotations Inventory, Distribution, and Sales) database. The QUIDS database was written in Microsoft FoxPro and contains over 30,000 products and 6000 customer entities. It enables tracking all aspects of HT business including sales, serial numbers and bills of material and profitability. The interesting feature of HT's online system is that the QUIDS database is common to all its key stakeholders. Suppliers and customers see the same information (pricing, stock availability, images and text) as seen by HT staff. For example, Tech Pacific, the company's main supplier, shares its stock availability and pricing with QUIDS each day via the Internet. Customers also interact with the database's inventory in the same way as employees make queries to the system. Web pages are generated upon request by assembling data elements associated with each product (e.g. images, texts, downloadable drivers and site links).

Using the integrated environment of the website, HT's employees can manage electronic transfer of stock and ordering information from all key stakeholders of the company (i.e. manufacturers, distributors, resellers, and end users). The facility also enable clients to scan product information, make orders, as well as track the process of delivery. Bank cheques, telegraphic transfer, and major credit cards can be used to make payment. Another interesting feature of the website is the 'live show room' which provides real-time snapshots of HT's physical showroom – www.ht.com.au

6.8.4 Scotland's Craft Brewers Co-operative (SCB Co-op)

SCB Co-op is an online SME made up of six Scottish SMEs and a bottling plant. The co-op was formed to deliver global sales and marketing functions for the participant enterprises that specialized in traditionally brewed Scottish beers in Lugton, Scotland. The distinctive feature of SCB Co-op is that all its beers are traditionally brewed using Scottish malt with no artificial additives. The Co-op was formed to pool the limited resources of individual SMEs to create a winning business image and a competitive product brand. Products of members are promoted under the Scotland Craft Brewer Co-operative brand name to large UK supermarkets. The Co-op's strategic objectives in going online are to access global markets, expand regional market share, create jobs and increase revenues. Through the website the Co-op has achieved significant performance growth that would have been difficult to achieve through conventional marketing strategies. Products of the Co-op have been submitted to the Canadian Liquor Board for sampling. As a result of online strategy, SCB Co-op is forecasted to create 75 new jobs within a year and then build a brand name to rival better known traditional brewers on a world scale.

In order to overcome the lack of technical skills and financial resources for developing an online infrastructure, the Co-op chose the IBM HomePage Creator service, which enabled it to establish the working website at a very low cost within a few days. The simplicity and low cost has made it possible for SCB Co-op to concentrate on its core operations of coordination and the participant SMEs, and developing a competitive global brand.

The site features product information, nutritional information and recipes and links to some of its major partners. One of the major business partners is ASDA, which is one of Britain's largest supermarket chains. The Co-op's site integrates seamlessly with that of ASDA. Clients in Britain, or those planning a visit, may also purchase the Co-op brand from any of the 31 ASDA stores across the UK. The ASDA website features an innovative search engine, Store Finder, for locating any ASDA store by entering the name of your location. Search results provide lists of nearby ASDA stores with details about address (including telephone and fax), distance from central location, and a map. All these extend the infrastructure commanded by SCB Co-op in developing its global marketing strategy – ww.lugton.co.uk

6.8.5 Leading Agents of Australia (LAA)

Leading Agents of Australia (LAA) is an example of a virtual alliance where participating firms maintain their independent websites. There is no common site representing their common interests as in the case of SCB Co-op, UK. LAA is a network of nine autonomous real estate SMEs operating across different states in Australia. Two key participating companies are Acton Consolidate Ltd, Perth, and Patrick Dixon Real Estate, Brisbane. Acton has a total of seven branches across the Perth Metropolitan Area and is one of the leading firms in the Western Australian real estate market. The other partner firms also enjoy significant market shares in their respective state markets. The members of the network share a common business philosophy, namely: 'commitment to the highest ethical standards and excellence in client service'. While each partner firm maintains autonomous business strategies for developing their competitive strategy, they join effort when it comes to making a deal in other states. For example, partners sharing market information and competencies. It is clear that the nature of the industry plays a part in choosing the collaborative strategy. In the real estate industry local information and knowledge about products are crucial in making a good deal. As stated on one of the affiliate's websites these firms 'are leaders in their respective markets and the interchange of property listings brings numerous qualified inter-state prospects' to their various operations. In relation to the management of their online business, the various partners maintain business links within the real estate industry and also with IT and e-commerce development companies. For example, Acton Consolidated reports a strategic alliance with The Globe.com.au and Spin Technologies in the development of their website ActonNet.

6.8.6 Sofcom

Sofcom is a Melbourne company acting as an electronic intermediary, which provides, in addition to other online content publishing, a virtual shopping mall for about 60 virtual storefronts. Sofcom may be described as an example of a virtual community. Members of the community engage in extensive linkages with each other and with a host of e-business service providers through Sofcom. The mall advertises over 4835 products in about 60 stores. There are ten categories of stores including: Apparel; automobile; business services; computers and electronics; gifts and collectable; home design; perfumery and jewellery; entertainment. Other electronic market services and facilities provided by Sofcom to its virtual community are: business information; Internet directories publishing; websites/ shop hosting; links to the Australian stock exchange; business newsletter; and advisory services.

Sofcom has an extensive online infrastructure to support its product lines and to manage the virtual stores of other businesses. All transactions at Sofcom pass through Sofcom's SSL secure server. The site offers an online Store Builder facility for potential online storeowners. The facility takes potential store owners step by step through the process of setting up a storefront at Sofcom and doing business online. There is a flat charge of AU$40 per month for stores available to the public and selling. Potential storeowners may develop and test run a store for free – www.sofcom.com.au

6.9 Mapping the transformation

Table 6.3 presents a mapping of some of the online processes from the perspective of both clients and focal SMEs to the key infrastructure components employed in delivering each functionality. Table 6.4 summarizes the case examples of business scope transformation resulting from the successful management of Internet-based infrastructures in a number of online SMEs.

In all cases, there is a common thread linking the strategic intents of the enterprise to go online and the choice of infrastructure components. While not all made explicit commitment to extend all the attributes defined in the framework, analysis shows that these were consistently modified directly or indirectly as a result of the application of the online infrastructure. Also, the benefits from virtual transformation of business scope always led to significant improvement in competitive performance even where it was not easy to quantify.

How can an SME considering entering this global market learn from these experiences?

6.10 Developing a strategic plan

Cragg (1998) identified four components of Internet strategy that may be useful for SMEs to consider when engaging in online commerce (see Table 6.5). The four components are *goals*, *content*, *process* and *functional*.

The *goals* component of an Internet strategy is sub-categorized into primary and secondary goals. An SME should incorporate both primary and secondary goals within the overall Internet strategy, in order to identify exactly what they expect from an online presence. The benefit of incorporating primary and secondary goals is a method for SMEs to recognize potential

Table 6.3 Mapping of online transactions to key infrastructure components

Process/ activity	Description		Key infrastructure components
	Client/stakeholders	**Focal online enterprise**	
Information search and data transfer	View/scan web pages, navigate multiple and widely distributed sources, submit request for information, exchange information	Capture and process online activity of visitors, develop profiles of products and stakeholders	• Browser/navigational software • Client/product profile database servers • Search engines • Data capture/transfer utilities • Multimedia communication facilities • Web authoring software
Selection and customization	Make choices, configure according to preferences, sample products, fill shopping basket		• Shopping cart software • Multimedia presentation software
Order placement and fund transfer	Fill out order form, provide details of credit/debit card, give details of preferred delivery location and date	Provide secure environment for online shopping and trading with partners, enable use of certificates and authentication procedures	• Software for secure online ordering and authentication procedures • Invoicing and billing applications • Negotiation and trading software for business-to-business processes
Product delivery	Online tracking of package delivery	Provide use of tracking software, manage relationships with courier services contractors online	• Package tracking software (e.g. DHL and FedEx tracking systems)
After-sales activities	Visit website to find out about product usage, upgrades and other offering, join user communities to discuss product quality and service needs	Develop feedback mechanisms on product quality and client support, provide upgrade details, information on new offers, create or sponsor product user groups	• e-mail filtering software
Online advertising	n/a	Gather and present advertising information from multiple sources, monitor responses to advertisements	
Work flow management and business relationship management	n/a	Automated coordination of activities of employees and partners across distributed locations and time regions	• Network management utilities • Process management/monitoring systems

Table 6.4 Application of SMALL: transformation of SME environments

Online SME	Transformation of attributes				
	Size	Market	Activities	Linkages	Locational diversity
Boots Online	Reduced physical assets, inventory and warehousing facilities reduced need to recruit more personnel to manage global clientele	Expanded market coverage local to global, increased sales from international clients Potential to develop new products in tourist information and hotel reservation	Increased simplicity, flexibility and automation of sales and distribution	Increased linkages supporting service providers (e.g. ISP and software companies, courier services – DHL)	Hardly changed
Hawaiian Greenhouse	Reduced need to recruit more personnel	Direct retail instead of through wholesalers, potential for new products and diversification	Automation of entire sale and distribution process, increased flexibility and market responsiveness and efficiency	Relationships with courier services and e-business solution providers (Datahouse and IBM)	Hardly changed, able to reach a worldwide market without need for regional branches
Best of Italy Sofcom	Expanded effective size of business, infrastructure and resources as a group of companies	Huge collection of diverse Italian products Worldwide coverage Prospects to develop other products, e.g. Happy Gift	Increased flexibility and efficiency through automation and enhanced information management	High and diverse links and e-business relationships among many participant firms, business services providers, e-commerce solution providers Also alliance with major global companies such as FedEx and Western Union	Reduction in locational scope of participating SMEs since operation from a single outlet
SCB Co-op LAA	Increase in effective size through pooling resources, and products of group of seven SMEs	Extended access to market from local to national and global; development of competitive global brand	Effective coordination of group of SMEs, enhanced efficiency and cost savings in marketing/ distribution of individual products	Development of strong business relationships among participant SMEs, effective management of business relationships with some of the major service providers (e.g. ParcelForce) and distribution channels (e.g. ASDA)	Concentration of location to one website as a one-stop for the participant groups

economic benefits, and to indicate that increased sales can only be considered as one indicator of success.

The *content* dimension of an Internet strategy identifies the main uses of an SME website. This component enables an SME to clarify what the site started with; its current major uses, what the site is for and future plans for the site.

The *process* component is basically a method to identify whether the initiation and leadership of the strategy was from the CEO level or further down the chain of command and whether the site was built utilizing internal or external expertise.

Finally, the *functional* component of Internet strategy examines the functions of the website. This could incorporate business-to-business electronic commerce, business-to-consumer electronic commerce, or the implementation of a method for increasing and retaining customers.

The majority of SMEs do not employ information technology managers or specialists and information technology decisions and operational factors tend to be relegated to the realm of the accountant, manager or owner/operator and are mostly seen as a peripheral and sometimes annoying business factor. This lack of internal IS expertise also impacts on the SME sector's ability to design, develop and promote websites. As such, SMEs tend to rely on external consultants to design and implement their websites.

Table 6.5 SME internet strategy (after Cragg 1998)

Goal	Example
primary	to reach an international market
secondary	to market site to potential customers
Content	
started with	e-mail, catalogue, order form
major use	marketing/promotion
WWW site for	product distribution
future plans	introduce new functions
Process	
led by	owner/manager
whose initiative	internal
built	external
Function	
functions of site	business-to-business, business-to-consumer

6.11 The consultant engagement process

It is estimated that by 2005 the global Internet consultancy market will be worth $US50 billion (Evamy 1999). In the UK alone, website design consultants' growth in earnings have increased from 76% to 133% involving millions of dollars in consultancy fees.

The success or failure of an SME engaging a website design consultant involves a number of issues. First, it may be the SME's first attempt at engaging an external consultant and the SME may lack the relevant knowledge and experience required for successful engagement. Second, website design consultants are often SMEs themselves, and in the current climate of accelerating growth in the electronic commerce area, website design consultants are often business start-ups and consequently may lack experience in negotiating successful contracts. Finally, consultants tend to view SMEs as one-off jobs and may consequently lack commitment to the project:

small firms were viewed as one-shot opportunities, offering no potential for establishing a long-term relationship. Consultants . . . would sell the small firms software and hardware, put together a network, and move on to the next company. (McCollum 1999, p. 46)

Prior to consultant engagement an SME should have a clearly defined Internet strategy but should also understand the need to align business processes with website strategy through the creation of a new e-business model. They should further identify the amount of time and effort the SME contributes to the project and the critical importance of maintaining a clear understanding of the role of the SME and the role of the consultant throughout all stages of the project. This means that the SME must review all the following steps:

- Identify and define Internet strategy.
- Align current business processes with new e-business model.
- Assess internal capabilities.
- Identify and address specific organizational roles.
- Accommodate evolving project objectives.

If the review of capabilities points to the need for an external consultant then the following steps must also be considered:

- evaluate internal resources available for the project;
- canvass the market for prospective consulting firms;
- develop a request for proposal (RFP);
- check references;

- evaluate proposals;
- assess self and consultant compatibility;
- select a firm;
- negotiate the contract (including deliverables, cut-off dates, penalties);
- announce the selection;
- continue review and refinement of mutual and individual responsibilities;
- continue monitoring and control of progress; and
- post-engagement evaluation of the service.

6.12 Summary

This chapter has outlined a framework for analysing an online SME based on the concepts of virtual organization and global information technology management. The *S-M-A-L-L* framework describes five dimensions of the business that may be transformed with the strategic application of information technology. These are the size of resources, market coverage, activities and processes, linkages and locational scope. Effective extension of the SME's environment along these dimensions should increase its access to resources and opportunities and enhance its ability to compete in the global market. The transforming factors are the firm's chosen business model, the technological infrastructure and the virtual infrastructure management strategy. Also corporate vision of the future, top management commitment, nature of business, and level of adoption of expertise with IT are relevant to the virtual infrastructure management approach to the global strategy of online SMEs. Once the small business has performed an extensive review of its current and extended global environment it can then develop a strategy for website development and engage a consultant where necessary for effective implementation. Following the stages suggested for consultant engagement does not guarantee success but will at least provide a structure enabling the SME to negotiate more effectively and a contract with specified deliverables. It has been our experience that even with this, however, the SME is still easy prey for the consultancy market.

<table>
<tr><td>**Appendix 1**</td></tr>
</table>

Case: Preparing to start an online business from scratch

Summary

This case presents a typical situation that faces many young entrepreneurs as they plan to enter the electronic business industry. Mostly, they are motivated by the popular stories about the phenomenal performance of some of the start-up online companies like Amazon.com which have grown to become large global businesses through innovative exploitation of online infrastructures together with winning business management strategies. There are, however, very important issues to deal with in developing an online business. Particularly, strategies to develop the appropriate organizational infrastructure and manage it successfully represent a critical input. In this case you are given the chance to apply the principles outlined in this chapter to help these entrepreneurs start right towards a successful global online business.

Introduction

Charles Evans and Dell Peterson are two young MBA graduates aspiring to develop an online business, which will eventually offer products worldwide. The company, which is yet to be registered as a corporation would be expected to be positioned in the information services industry. Particularly, they hope to deal in specialized information and technology solutions for the small travel agencies and associated travel, tourism and hospitality companies.

Dell, an immigrant from Netherlands, studied Finance for her MBA degree and is currently employed in a home finance company in Adelaide. Her employer is a national company with branches in all the states of Australia. As a financial analyst her work involves regular interaction with the various branch offices both through electronic communications systems as well as planned meetings every quarter in one of the states.

Evans currently works with an international organization in the IT consulting business in Australia. His job includes researching e-commerce solutions for SMEs. Having studied computer engineering and information systems for his first and second degrees respectively, he feels he has the background expertise to develop a global SME based on the Internet. Particularly, Evans plans to develop a niche business in strategic management consulting for SMEs in Australia. Product offerings of the company would include electronic market research, infrastructure management solutions and business alliance brokering. Evans is keen to learn about the appropriate strategies with respect to aspects such as the business location, number of branch offices across the country, IT equipment and online infrastructure, and the types of alliances to form in order to make his business successful. He is also interested in developing a business value chain that is effectively aligned with the chosen industry and the electronic market environment from the beginning.

They plan to run the business from Melbourne, Australia, where in their estimation there exists a vibrant e-commerce industry and therefore cheaper access to Internet resources. They also planned to work with a team of about eight persons, mainly with backgrounds in information systems, technology management, and finance. They intend to recruit a couple of others for routine administrative support. In the bid to get going, Evans has already applied for a website address with the international Internet registrar, InterNic. That means that very soon the company must decide on a web hosting service provider with the possibility of providing a total e-business infrastructure solution.

Questions

1 Briefly outline the opportunities in the chosen industry for the prospective enterprise.
2 What opportunities can the company take advantage of in developing some Internet presence and later exploiting some online infrastructure as part of its routine business?
3 State with appropriate examples the key issues associated with an online business in the chosen area, specifying what must be considered as core competencies of the start-up firm.
4 Using the five attributes of a typical SME, discuss the relative merits of (a) doubling the proposed number of staff, (b) having employees working from locations in three states – WA, SA and ACT – and (c) increasing the number and complexity of business relationships within industry.
5 What Internet technologies and systems would you recommend to form the core of the start-up business. What are some of the foreseeable developments in infrastructure as the business grows.

6 What would you advise as the minimum level of information management competence of any future employees of the company?

7 What strategic reasons might there be for joining or forming an alliance with other businesses?

8 How will these reasons change in the near future and in the long term?

9 What are the key lessons from the Harris Technology and Boots Online companies for the new enterprise?

| Appendix 2 | DiBLOCKKA.com: Building a successful online business on the Internet |

A Teaching Case on Online Business Infrastructure Management

The authors gratefully acknowledge the assistance of Emmanuel Tetteh in preparing this case.

Abstract

This teaching case provides material for discussing the key aspects of strategic management of Internet infrastructure and e-business strategies in knowledge and business services organizations. The case focuses on a small firm with a global orientation, seeking to build and develop profitable operations through the exploitation of an Internet-based infrastructure to access extensive and cheap resources from diverse global sources. The basis of strategic management for such firms is an understanding and effective management of virtual values of the global electronic economy.

Introduction

The DiBLOCKKA Research Company Ltd is a young technology research organization established in mid-1996 in Durban, South Africa. DiBLOCKKA specializes in research consulting in technology innovation and management. With an annual revenue of US$2.5 million and total digital assets worth US$7 million for 1999, the company aims to become a global player in an exciting industry sector with others like Forrester Research Inc., Jupiter Communications Inc., and Nua Ltd. It, however, recognizes that the key to success lies in the exploitation of its knowledge assets and knowledge management competencies as well as innovative management of virtual values associated with an Internet-based business infrastructure. Particularly important is how the business manages its widely dispersed employees and business infrastructure spanning five continents.

DiBLOCKKA Research is the brainchild of a young computer systems engineer, Dan Blocks, who holds degrees in Electrical Engineering and Business Administration with a major in Information Systems. Since graduating in 1989, the CEO has aspired to develop a career in research and consultancy through the exploitation of skills in information and communications technology. The company is the realization of that dream after a number of years working for a computer systems reseller and later national technology policy institute, both in Durban. An important factor in the development of the company from a 'network of collaborating professionals' to an active profit-orientated online company is, as Blocks puts it, the capacity to 'learn-by-doing on the Internet'. The Internet, according to CEO Blocks, 'provides a global environment with huge resources and opportunities for the information capable and visionary play-ers'. Also, most of the members including the CEO have had extensive exposure to state-of-the-art applications of IT during their continuing education in western countries. For example, the Vice President, Kennett Musenge, worked with the national electricity company in Durban as systems planning officer and maintains an active interest in computer technology systems both at work and privately.

Organizational structure and work arrangement

DiBLOCKKA wants to remain a small firm comprising knowl-edge workers who enjoy significant autonomy in terms of work style, time–space management and culture. Currently, there are 12 staff members including 11 professional partners and one logistic management officer in charge of supply of materials needed on project-by-project basis. The company's Durban office has four staff members, including the CEO and the logistics management officer. The firm maintains a flexible management environment where partners enjoy near equal authority. Members who are located in different international cities agree to meet in project teams (either physically or electronically) to discuss issues and share notes on progress in current projects. Each of the partners has extensive experience in varied professions, for example a director in a public policy organization in Europe, a systems manager in a national electricity company in Africa, a university professor in informa-tion systems in Singapore and a computer systems engineer in the United States of America.

Work is organized as task-orientated projects around teams made up of organizational members and other partners and collaborators in other companies. For example, one of the current projects is the development of a national infrastructure assessment and strategy (NIAS) for an East Asian country. The project involves three staff members of DeBLOCKKA located in the Asian region. The NIAS project team also involves external partners including two technology policy workers from the client country, a local telecommunications expert and a World Bank economics expert on Asia also based in that country.

Business infrastructure

The common denominator of the organization's global business orientation is its application of network computer and communications technologies with all members possessing advanced user skills. The company runs virtually on the globally dispersed network of personal computers used by organizational members who live and work across the globe. The core infrastructure components, comprising the company's two Internet server computer and workstation resources (including printers, scanners, fax machine and photocopiers), are located in the company's office in Durban.

At present the company has installed an electronic business system over an Internet website. The website features a rich presentation of content on product offerings as well as business tools for online ordering of the company's publications. The online ordering system employs data encryption and digital signature protocols based on the Secure Electronic Transaction (SET®) standard. In the near future it hopes to run its site as the common interface for all interactions with its stakeholder community (employees, external partners, clients, suppliers, etc.). In that connection the company is planning to install facilities to support collaborative work among its employees and external partners.

Business activities

The core business activities of the company are knowledge intensive. They include information search and management, research, group discussions, analysis of data, synthesis of ideas, development of policies, strategies as well as preparation of reports and other publications.

The use of networked information and communications systems largely on the Internet platform enable collaborative effort such as group discussions, information sharing, collaborative authoring of publications, remote participation in project management activities, and relationship management among external business partners and individuals.

Product portfolio

The main value offerings of DeBLOCKKA include:

- Business and national information infrastructure research in the area of telecommunications (landline and mobile technology), Internet and e-commerce systems.
- Technology innovation management consulting.
- Training and consultancy in technology policy development in developing and newly industrialized economies.
- Industrial design and intellectual property (IP) services.

Currently much of the firm's activities are in the first three areas and these are targeted for an urgent agenda to establish a global clientele.

As a foundation project, the company undertook a two-year study on the technology management practice in one of the African countries with a Danish Government financial grant. This project provided significant exposure to the international community in technology services consulting as well as helping the company to build a wealth of strategic business partners around the world. The National Infrastructure Assessment and Strategy (NIAS) project, still in progress, is another example of a widely distributed work arrangement employed at DeBLOCKKA which is only made possible by the availability of a global inter-organizational system built on Internet technologies.

Business performance and profitability

DeBLOCKKA has made great strides in performance considering its size and resources. Over the last four years, it has built a reputation as one of the most successful small technology research consulting companies especially in developing countries. It has accumulated a huge collection of digital and knowledge assets, e.g. publications, industry survey data and country specific research data on developing economies. Revenue for the year 1998–1999 was double that of the previous financial period and was about US$2.5 million. The company, currently negotiating three major projects in Africa with World Bank funding, is set to achieve a profit of about US$1 million by the end of 2002.

Future developments

In the next few years the company intends to increase its visibility on the global marketspace through a proactive strategy involving innovative online marketing and distribution of its products. DeBLOCKKA will also seek new partners with whom it can widen its product mix and increase its market share in the region. While planning to remain a small company, strategic partnering with other businesses founded on the use of networked information infrastructure should enable it to build up its effective resource base and also expand its access to market opportunities around the world. Part of the subsequent developments in infrastructure will be to provide varied access levels for the stakeholder community to its online databases and resources in support of collaborative work with its strategic partners.

The training portfolio is especially targeted as a cash cow for the company in the next five years. The company has decided to develop an international training package on technology management for national clients in the developing economies. In the longer term, the company hopes to lay the foundation for industrial design and intellectual property consulting services in the developing countries.

Questions for case analysis and discussion

(In providing answers to the following questions, your ability to locate discussions within contemporary literature on the subject will be a plus.)

Strategic management issues

Deciding on global orientation raises a number of strategic issues for the company. The following questions are intended to stimulate discussions on infrastructure management strategies in DeBLOCKKA.

A. General

1 List some of these issues especially focusing on their relevance to the relative size of the company and how it will manage access to resources, clients and technological facilities?
2 How would you expect the company's high virtual profile in relation to the small physical presence (i.e. a single business office in Durban) to affect the credibility of the company in the eyes of some its clientele, especially in international projects involving national governments? What would you suggest as possible solutions (either technical or other) to this problem?

3 What do you think about the legality of the operations of DeBLOCKKA, especially in relation to partners maintaining other employment? Do you see this as becoming a dominant approach to work among professionals that may be facilitated by the Internet?

B. Skill base

1 Identify the relevant skills in the company and discuss how these may prove useful for achieving the core objectives as well as support its business infrastructure management.
2 With respect to the knowledge intensity and extensive collaborative effort involved in the core business activities, suggest examples of enterprise-wide solutions for managing work in the organization.

C. Choice of virtual markets and e-business models

1 Analyse the virtual market and identify an appropriate market model for the company.
2 What would you recommend as the e-business model to start with and also discuss possible migration along the broad classes of online business models?

D. Contribution of Internet and management of business infrastructure

1 Discuss the main advantages presented by the Internet to the company's global strategy.
2 With reference to the NIAS project, list and explain the nature of intra- and interfirm relationships and how each may be enabled by the companies Internet infrastructure.
3 Based on your own experience and also from assessment of websites of other e-business companies, present at least two different practical scenarios of development of DeBLOCKKA's business infrastructure using mainly available Internet technologies and e-commerce solutions. You will need to note the company's organizational structure and working arrangements and its need to link up with many others in sharing resources (mainly soft), business opportunities, collaborative effort.
4 Note: It would be useful to develop a taxonomy of 'infrastructure component'/'business environment impact' for each scenario of Internet infrastructure deployment that you propose.

E. Alignment of business value chain with infrastructure management strategy

1 Discuss the options for optimizing the alignment of e-business strategy with the infrastructure management strategy.
2 Apply a *business value chain analysis* or *supply chain management analsyis* approach to strategic planning for future e-business.

References

Cragg, P.B. (1998) Clarifying Internet strategy in small firms. Paper presented at the Proceedings of the 9th Australian Conference on Information Systems, NSW.

Evamy, M. (1999) Web clients pursue design strategies, Marketing 1 July, 1999, 38–41.

Henderson, J.C. and Venkatraman, N. (1993) Strategic Alignment: Leveraging Information Technology for Transforming Organisations, *IBM Systems Journal*, **32**(1), 4–16.

McCollum, T. (1999, June 1999) Tailored solutions for growing firms, *Nation's Business*, **87**, 42–44.

OECD (2000) Realising the Potential of Electronic Commerce for SMEs in the Global Economy, Bologna, Italy.

OECD (1998) A Borderless World – Realising the Potential of Global Electronic Commerce, Ottawa, Canada 7–9 October, Organization for Economic Co-operation and Development – http://www.oecd.org//subject/ecommerce/index.htm

Tetteh, E. and Burn, J.M. (2001) Global strategies for SMe-Business: applying the S-M-A-L-L framework, *Journal of Logistics and Information Management*, Vol. 1.

Ticoll, D., Lowry, A. and Kalakota, R. (1998) Joined at the Bit, in: Don Tapscott, Alex Lowy and David Ticoll (eds), *Blueprint to the Digital Economy Creating Wealth in the Era of E-business*, McGraw-Hill

Venkatraman, N. (1994) IT-Enabled Business Transformation: from Automation to Business Scope Redefinition, *Sloan Management Review*, Winter.

Venkatraman, N. and Henderson, J.C. (1998) Real Strategies for Virtual Organising, *Sloan Management Review*, **4**, 33–48.

Developing knowledge-based strategies for a virtual organization

The Art of War: 'Know your enemy and know yourself, one can go through one hundred battles without danger.

Know not the other, yet know yourself, the chance of victory is only half.'

(Sun Zi)

7.1 Introduction

This chapter examines strategies for managing knowledge and how these can be used to make the transition through e-business to a virtual organization. In particular this chapter considers the role of knowledge as capital and the value of knowledge assets to the organization and the online community. Strategies for knowledge management are reviewed and linked with strategies for change. Being virtual is a strategic characteristic applicable to every organization, and virtual organizing is a specific approach to allow for the leveraging of business competencies and expertise for business competitiveness. This approach covers virtual encounters, virtual sourcing, and virtual expertise and knowledge. Finally the issues or actual execution of strategies are considered and suggestions are made for the development of an action framework.

7.2 Developing knowledge-based strategies for a virtual organization

In the e-business of today, knowledge is the most strategically important resource and learning the most strategically important capability. However, initiatives being undertaken to develop and exploit organizational knowledge are of little value if they are not explicitly linked to the overall business strategy. In turn, the strategic process must reflect the continual learning capabilities of the organization. The solution is to develop a perpetual strategy process that will embed knowledge and competitive intelligence into a continual monitoring of the external and internal environment and allow managed change and continual reengineering of the organization in line with shifting demands.

This strategy needs to be resource-based: emphasizing distinctive, firm-specific and hard-to-copy assets, skills and knowledge. These are generally referred to as core competencies or distinctive capabilities that confer competitive advantage on the business.

Strategic management or management of strategic innovation is the planned use of such organizational skills and knowledge. These strategies, however, are not so easily implemented in an online or virtual community where concepts such as assets, skills and knowledge may not be the sole property of a single company: they may derive from the overall combination of multiple organizations networked in the virtual chain. It is nevertheless vital – as organizations become more virtual – that experience, information and expertise are coherently managed and used to support future e-business initiatives and enhanced virtual alliances. With the increasing amount and value of information needed by every firm, the task of transforming this into a body of knowledge available as and when needed is becoming a paramount necessity for survival.

In this chapter we shall be looking at the knowledge difference in terms of the concepts of knowledge management and the benefits that an organization gets from it. We then consider suggested approaches to knowledge-based strategy development. Using a virtual organizing framework, the strategies for implementing knowledge-based management are reviewed and considered in relation to the likely problems that will arise. Finally, we look at whether and how we can find new ways to measure successful performance in a world of commerce that is playing by new rules.

7.3 Knowledge management – what it is and what it isn't

Knowledge management is a fashionable term today in business circles. Look at the website http://brint.com and see a sample of the hundreds of papers generated in the past few years. Then try a search for the term 'knowledge management' in a couple of search engines – the amount of information generated about knowledge is amazing but also inevitably confusing. Here we try to give a more user-friendly view.

Broadly, the term knowledge management is used to describe the entire business of recognizing and managing all of an organization's intellectual assets to meet business objectives. These intellectual assets may be information passing through channels, skills and tricks picked up and shared between employees, or the structured dissemination of regulations, procedures and the like.

Knowledge management looks at how an organization adapts to changing conditions to survive in the same way that animal and plant species change over time to adapt to changing conditions – or, like unsuccessful firms, they die off or are swallowed up by more successful competitors. With advances in technology, communications, transport and shared worldwide media, the business environment is increasingly sensitive to things happening far away. The speed at which events change the business environment is also far faster than ever before. This means that business success and survival is increasingly a chancy business with more opportunities for failure at every step.

Essentially, the idea of knowledge management is that it actively tries to find and create organizational processes that capture and create useful combinations of:

- data;
- information processing;
- all information and communications technologies; and
- the creative and innovative capacity of human beings.

Knowledge does not just happen along as a result of processes or activities; it comes from people and communities of people. An organization needs to know what knowledge it has and what knowledge it requires. Here it is important to recognize that not all knowledge is ready to use and even to be recognized. While much information can be gathered and collected for analysis, it is a much harder task to capture the skills and experience that lie in a person's mind. Most of us learn by doing things, and often know when something is a mistake – because we have seen it before. It is not always easy to recognize where this knowledge lies in an organization, and the loss of knowledge when employees change jobs can be a significant factor in a firm's performance.

David Skyrme and Associates (http://www.syyrme-.com.km.html) have developed a specific definition of knowledge management as: 'Knowledge Management is the *explicit* and *systematic* management of *vital* knowledge – and its associated *processes* of creation, organization, diffusion, use and exploitation'. This identifies some critical aspects of any successful knowledge management programme:

- Explicit – surfacing assumptions, codifying that which is known.
- Systematic – leaving things to serendipity will not achieve the benefits.
- Vital – you need to focus; no-one has unlimited resources.
- Processes – knowledge management is a set of activities with its own tools and techniques.

It is important to note that knowledge encompasses both tacit knowledge (in people's heads) and explicit knowledge (codified and expressed as knowledge in databases, etc.) and the programme will address the processes of development and management of both these basic forms.

To address knowledge management issues, we need to ask questions about: 'Who knows about what? Who needs to know? How important is it to us to get it right? What do we stand to lose if we get it wrong?' and so on. The goal of a knowledge management strategy should be to understand that there are communities and groupings that share a pool of knowledge, and to understand how the processes and channels for pooling this knowledge operate. We then need to look around for the right tools (often ICT tools) to facilitate the capture, transfer and use of knowledge about all aspects of the business.

This process of knowledge capture and use takes place at the level of the individual networks of knowledge within the organization and community networks. This can be described as:

- knowing individually what we know collectively and applying it;
- knowing collectively what we know individually and making it (re)usable;
- knowing what we don't know and learning it;

Knowledge management is both a discipline and an art. There are techniques that can be defined, taught, learned, replicated, customized and applied to yield predictable outcomes, but it's the art part that counts. Emphasis on the human nature of knowledge creation has moved knowledge management away from its early technology-centred interpretation towards a view that can provide multiple, diverse and contradictory inter-pretations. This has been described as 'the *sense-making* view' and is one that promotes continual challenge to the current way of doing things within a company and also forms a basis for a continual challenge against procedures that would otherwise become a different set – congealing and outliving their useful-ness, perhaps.

Skyrme and Amidon (1997) specifically identify three new aspects for the knowledge agenda:

1 Making knowledge and knowledge processes more explicit.
2 The development of strategic frameworks to guide the exploitation of knowledge – in products, services and processes.
3 The introduction of more systematic methods to the manage-ment of knowledge.

These are the issues we will be addressing in the remainder of this chapter.

7.4 Knowledge as an asset

We would all agree that knowledge is an asset – whether it is knowing how long you can leave your car outside a building before getting a ticket, or knowing enough to get an Open University degree that will give you a better job. But knowledge is an asset in a different way from the way in which having cash in the bank, good health, or a rich father is an asset. We may usefully consider it as having four distinguishing characteristics:

1 Extraordinary leverage and increasing returns – unlike most assets, knowledge is not subject to diminishing returns but grows in value.
2 Fragmentation, leakage and the need for refreshment – as a collected body of knowledge grows it tends to branch and fragment. The pieces may lose touch with each other. This means that sometimes a lot of effort is put into creating an area of knowledge that is already known but by people in other places whom we didn't think to ask. For this reason we need to keep refreshing our communication channels and knowledge reserves.
3 Uncertain value – the results of knowledge gathering or sharing can be extremely difficult to estimate or measure and may not come up to expectations or equally may exceed them.

4 Uncertain value sharing – unlike gold coins or share certificates, much knowledge is tacit and/or communal. For this reason, ownership is controversial and difficult to trade, share out or copyright.

These complex issues mean that it is not surprising that organizations have not always seen it as obvious that there can be value created by capturing the knowledge lying around in their activities. Today, however, most large organizations are becoming convinced that the returns from successful knowledge management far outweigh the risks. Shining examples such as Glaxo Wellcome, McDonald's and Oticon are leading the way in this field – a web search for case studies, papers, corporate reports and other discussions of the activities of these companies will illustrate the point.

Typically, huge returns come from collaborative knowledge sharing along the supply chain. This is not just about sharing sales and forecast data but knowing:

- what material is available for components and how the different materials work;
- how the plants operate and equipment compatibility;
- about the competition, the market and potential suppliers; and
- what impacts all of these (from multiple sources across the supply chain) may have on production and on the business.

A knowledge management strategy has to embrace all of these aspects. If the knowledge management procedures do not extend beyond the traditional boundaries of the firm, then they cannot be effective. For this reason, knowledge management directly bears upon new organizational forms in general, and on virtual organizations in particular.

Surprisingly, when we know how easy it is for machines and systems to let us down, the technology is the easy part of the procedure. Knowledge can be delivered and accessed through the enterprise network. The hard bits are the organizational and cultural ones – deciding what knowledge to put in the system, how to clean and apply it and how to convince all members of the value network *that sharing personal knowledge assets will bring individual as well as corporate benefits.*

7.5 Knowledge classification

Knowledge can be classified at a strategic level according to whether it is core, advanced or innovative.

The term core knowledge refers to the minimum required just to play the game and is commonly held by members of an industry. Advanced knowledge enables a firm to be competitively viable while innovative knowledge is that which allows an organization to move away from the pack and significantly differentiate itself from its competitors and even change the rules of the game. Since knowledge is dynamic, what is innovative today may well be the core for tomorrow. Competitive and strategic advantage is notoriously difficult to sustain, and this holds as true for knowledge-related issues as it does for purely technical advances such as improved engine design or the use of automated teller machines as a part of branch banking.

At the operational level within the organization, knowledge needs to be defined and understood within the contexts of content, community and computing technologies.

7.5.1 Knowledge content

Content can be described and classified in a variety of ways:

- tacit, explicit and meta;
- procedural, declarative, causal, conditional and relational;
- know-how/what/why/that/what was; and
- symbolic, embodied, embrained, and encultured.

Many definitions are given for these with frequent disagreements over terminology but for our purposes, explicit, procedural, know-what and know-how are readily identifiable and can be expressed in a recognizable range of forms. We can capture, share and apply this knowledge.

Tacit knowledge often takes the form of a mental model and can be a mix of facts and perceptions typically answering the why/that issue. This is frequently encountered in the attitude expressed as 'We do that because we have always done it that way, and it works.' Tacit knowledge is often very hard to formalize and communicate to others and also may be an unacceptable answer to the 'Why?' question. But nevertheless this is a common attitude toward the existing and perceived knowledge within a certain community.

7.5.2 Community knowledge

We live and work at the intersection of several communities and take these for granted – we may identify with a family group, a church group, an alumni group, a Rotary Club group and so on. In everyday living, we take these different community groups and their different perceptions and expectations for granted, and we change our activities and behaviour accordingly – often without realizing it. But in a business context it makes sense to pay particular attention to these communities, their rules, and shared assumptions and knowledge.

Community is largely about collaboration and, in the context of our interests as system managers, will generally but not necessarily centre on a common business interest. Community knowledge comes inextricably bound up with culture, which is a specific shared knowledge area in which the movement and transformation of knowledge occurs.

In our discussions, the term 'culture' has a broad meaning. We use this term, not merely in the narrow sense that we talk of as national cultures, Asian or Western culture, but to refer to the shared values, perceptions and concepts within any group. These shared values, beliefs and ways of evaluating the worth of activities and so on are extremely important for understanding what can be done within an organization or community. In this sense we refer to a company's culture, a government culture, a youth culture and so on.

It is becoming increasingly recognized that it is useful to be aware of and regard culture as a knowledge asset within the information space. We, as managers, must recognize the place and value of technological and organizational systems as extensions of culture. This community knowledge is place and time dependent, socially constructed and defined in terms of what is understood as useful and supportive within that context.

Organizational tensions and paradoxes will arise from collisions of cultures as different communities interpret 'knowledge' in different contexts and at different rates of learning. Cycles of social learning take place and it is this process of 'knowing' that is of greatest importance to the organization rather than a static abstract snapshot of knowledge.

Three particularly important characteristics of community knowledge as opposed to personal knowledge are:

1 The degree to which it can be codified and so move from tacit to explicit.
2 The degree to which it can be generalized or abstracted.
3 The degree to which it can be shared or diffused throughout and beyond the organization.

Table 7.1 The computability of knowledge management

Ease of computing	Codification – is the knowledge	Abstraction – is the knowledge	Diffusion – is the knowledge
HIGH	Easily captured: Figures or formulae? Standardized? Easy to automate?	Generally applicable? Fact or scientifically based?	Readily available?
MEDIUM	Describable? Words or diagrams? Document based?	Applicable to few? Need adaptation to contexts?	Available to few?
LOW	Hard to articulate? Easier to show than tell?	Limited to single sector? In need of extensive contextual adaptation?	Highly restricted availability?

7.5.3 Knowledge computability

This can be regarded as the computing factor – the gathering, storage, dissemination and maintenance, of content to the community. However, the higher the ease of computing, the less valuable knowledge generally is since it is generally accessible to all. This represents the paradox of knowledge value.

Note that consultancy firms make a living by advising firms on knowledge management to commonly adopt two different approaches.

The first may be described as the codification or 'reuse' approach where a conscious effort is made to restructure processes and communications so that knowledge is stored for universal access. The second, recognizing the difficulty of extracting and formulating knowledge exactly in a commonly intelligible and accessible form, adopts the 'personalization' method in which knowledge remains tied to the creator. Sharing of knowledge, in this model, relies on striving to improve and form person-to-person contacts. This latter way of going about things is appealing to generators and creators of knowledge who may consider themselves the possessors of this asset. This is appealing in cultures in which self-esteem is enhanced by being viewed as 'the person to ask', and in which there is time to be available and freely share knowledge on demand.

These two strategies for sharing knowledge can be incompatible, and trying to pursue an approach toward which a culture is not inherently sympathetic can lead to quite unintended and unfortunate consequences.

These three factors – content, community and computing – are all interrelated but are also in a state of tension with each other. Achieving a balance between them is the main focus of any knowledge management strategy.

7.6 Strategies for managing knowledge

Competitive strategy must drive knowledge management strategy but categorizing what an organization knows and should know about its industry or competitive position is not easy. If it were easy then competitive advantage would be unsustainable. Many programmes start by focusing on the thrust of better sharing of *existing* knowledge, e.g. sharing best practices, but it is the *creation and conversion* of new knowledge through the processes of innovation that gives the best long-term pay-off.

7.6.1 Strategic thrusts

As a first step the organization needs to determine the value of knowledge to its business. In other words it must align its knowledge resources and capabilities to the intellectual resources of its strategy. This should be measured against two dimensions and related to knowledge aggressiveness. The first dimension addresses the extent to which an organization is primarily a creator or user of knowledge and the second addresses whether the primary sources of knowledge are internal or external. These together will provide the strategic framework in which knowledge management strategy needs to be developed.

The first dimension seeks to measure and report on the extent to which an organization is primarily a creator or user of knowledge. The second dimension seeks to determine where it gets the knowledge it uses – does it look for and find this resource outside the organization or does it generate it from within? These two dimensions combine to provide the strategic framework in which knowledge management strategy needs to be developed.

Internal knowledge is obviously especially valuable (as we know from insider knowledge of companies and the effect this has on share trading). Internal knowledge always arises when a firm knows its business – and the fewer competitors it has in its area, the more rare and hence valuable is its knowledge of how its business works and so on. This must certainly be given a priority of use – to ignore it is to discard assets that, although valuable, have cost relatively little to acquire as they develop or evolve in the normal course of business. In today's competitive markets, however, most positions of market dominance attract intense attention and competition, so this is not a common occurrence.

Where firms collaborate closely, or virtual organizations form to bind 'several as one' for advantage, exploitation of external knowledge can take place through the value chain network to create knowledge advantage within the group situation. This can be further extended along the supply chain to capture knowledge from environments. These typically might include potential and actual customers who, to a greater or lesser extent, do or can be persuaded to share information and knowledge for mutual benefit. Commonly used ways of achieving this are becoming ever more common and include user groups, joint ventures, beta-testing, websites, electronic mail, toll-free numbers, customer care centres, customer advisory boards, conferences and even social gatherings.

Combining the knowledge exploitation versus exploration orientation of the organization with its internally versus externally acquired orientation towards knowledge strategy gives a framework for the knowledge-based virtual organization as shown in Figure 7.1.

Exploration and exploitation typically occur in different parts of the organization and are often separated temporally (by time) and culturally as well as organizationally. Balancing these requires a knowledge culture, transfer and integration capability

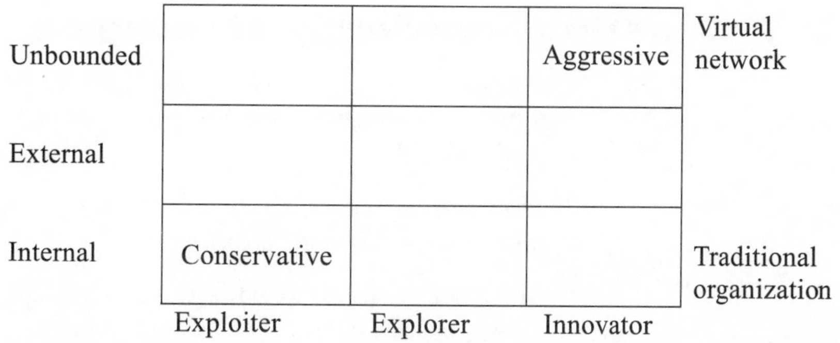

Figure 7.1

Framework for knowledge strategy (adapted from Zack 1999)

				Virtual network
Unbounded			Aggressive	
External				
Internal	Conservative			Traditional organization
	Exploiter	Explorer	Innovator	

that is itself strategic and subject to constant re-evaluation. The choice of exploitation, exploration or innovation reflects the overall competitive business strategy of the organization. Strategic positioning within this framework reflects the knowledge management strategy in alignment with the business strategy. These two together can radically change the organization and the way it is positioned within the marketplace.

7.6.2 Strategic Levers

The successful virtual organization will be the one that works out a series of procedures for getting or capturing the most value from its strategic inter-organizational alliances. In this way, it moves beyond the boundaries of its own organizational form as a source and container of knowledge and moves towards the model of unbounded innovators. This aggressive strategy has been shown to outperform more conservative ones in knowledge intensive industries. In any one organization, however, it is likely that value will be leveraged by concentrating on just a few of the strategic levers for knowledge management such as:

- Customer knowledge – the most vital in most organizations.
- Knowledge in processes – applying the best know-how while performing core tasks.
- Knowledge in products (and services) – smarter solutions, customized to users' needs.
- Knowledge in people – nurturing and harnessing brainpower, the most precious asset.
- Organizational memory – drawing on lessons from the past or elsewhere in the organization.
- Knowledge in relationships – deep personal knowledge that underpins successful collaboration.
- Knowledge assets – measuring and managing intellectual capital.

7.7 Creating knowledge strategies

There are ten vital issues that must be considered if an organization wants to use the potential of the new dynamics of virtual markets:

1 *Strategy – pursue strategies of change, not merely seeking to defend an established position*:

- Learn to think 'outside the box' by questioning constraining assumptions

- Trust people to think and act strategically; by informing of them of long-term goals and encouraging input, you involve them in the search for success.
- Build up the identified core competencies and avoid rigid thinking about them that prevents adding to or altering your perception of these.
- Leverage value through strategic alliances and economic webs – see the success of others as something to be helpful to your business and do not strive against the entire world.

2 *Customer value – match what you can deliver to the groups of customers who want your products or value*:
- Think like your customers and question whether you are working for joint benefit, or yours alone.
- Choose the right value proposition and build the right operating mode (difficult!).
- Evolve the model continually – do not be afraid to improve on successful models or test the market for changes in direction. Many failures have emerged from concentrating on satisfying a defined need and not seeing where new needs were arising.

3 *Knowledge management – leverage knowledge for competitive advantage*:
- Learn how to define and acquire knowledge.
- Know who the knowledge workers are: encourage and keep them.
- Learn how to learn – an informed staff can contribute more.

4 *Business organization – organize around networks and processes*:
- Move from hierarchies to networks that aim to get the job done for the customer, not the internal boss.
- Emphasize processes and teams because these work better.
- Recognize the organization as a social structure.

5 *Market focus – find and keep strategic, profitable, and loyal customers*:
- Build the value of customer capital.
- Find out which customers are worthwhile.
- Acquire and keep the right customers; it costs less to fill repeat orders than to find new customers or take them away from a competitor.

6 *Management accounting – manage the business, not the numbers*:
- Know how to analyse product and service profitability.
- Use accounting to help improve processes.
- Move towards more relevant accounting systems.

7 *Measurement and control – strike a new balance between control and empowerment*:
- Beware of the behavioural implications of budgets.
- Implement a strategic measurement system such as the Balanced Scorecard.

8 *Shareholder value – measure the new source of wealth creation: intellectual assets*:
- Understand the changing shape of share values and the need for new yardsticks to measure performance.
- Seek solutions to the problem of valuing intangible assets such as intellectual capital.
- Ensure that capital expenditures go beyond managing information to improving its productivity.

9 *Productivity – encourage and reward value creating work*:
- Beware pursuit of the lowest unit cost.
- Adopt pursuit of value adding work.
- Look for new ways to measure productivity.

10 *Transformation – innovation*:
- Create perpetual strategy processes.
- Question the value of management education.

Some of the more common practices and processes used are summarized in Table 7.2.

These practices can be supported by a large number of tools (Skyrme identifies over 80 categories), many of which are themselves computer based. All of these strategic processes are knowledge based and must form part of a perpetual strategy process that is continually fed by a competitive intelligence process. This may result in frequent changes in strategy, in tactics and in constant reengineering of the organization.

7.8 Dynamic strategies for virtual organizations

Knowledge is so dependent on individuals that a rigid distinction between strategy and organization is inappropriate and, indeed, successful knowledge strategies involve almost every aspect of a company's organizational design. This is not something that can be lightly undertaken according to a simple set of rules that fits all circumstances. But this policy can be part of a staged growth development that should be implemented through an ongoing process of trial and testing, of experimenting with products and processes, of seeking to adapt for the better rather than keeping a model that proved its worth once.

Table 7.2 Knowledge management practices

Creating and discovering	Creativity techniques
	Data mining
	Text mining
	Environmental scanning
	Knowledge elicitation
	Business simulation
	Content analysis
Sharing and learning	Communities of practice
	Learning networks
	Sharing best practices
	After action reviews
	Structured dialogue
	Share fairs
	Cross-functional teams
	Decision diaries
Organizing and Managing	Knowledge centres
	Expertise profiling
	Knowledge mapping
	Information audits/inventories
	Information resource management
	Measuring intellectual capital

1 *Find out where, how and why knowledge matters in the organization.* Brainstorm, ask diagnostic questions such as 'Could we cut costs, reduce time to market, improve customer service, or increase margin by sharing best practices more effectively?' In many cases the simple act of performing a SWOT analysis will help to uncover vital information needed to find out important starting points for change. Important questions that can be raised and explored in this process start from such innocent sounding, but sometimes difficult to answer, questions like: 'How do we want to play the game we are in?', 'What do we need to find out in order to improve?', 'What do we know already that we haven't found a way to use in our work?', 'What is the gap between what we know and what we need to know?'. Apply this questioning approach internally and externally on a regular basis.

2 *Continually go over the nature and extent of your current market alliances, customers, suppliers and competitors and evaluate their worth.* Apply the SWOT analysis as above and identify knowledge-based partnerships of advantage.

3 *Set the vision for value creation through knowledge management.* How will the organization use knowledge management to bring value to the organization, to customers and to the organizational stakeholders? How will it measure these assets and their value and create a knowledge sharing culture? What will your knowledge strategy be – exploiter, explorer or innovator? How can multiple views be integrated and change over time?

4 *Establish how an integrated view of knowledge management can be developed and maintained.* Identify the organizational learning cycle and evaluate it against competitors' and industry learning cycles. Develop capabilities for guaranteeing the availability of high quality content within specific knowledge communities and the appropriate technology to support these. Evaluate these across your full network of alliances on a regular basis.

5 *Understand the implications of knowledge for organizational and network design.* The need to foster, share and retain tacit knowledge, for example, imposes a natural limit on the size of operating units. Small knowledge-based work groups working in a matrixed network rather than a hierarchical structure are generally more helpful to people and work processes when they rely on effective cooperation than in a hierarchical reporting structure. IT helps to identify the core alliances along the virtual value chain and communication channels, and be prepared to continually change the way people and processes interact to take advantage of changing circumstances and get the best out of all resources.

6 *Experiment, prototype and fine tune.* These are all part of the iterative strategy whereby initiatives that evolve from experimentation should build upon each other, eventually involving multiple communities.

7 *Adjust the organization's external posture and conduct and build value through innovation.* Innovate faster and get new products and services deployed within the organization and to customers or suppliers – for example, codified knowledge might be given away as a customer retention strategy or to tie in suppliers.

8 *Continually measure and monitor knowledge.* Most measurement systems such as financial accounting are inappropriate for intangible assets such as knowledge management, but methods such as Balanced Scorecard, economic value added (EVA) and inclusive valuation methodology can all be applied. Continually monitor stakeholder actions and options.

This perpetual strategy process can be described as creative abrasion – it means a constant wearing away of the way things have been and are being done. This is necessary to prevent harmful build-up of procedures that have outlived their usefulness. A process such as this is an essential part of the development of an effective competitive intelligence system. Such development is essential to create and sustain the virtual links and processes that can change a company into the optimal form for the time and allow it to feel comfortable with an environment of dynamic change in the virtual marketplace.

Critical to the success of a knowledge management strategy is effective knowledge leadership generating a knowledge sharing culture, supported by systematic processes including clear measurement of business benefits and success.

7.9 Knowledge management in the virtual organization

Developing a strategy for knowledge management involves every aspect of an organization's design and may well require the development of a very different knowledge-based business model for the virtual organization. Venkatraman and Henderson (1998) have defined a business model for the knowledge

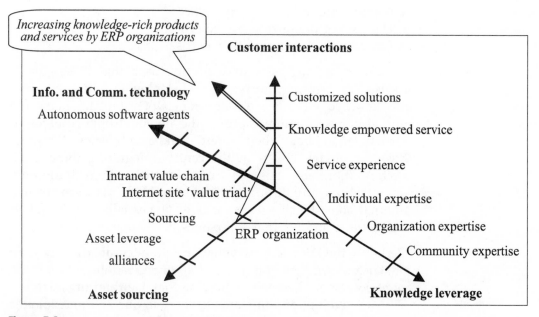

Figure 7.2
Knowledge through virtual organizing in an ERP organization

economy that promotes harmony over three vectors – customer/market interaction, asset sourcing and knowledge leverage supported by a strong ITC platform. They see this as the virtual organizing model for the 21st century and as such a strategy in itself.

Figure 7.2 gives a view of an organization using an enterprise resource planning (ERP) system such as SAP, as an integrated system to enable knowledge management across the three vectors of the organization.

Virtual encounters (customer interaction) refers to the extent to which you virtually interact with the market defined at three levels of greater virtual progression:

- Remote product/service experience.
- Product/service customization.
- Shaping customer solutions.

Virtual sourcing (asset sourcing) refers to competency leveraging from:

- Efficient sourcing of standard components.
- Efficient asset leverage in the business network.
- Creating new competencies through alliances.

Virtual work (knowledge leverage) refers to:

- Maximizing individual experience.
- Harnessing organizational expertise.
- Leveraging of community expertise.

Virtual organizing is a strategic approach that is singularly focused on creating, nurturing and deploying key intellectual and knowledge assets in a complex network of relationships. No one vector adequately captures the potential opportunities of virtual organizing: their interdependence creates the new business model. ITC is at the centre, integrating these three vectors (normally quite discrete functions in a traditional organization), and through an interoperable IT platform ensures internal consistencies in the profile of virtualness relevant to competitors and referent companies in the marketplace.

Certainly the knowledge leverage has to integrate directly with the customer interaction in a virtual organization and with the asset sourcing. However, it may be that a virtual organization chooses to adopt an innovator strategy in one and an exploiter strategy in another such that the knowledge management while still integrated and aligned will reflect different stages of vector development. An innovative approach to customer interaction would have to be supported by a knowledge management system which fully leveraged community expertise. An asset sourcing strategy focused on efficient sourcing of components could be supported by a knowledge management strategy that maximized the individual supplier experience and was directed to tying in that company as a joint partnership.

Reaching the third levels in all vectors would reflect a fully integrated virtual organization with an 'information rich' product and the highest degree of use of ICT. If we view this as the virtual culture of the organization then this needs to be articulated through the strategic positioning of the organization and its structural alliances as introduced in Chapter 3. It also needs to be supported by the knowledge management processes and the ICT. These relationships are depicted in a dynamic virtual organization change model as shown in Figure 7.3.

7.10 Virtual change management

As previously discussed, the virtual organization has three choices for strategic direction, exploiter, explorer and innovator and these represent the entrepreneurial domain. The engineering and administrative domains are change factors that need to be integrated into the overall strategy and maintained in

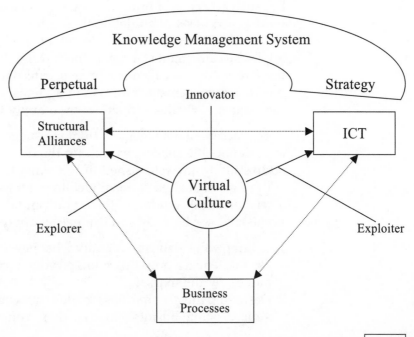

Figure 7.3
Virtual organizational change model (Burn and Barnett 2000)

alignment. The degree to which virtual organizing can be applied in the organization will relate to the extent to which the change management factors are in alignment. When these are not aligned then the organization will find itself dysfunctional in its exploitation of the virtual marketspace and so be unable to derive the maximum value benefits from its strategic position.

Figure 7.3 revisits the VOCM introduced in Chapter 3 and integrates the e-business strategies – exploiter, explorer and innovator – into a knowledge management framework for change management. This can be used by the organization to identify those factors where their greatest focus is required:

- the exploiter strategy will focus on maximizing the effectiveness of business processes along the value chain through ITC;
- the explorer strategy will extend market reach by strengthening structural alliances and interorganizational partnerships along the supply/demand chain; and
- the innovator will be attempting to integrate all these processes into a virtual value chain and to move into new virtual markets.

7.11 Strategies for transition

It is all very well to say that a firm must look for ways to change, but such advice is of little consequence unless we can provide a more practical set of guidelines that can be followed. This is not to say that there is any single set of guidelines that can be applied to all circumstances. If there were, then nobody would need to study management or seek effective means of implementing management information systems – we could all buy the same set of rules and sit down to apply them.

Recent accepted management thinking suggests that nine useful and identifiable challenges sum up the difficulties that must be addressed by any established firm looking to take advantage of adopting a virtual business model. In so far as we can formulate a set of rules of guidance, then, you can take these as starting points and see how far you can get by applying them:

1 Shifting value drivers – identify what new or emerging factors are influencing how the value of your product or process is judged by the market.
2 Designing the new business model: first you must be aware of your existing business model, then you must look to see

whether it is and will be an appropriate response to changing circumstances.

3 Governing beyond outsourcing – how far can you influence and control activities and attitudes of those on whom you depend for related business activity, but do not control by contractual relations.

4 Interacting with customers for knowledge leverage – if you assume that your customers know the most about what, when, why and for how much they are willing to buy or use your product, you should look to ask them for answers and seek to interpret their behaviour. This policy is at odds with the idea of first deciding what you can make or do and then looking for ways to persuade others to pay for your creations.

5 Navigating across multiple communities – you must seek to extend your relations with all players in the business and consumer arena to play an active part throughout to your advantage.

6 Deploying an integrated IT platform – you can no longer have systems that do not integrate with each other or those systems of your clients, partners, and all other interested parties.

7 Allocating resources under increased uncertainty – managing with the expectation of change yields different strategies than managing under the assumption that next week will resemble last week.

8 Designing an organization for knowledge leverage – the capture, collation, collection and spread of knowledge and information must be a priority when designing your ICT and social systems.

9 Assessing performance along multiple dimensions – you cannot expect all returns on your investment or efforts to be measured along a single scale (ROI, for example) as you cannot measure all important events and outcomes.

The majority of these challenges have been addressed in the framework for perpetual strategies for knowledge management. However, it is worth highlighting issues 3 and 9 from the above list. These are both critical areas of current concern for practitioners and researchers.

Companies are looking to get rid of some internal functions, in particular the management and technology of the IT/IS departments at an unprecedented rate at a time when technology and its effective management has never been more critical to business success. There are many reasons for this, not all of them bad. These include:

- the problem of managing IT/IS personnel with a different culture from the mainstream activities;
- the difficulty for managers to accurately forecast and control costs in areas with which they are not familiar; and
- the fluctuating demand for IT/IS services internally.

In addition, the difficulty of attracting, training, and retaining IS staff all have a part to play in this.

Having recognized these very real factors, we must still be aware that strategies for outsourcing need to be very closely aligned to the overall knowledge management strategy and not based solely on cost reduction. For many enterprises, some adoption of virtual organizational form may offer a solution to be tested in this area. Virtual organizations offer a way to source the best knowledge resource through virtual alliances without the addition of further management layers for coordination and control. In order for this to work effectively, however, the recognition of what is happening must be clearly stated and recognized as an integral part of the virtual strategy and it must achieve the strategic intent. This intent must be recognized and expressed as a goal of IT/IS improvement (most common), business improvement or commercial exploitation. A failure to set out clear reasons for policy is to throw away any chance of measuring its success.

Performance and value measurement has to move away from static measures such as market share when new markets with very different rules and games are being developed on a regular basis. It is well known that Amazon.com cannot be measured against traditional market values since it has yet to record traditional profits and is not pursuing a policy of doing so in the short term. New approaches such as economic value added (EVA), market value added (MVA), and benchmarking give much wider definitions of value and need to be incorporated into the organization's portfolio management. An analysis of industrial and business wealth creation today might well be based on the role of intangible assets and dynamic capabilities.

There is also one further issue to be added to the above list – in our opinion. We maintain it is of critical importance to any knowledge management strategy, and that is *how to look after and manage the people on whom the organization depends*. We encourage you to think in terms of what the social structures, attitudes and reward mechanisms are – or that should be in place – to move toward effective knowledge management and create a real knowledge-based culture in the organization.

7.12 Summary

The virtual organization is recognized as a dynamic form of interorganizational systems and hence one where traditional hierarchical forms of management and control may not apply. Little, however, has been written about the new forms which management and control might take other than to espouse a 'knowledge management' approach. We are entitled to ask – managing knowledge about what?

In an organization where change is the only constant, then there has to be a system that can *capture* the organizational core competencies and *leverage* these to provide strategic advantage. This may be a competitive advantage or a strategic advantage in collaboration with the competition.

Knowledge has become the major asset of the organization. Consequently its recording, communication and management deserve attention. Without the ability to identify who has the key information, who the experts are, and who needs to be consulted, management decisions are unlikely to be as good as they could be even if they are not completely wrong. Both the importance and the difficulty of the issue are magnified by the changing nature of the firm itself. We see on every hand that change – most frequently incorporating aspects of virtuality – is occurring daily in every industry. We see the move in every industry toward larger companies and organizations, decentralization and dispersion, empowerment and continual change. In the resulting complex interdependent organizations, the synergy of knowledge might be the principal benefit of this interdependence and so the issue is magnified further.

More conscious efforts and explicit procedures are needed in *dispersed* organizations. Skills may not be available where they are wanted, data might not be shared or they might be used inefficiently or wrongly. New skills need to be developed quickly and employees will have to take personal responsibility for their own knowledge development. This implies that the virtual organization will need a number of managers with converging expertise in the areas identified within the virtual organizing change management model (Figure 7.4). There may no longer be a separate ICT or knowledge management function. Indeed there may no longer be any management function that does not explicitly demand expertise in these areas.

The implications for you, as IS professionals, are quite frightening. Whole areas of new skills need to be acquired and these skills are themselves constantly in a process of development, demanding continual updates. We are still struggling with the information age as we are being thrust into the knowledge age but we haven't yet developed the intermediation services to support this. Opportunities abound for skilled IS professionals at every level of the organization, but these professionals must be supported by an ongoing education programme at the heart of every organization. The virtual organization that succeeds will be the learning organization where people are regarded as their greatest core asset.

References

Burn, J.M. and Barnett, M.L. (2000) Emerging Virtual Models for Global E-commerce – world wide retailing in the e-grocery business. Special issue on Global E-commerce, *Special Millennium Issue of Journal of Global Information Technology Management*, Vol. 3, No. 1, 18–32.

Skyrme and Amidon, (1997) 'The Knowledge Agenda', *Journal of Knowledge Management*, Vol. 1 (1) 27.

Skyrme and Associates (http://www.skyrme.com.km.html)

Venkatraman, N. and Henderson, J. (1998) Real Strategies for Virtual Organizing, *Sloan Management Review*, Vol. 40, Fall, 37–48.

Zack, M.H. (1999) Developing a Knowledge Strategy, *California Management Review*, Berkeley, Spring.

8 Evaluating strategies for e-business change

> It takes all the running you can do to keep in the same place.
>
> (The Red Queen, in *Through the Looking Glass*, Lewis Carroll)

8.1 Introduction

Global, fast, cheap, communication technologies coupled with new, innovative, management practices bring both new opportunities and threats. For many organizations the threats – rapid market change, new and more agile competitors and diminishing control over organizational changes – outweigh the opportunities which themselves require a dynamic approach to change. An organization that is responsive to change and capitalizes on new alliances, better customer and supplier relationships and new markets, products and services needs to have a different strategic planning and management process in place which is associated with an effective value measurement system. The majority of measurement systems imply static value measurements based on financial returns and do not reflect the holistic view of an enterprise that is needed to support the transition to a virtual organization.

Before considering the specific application of an e-business plan, each organization seeking to gain advantage from the emerging ICT and Internet tools should strive to gain an understanding of its current and potential position in the universe of business. There are many ways of doing this, and many ways of translating the results into action, several examples are given throughout this book at appropriate stages. This doesn't mean that there is one right model, or that you should necessarily move from one model to another when considering systems thinking and needs at different levels. Rather that there are many useful ways of looking at the business world, and that each organization stands at a unique intersection of these. If this were not the case, management and systems strategy discussions would not be needed.

8.2 Coevolutionary strategies

There are many traditional models of business strategy such as Porter's competitive forces model and yet few examples of organizations applying these well-defined models to secure competitive advantage in the current environment of constant change. Are such strategic models redundant? What is needed is a model of a world where innovation, change and uncertainty are the natural state of things. In a system of coevolution, when the predator learns to run faster, the prey starts to climb trees and then the predator develops alternative means of transport and so on. Long-term sustainable advantage isn't possible without continual adaptation. Strategy is full of contradictions and dilemmas as evidenced by the Red Queen effect. A study of the performance of more than 400 organizations over 30 years reveals that companies find it difficult to maintain higher performance levels than their competitors for more than about five years at a time (Beinhocker 1999).

Advantage tends to be competed away quite quickly and increasingly so in this new global market. In a system of coevolution, adaptation can be seen as the attempt to optimize systems riddled with conflicting constraints. Strategy is all about adaptation – reconciling opposing issues in tension or dilemmas or polarities. Strategy answers two basic questions: 'Where do you want to go?' and 'How do you want to get there?' Traditional approaches focus on the first question and

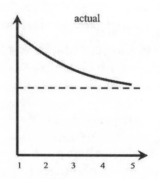
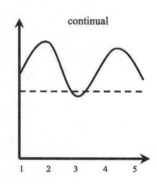

Figure 8.1
The Red Queen effect (after Beinhocker 1997)

only later, if at all, is the second question addressed. Even combined, these approaches are incomplete since they over-emphasize executives' abilities to forecast and predict in a highly competitive, high-velocity market and underemphasize the challenge of actually creating effective strategies. Traditional strategy focuses on a single line of attack – appropriate for short-term niche domination but insufficient in the longer term. Given uncertain environments, strategies must also be robust and allow for the organization to pursue a package of potentially conflicting strategies at the same time. A robust package of strategies can be likened to a portfolio of real options and as with financial options, the greater the uncertainty, the greater their value. The value of an option represents the potential benefit a firm may reap in the future beyond a value that can be estimated using the current organizational capabilities and knowledge in the market. Hence a strategy is a path of related options and there is no such thing as a well-thought-through overall strategy. Companies need to cultivate evolving populations of strategies.

EXHIBIT 1

A fitness landscape

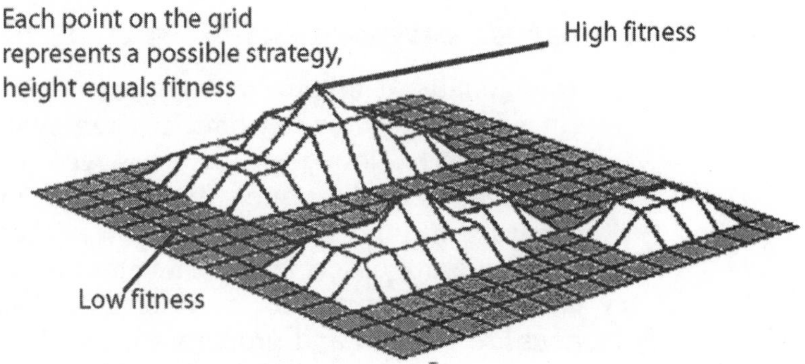

Each point on the grid represents a possible strategy, height equals fitness

High fitness

Low fitness

Figure 8.2
Fitness landscapes

Kauffman (1995) refers to this evolutionary process as the development of fitness landscapes where the corporation will search for the high points on their fitness landscapes which can assume various forms with multiple landscapes and strategic teams employing different techniques to explore the terrain.

Such strategies force people to deal with ambiguity and accelerate constructive conflict and this requires the development of a new mindset that will encompass the following:

- Invest in diversity.
- Value strategies as if they were options.
- Categorize the mix of strategies.
- Stress-test strategies.
- Bring the market inside.
- Use venture capital performance metrics.

Successful adaptation also implies coevolution between the organization and the strategy model. Not only must strategy models be adapted to fit the unique characteristics of an organization but also organizations need to evolve to benefit from the lessons incorporated into the strategic model and so both the organization and model continually change. These change factors cannot be solely measured on financial data but require an integrated view of organizational innovation and change. One of the most commonly adopted approaches to this coevolutionary process in recent years has been the application of the Balanced Scorecard (BSC) as a strategic management and performance evaluation system. Before examining the application of the BSC we will look at some of the opportunities and threats presented by e-business and the limitations of typical measurement tools.

8.3 e-business: opportunities and threats

Traditionally – in our terms over the past 20 years! – the emerging e-business economic environment has been created by a strong technology push. This has seen the rise of channels of electronic communication between businesses, government departments, and individuals on an unprecedented scale. This digitization of ordering, reporting and product information has created opportunities for major change, if the business implications are grasped and properly managed.

The value of products is rising, often directly as a result of the increasing use of information; the digitized capture of information regarding electronically based transactions allows for ever more sophisticated customization of products by smart information management. There is posited the goal of mass customization: the tailoring of a product specifically for an individual consumer, based on his or her needs. The key to this is the ability to customer preferences and behaviour compactly and efficiently. This information is relayed to a flexible manufacturing process allied to a responsive network of suppliers or other intermediaries.

Dell Computer is a good and often quoted example of a supplier that uses electronic trading networks. It does this to collect and analyse customer orders and to control the creation and delivery of made-to-order goods to their customers, normally faster than conventional competitors and with a rich layer of value in the form of information supplied.

Not only can the product advertised be supplied more effectively using attention to personal demand and circumstance using electronic information flows, but the potential also arises for the sensing and testing of demand for new goods and services that can be exploited by electronic means. Would a customer already on a website react positively to tailored news casting? Database access? Free chips in an online casino? And so on.

We readily see that new electronic information flows dramatically alter sales and distribution channels, having impact on two categories of primary flows: physical goods and virtual goods.

The physical goods may be advertised and ordered online yet delivered traditionally, whereas virtual goods may be advertised, customized, ordered, paid for, and delivered online without the customer moving from his/her chair. In the first category e-business comes into its own in markets in which information (for example, an array of choice) forms a significant component of value, rather than in commoditized and well-known products.

The second category consists of products that can be digitized – books, banking and investment transactions, insurance and travel contracts, off-course betting and so on. For virtual goods the world of e-business provides a new distribution channel, for example by means of the Web. We do not need to visit the racecourse to place a bet or collect our winnings if we have a remote terminal or an account which can be accessed by our electronic device – be it phone or PC. This category is obviously in use and examples will be familiar to you all: you may even have downloaded your own selection of music from a website, checked online travel agents or investigated online banking. While visible to the consumer, these are but tiny fragments of the vast amount of business-to-business currently conducted electronically and changing the ways in which firms think and operate.

Are there any drawbacks to this apparently simple way of transforming the economics of doing business? Of course there are, and they are industry specific and not yet fully apparent. For example, it will become apparent that e-business enables and requires new product capabilities and new services. This opens opportunities for those already in business, but equally opens the way for new entrants. The positions of current players are threatened, especially those who act as intermediaries.

As a result we see a trend for e-business to bring producers closer to the consumer, leading to the reduced need for intermediaries (wholesalers, distributors and the like). This trend toward disintermediation has been observed in the financial markets and is being followed by developments in the insurance and travel industry. Does this mean less employment? Probably not, but it does imply that different forms of employment will prevail.

On the other hand, we may also observe the opposite trend in action at the same time. There is a process of reintermediation occurring as e-business creates the possibility of new and different forms of intermediary – the bookseller Amazon.com being the world's largest and best known example. These very different opportunities and threats cannot be evaluated through simple cost – benefit analysis tools and present a significant challenge for investment and risk analysis.

8.4 Return on investment and risk analysis

Some EC initiatives could be strong revenue generators but may not create new markets; others may create new markets but will not return a significant profit. Some may create a competitive advantage in the short term but lose this on the emergence of a new competitive initiative in e-business. Resources required to create additional value through e-business need to be examined with respect to their likely return on investment in order to develop a compelling business case. This is not so simple as it sounds, however. Traditional measures such as discounted cash flow (DCF) and net present value (NPV) do not take into account the values of benefits such as knowledge of customer needs. Calculating any rate of return on investment (ROI) from e-business cases requires an assessment of increased revenue as well as decreased costs; customer value variables, stakeholder value variables and competitive capability variables. One approach suggested by Parker (1996) and referred to as information economics attempts to address some of these issues by classifying values and risks as (a) values: financial, strategic and

Table 8.1 Information economics – value-based approach

Traditional ROI (+)

+value linking (+)
+value acceleration (+)
+value restructuring (+)
+innovation (+)

= Adjusted ROI	*Business value	+IT value
	• Strategic match (+)	• Strategic IT architecture (+)
	• Competitive advantage (+)	
	• Competitive response (+)	
	• Management information (+)	
	• Service and quality (+)	
	• Environmental quality (+)	
	• Empowerment (+)	
	• Cycle time (+)	
	• Mass customization (+)	
	• Business strategy risk (–)	• IT strategy risk (–)
		• Definition uncertainty (–)
	• Business organization risk (–)	• Technical risk (–)
		• IT service delivery risk (–)

= VALUE (business contribution

---

stakeholder; and (b) risks: competitive strategy, organizational strategy and uncertainty.

Even at the simplest level – financial values there are still many factors which are difficult to quantify. e-business increases revenue in at least three ways, by decreasing costs, by accessing new markets and additional segments of existing markets and by redefining the market through new, better and readily available information. In each of these areas there are many different values to be measured against selected value drivers. Deise *et al.* (2000) identify seven variables related to customer value and competitiveness as:

• Services – expanded and improved.
• Price – more rational and dynamic.
• Quality – improved and more attractive.
• Fulfilment time – reduced.

Table 8.2 Value drivers matrix

Value drivers	service	price	quality	Fulfilment time	agility	Time to market	reach	Net driver effect
Revenue growth								
Operating margin								
Working capital								
Capital expend								
Cash tax rate								
Cost of capital								
Competitive advantage period								

- Agility – increased flexibility.
- Reach – global expansion.
- Time to market – reduced time and increased products.

Against these seven variables an e-business should measure seven value drivers:

- Revenue growth
- Operating margin
- Working capital
- Capital expenditure
- Taxation
- Cost of capital
- Competitive advantage period

Not all of these value drivers will be impacted by improved customer or competitive values but a business can identify where the major impacts are going to be and the net driver effect overall by examining these on a simple matrix and then evaluating these as overall opportunities and threats.

8.5 Development of the Balanced Scorecard (BSC)

8.5.1 The BSC approach

The Balanced Scorecard was developed by Kaplan and Norton in a series of articles published in the *Harvard Business Review* from 1992 onward. It is offered as a tool to evaluate a company's efficient implementation of IT within the business context, and it does so by combining four perspectives on a project. These are the financial perspective, the client's view, internal processes, and innovation (Figure 8.3).

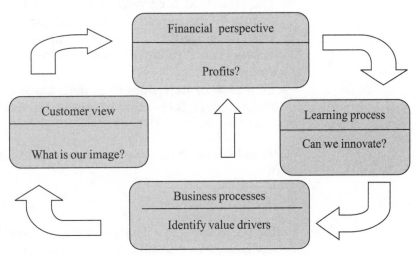

Figure 8.3
The Balanced Scorecard (BSC)

Each of the four perspectives must be operationalized into measures of the current situation. The measurements will then be repeated periodically and matched against goals set beforehand. In general, it is accepted that there are three principles which must be kept in mind when proceeding with the implementation of a scorecard policy.

- Principle one states that cause and effect relationships between the components must be built in and understood in order that the quantifiable effects of quantified causes can be readily appreciated. For example, 'what actions will influence our customer image?' and 'how will our customer image be measured?'

- Second, there must be drivers of performance (training, incentives and the like) demonstrably affecting operational outcomes. For example, 'what training is required to improve our delivery to customers?' and 'how will we measure the effectiveness of such training?'
- Third, there must be direct linkage to financial outcomes – in other words, the success or otherwise of projects and initiatives must be realized on the balance sheet. Where this does not occur, the scores are not being kept for important items. For example, 'what net margin return do we expect for success?'

This method stresses the use of measurable goals and measurement of strategies to drive it, framed within a three-tiered structure:

- The mission as conceived as the overarching and driving force (e.g. to be the industry's preferred supplier).
- Objectives derived from the mission (e.g. to introduce appropriate products as needed and before our competitors).
- Performance indicators (e.g. percentage of customers giving repeat orders; proportion of profits derived from products less than two years old).

A simple table outlining this approach might look like Table 8.3:

Table 8.3 Example of a Balanced Business Scorecard

Perspective	Goals	Indicator
Financial	Revenue Net margin	US$30 million p.a. 16%
Customer	Satisfaction per sale % of clients retained	8.4 out of 10 80%
Learning	Training hours per employee	40 p.a.
Processes	Productive: non-productive hours	81%

In practice, a company looking to build a scorecard would first secure the understanding and support of business and IT management who must be committed to the integration of business and IT strategies to lead to success. Following this, data would be gathered on measures and metrics in place which can be used – much performance measurement and assessment of drivers will probably already be in place. Third, the company-specific scorecard is to be developed.

The emphasis of the BSC is to capture real meaning by including both quantitative and qualitative information on a mix of outcomes (lag indicators) and performance drivers (lead indicators). The portfolio of measures thus created offers an alternative approach to the use of incentive compensation payments tied to traditional simplistic formulae of past performance. A well-constructed scorecard will contain a good mix of measurable outcomes and performance drivers. Outcomes such as productivity measures alone, without linked performance drivers, will not show how these outcomes are to be achieved. Similarly performance drivers put in place with no links to outcomes may indeed result in short-term improvements, but will not show any correlation between resources put into these and financial outcomes. This latter is imperative for the success of this method: 'A failure to convert improved operational performance into improved financial performance should send executives back to the drawing board to rethink the company's strategy or its implementation plans' (Kaplan and Norton 1996).

8.5.2 Implementing the BSC

Ten steps are suggested for successful implementation of a Balanced Scorecard approach:

- Focus on the strategic direction: all business units should be aware of the overall strategy and organizational mission.
- Use a grassroots approach: the smallest viable strategic business unit (SBU) should be the locus of implementation.
- Use a less-is-more philosophy: choose between six and eight key performance indicators (KPI) for each SBU rather than 30.
- Link performance measures to key success factors: ensure that you have identified reasonable and achievable measures for success.
- Treat the Balanced Scorecard implementation as a strategic initiative: this is not a control system.

- Search for leading indicators: emphasize lead rather than lag indicators.
- Search for cause and effect links: altering one part of the process may have hidden effects on another process.
- Link key performance measures to compensation: reengineer your reward systems to link in with KPI achievement.
- Use the scorecard as an everyday management tool: make this part of corporate policy such that all employees are familiar with the measures.
- Continuously improve your system; today's improvement becomes tomorrow's norm – it is important to maintain a living evolving system.

In essence, the scorecard becomes a cybernetic or feedback system of if-then statements linking financial, customer, business process and learning objectives. This will only be an effective mechanism if it also incorporates a new system of measurements.

8.5.3 Measures of success

The Balanced Scorecard establishes a framework for performance evaluation but the actual measurements applied remain at the discretion of the particular organization. There are four specific areas in the Balanced Scorecard where dynamic and strategic measurements need to be applied:

- Measuring corporate contribution.
- Measuring user orientation.
- Measuring operational excellence.
- Measuring future orientation.

Short-term financial evaluations such as control of IT expenses and third party sales need to be considered as part of the corporate contribution along with longer-term business value of new IT projects and the business value of the whole IT function. The type of financial measures that can be applied to ascertain these figures are exemplified by the information economics approach, using a scoring technique for value and risk.

Similar measures need to be developed for user orientation, operational excellence and future orientation and performance drivers related to outcome measures. Examples of other approaches include the incorporation of activity-based costing (ABC) into the BSC, economic value added (EVA) and market value added (MVA) and inclusive valuation methodology as a knowledge asset evaluation approach. None of this is easy.

In truth very few examples can be found of organizations who apply a fully comprehensive approach to measuring value – particularly in regard to intellectual assets. Whatever the approach, consideration should be given to the organizational level of implementation. Generally it is most successful at the smallest replicable unit in the organization. This can be a process rather than a functional department. Micro-units permit the highest possible degree of segmentation, strategic fine-tuning, value added and customer satisfaction at the lowest cost. The larger the organization the more refined are these replicable units and the greater their leverage for creating added value.

8.6 Value measurement

8.6.1 Strategic value analysis (SVA)

Competitive advantage in the marketplace ultimately derives from providing better customer value for equivalent cost or equivalent customer value for a lower cost – the standard differentiation or lower cost strategic choice. Occasionally, but rarely, a company achieves both by providing better value at a lower cost such as in the case of Microsoft with Windows 95. Regardless of strategic focus the organization needs to measure the added value across the whole value chain to determine exactly where in the chain customer value can be enhanced or costs lowered. This includes linkages upstream as well as downstream in the overall value alliance. The value chain analysis will break down the chain from basic raw materials to end-use customers into strategically relevant activities in order to understand the behaviour of costs and the sources of differentiation. Since no two companies compete in *exactly* the same set of markets with *exactly* the same set of suppliers, the positioning within the overall value chain for each company is unique.

SVA is a technique for quantifying business issues and opportunities across the entire value chain for an industry and differs in two important ways from traditional business analysis:

- SVA disaggregates activities into the fundamental building blocks of the full value chain, from suppliers to consumers, and then groups these activities consistent with the way markets actually work.
- SVA evaluates each stage of the chain on an economic value basis eliminating problems caused by historical cost, transfer prices and accrual-based accounting.

In order to determine whether SVA would be a useful framework for strategic analysis in your organization there are four tests that can be applied:

- Are there new or emerging players in the industry (within any part of the value chain) who may be more successful than existing players?
- Are these companies positioned differently in the value chain from current players?
- Are new market prices emerging across segments of the value chain? Are these markets sufficiently deep to reflect arm's-length trading?
- If we used these market prices as transfer prices in our company would it fundamentally change the way that the major operating units behave?

If the answer to any of these questions is 'yes' then SVA will be of far greater benefit than a standard 'value-added' (revenues minus purchases) approach. Applying these four tests will provide an explanation of the relative position of your company in an industry and then can be used to guide a plan for management action with regard to overall structure, markets and assets and reporting relationships most likely to succeed in specific parts of the industry.

In this way SVA is uniquely helpful in understanding restructuring processes that may be required in periods of dramatic change. The next step is to evaluate a specific e-business opportunity.

8.7 Identifying the economics of e-business

For an organization considering whether to enter into a new e-business value proposition a simple matrix such as that suggested by Riggins (1999) can provide the first step. This framework seeks to display, in a simple form, how factors combine to allow a single organization to plot itself in respect of the opportunities offered by contemporary e-business. The value of this matrix lies in the fact that each business can allocate their own value and weighting to the factors leading to comfortable development of their enterprises, and position themselves accordingly.

The EC Value Grid offers a means to order and categorize the different features offered by forms of online storefronts – to use the grid, managers are recommended first to determine which of the five dimensions of commerce to target with an online presence.

It is a business decision, not a technical one: should an Internet presence be used to reduce the time taken to deliver products, services and information? Are distance impediments those most likely to succumb to virtual presence and yield advantage? Can industry relationships be altered to your advantage by using ICT to alter the intermediation chain favourably? Would an Internet presence enable you to deal in an entirely new product or service? And so on.

Once questions along this dimension have been answered, you might want to consider the *type* of value that is to be created for the customer. Is there a need to work more efficiently? Improve the client's effectiveness? Or create and maintain long-term relations with other parties? It is a truism that in every industry examined, it costs more to gain a customer than to keep an existing one.

Once these two sets of questions have found answers, the Value Grid shown in Table 8.4 is suggested to bring about

Table 8.4 The Electronic Commerce Value Grid (after Riggins 1999)

	Value creation	⇨	⇨
5 dimensions of e-commerce	*Efficiency*	*Effectiveness*	*Strategic*
Time	Accelerate user tasks	Eliminate information float	Establish 24 × 7 hour customer service
Distance	Improve scale to seem large	Present single gateway access	Achieve global presence
Relationships	Alter role of intermediaries	Engage in micro-marketing to look small	Create user dependency for repeat business
Interaction	Use extensive user feedback	User controls detail of information accessed	Users interact as online community
Product	Use software agents to automate tasks	Provide online decision support tools	Bundle information, products and services

business change by transferring work into an area of new business value for you. In addition, the grid may be used to act as a template against the activities of your firm and that of competitors may be plotted for comparison. The extent to which a website incorporates several cells in the grid becomes a measure of the site's effectiveness – and an obvious strategy for improvement is to seek to extend one's reach by moving into neighbouring cells. In this way an examination of possible advantageous next moves within the grid will prompt an examination of the preparedness of the organization to effect those changes.

The manager's goal should therefore be to move from a simple online presence which reduces time and distance barriers, to move toward adding value through increased efficiency and effectiveness, and considering moving further by changing industry relationships and new partnerships, perhaps with new products.

8.8 Reviewing organizational readiness for change

Any organization wishing to maximize its effectiveness and profitability as an e-business needs to recognize how virtual it is, how virtual it should be and how it should manage the opportunities and problems that arise. The ACHIEVE Working Group (Impact Programme, 1998) identified four primary characteristics of virtual organizations as:

- Dispersion (multiple locations).
- Empowerment (devolution of powers).
- Restlessness (acceptance, even enthusiasm for change).
- Interdependence (cooperation and synergy between and within organizations).

These four characteristics can be used as a measurement scale where an organization chooses a number of characteristics that are important to it and defining a number of identifiable levels of virtuality for each characteristic. For example, the degree of dispersion could be measured on the following scale:

A – there are no physical locations, staff scattered throughout the world, e.g. Institute of Catalysis.

B – there is one HQ building, staff are scattered throughout the world, e.g. Interpol.

C – there are many physical locations where staff are employed, e.g. BP.

D – the majority of staff work in one central location, e.g. Bank of England.

The organization can then measure and plot its level of virtuality and that of its major competitors and assess the impact of changing or not changing. Criteria that might be applied are identified in Table 8.5.

The ACHIEVE group emphasize that there are four main management concerns when overseeing such change:

- Managing and changing culture.
- Communication, internally and externally.
- New approaches to control.
- Managing and refreshing knowledge as a major asset.

None of these are easily solved but they must be given priority over technological change.

Table 8.5 Criteria for measuring virtuality

Dispersion	Empowerment	Restlessness	Interdependence
No. of locations	Degree of definition of accountabilities	No new products/ services; markets; processes; job profiles per year	No formal alliances with external organizations
Personal workplaces	No. of decision levels	Level of staff education	No. and importance of informal alliances
Amount of hot-desking	Degree of risk acceptance	Level of openness to change	Level of influence on external organizations
Extent and quality of reach	Investment in workplace skills	Rate of change of appraisal criteria	Proportion of staff to line functions
Degree of political/ economic support in any one location	Complexity, magnitude and scope of decisions by customer facing staff	Degree of anticipation to changing markets	Degree of contact between sister companies
Degree to which dispersion is visible to the customer		Level of stress in workforce	Use of cross-functional/process teams and interactions

8.9 Demonstrating the need for an action plan

It helps to begin a change effort with an action plan. Although each action plan will be different, you should consider incorporating the following minimum components:

- strategy – a planned course of action and allocation of resources to meet stated change goals;
- project organization – a clear designation of the authority, responsibility and relationships that will see the plan through;
- roles and responsibilities – a discussion of who will contribute exactly what to the project;
- systems – the procedures and processes that will be used throughout the organization;
- training – teaching the specific skills that people need to enable the change;
- style – the shared expectations of management style between employees as they work toward common goals;
- common mission – the agreed statement of the direction all will work to achieve organizational goal; and
- technology – the IT/IS and technical platform that will underpin the way work gets done.

A close examination will show you that, while this advice appears simple, turning it into effective action steps is not so obvious. A web search on 'organizational change' will yield many different plans and detailed advice, much of it provided by consulting companies eager to work with you to provide their favoured methods for implementing change according to their favoured strategy. It is recommended that, before selecting a change management partner, an organization tries to work through some of the issues itself. You may not identify a complete plan for change, but any areas identified which remain problematic after serious consideration will identify the extent to which this organization is ready to implement a change strategy at this time, and hopefully will identify groundwork to be completed.

If the matrix (Table 8.6) can be completed to the agreement and satisfaction of interested parties, then you may want to move on to consider the major issues that will arise once the decision to go ahead with a change is made. Again, you should consider the matrix (Table 8.7) and ensure that agreed responses can be supplied in the right-hand column to match the queries raised on the left.

Table 8.6 Matrix for preparing to manage change

Major issues	Response identified
Why do we need to change now?	
Can we describe the present state?	
What is the future state we want to see?	
What will change?	
What will remain constant?	
What vulnerabilities will we create during the change process?	
State the critical success factors for successful change	
What are the major impediments to change?	

Table 8.7 Matrix for beginning change implementation

Major issues	Planned response
Can we define our change strategy?	
List the operational definitions of desired change	
Have we positioned changes as a desirable challenge to affected staff?	
How do we best use our advantages to assist in change?	
How do we minimize adverse effects on staff and operations?	

The checklist for items of interest and action may work well when applied by an experienced group of practitioners, but a discussion with colleagues may reveal that reaching consensus on open-ended questions is a lot more difficult than might be supposed. For this reason there has been a move to introduce systematic thinking to the measurement and improvement of corporate information technology.

8.10 Summary: evaluating strategies for e-business

This chapter has explored the stages involved in the development of an e-business strategy. These are:

- *assessing organizational readiness for change* helps the organization to focus on where the organization is currently and where they should be heading in an e-business environment;
- *identifying the economics of e-business* helps the organization to compare various different e-business opportunities by evaluating their net value effect against various shareholder values;
- *evaluating the needs for change and performance measurements for the future* – employing the BSC technique allows the organization to assess all four levels of organizational interactions and to establish an integrated performance evaluation system to achieve the new e-business mission;
- *developing a strategy for e-business* is the final stage where the business decides how it is going to package these new values into products, services or experiences.

Developing strategies for e-business is not a straightforward sequential process but rather a perpetual and iterative learning process where the organization needs to have a built-in learning and relearning capability.

References

Beinhocker, E.D. (1997) Robust Adaptive Strategies, *Sloan Management Review*, Vol. 40, No. 3, 95–106.

Deise, M.V., Nowikow, C., King, P. and Wright, A. (2000) *Executive's Guide to E-Business – from tactics to strategy*, Wiley, Chapter 11.

Kaplan, R. and Norton, D. (1996) *Translating Strategy into Action: the Balanced Scorecard*, Boston: Harvard Business School Press.

Kauffman, S.A. (1995) Escaping the Red Queen Effect, *The McKinsey Quarterly*, No. 1, 118–129.

Riggins, F. (1999) A Framework for Identifying Web-Based Electronic Commerce Opportunities, *Journal of Organizational Computing and Electronic Commerce*, Vol. 9 No. 4, 297–310.

9 Outsourcing, partnering and the virtual organization

'I've had plenty of practice,' the Knight said very gravely, 'plenty of practice!'
(*Through the Looking Glass*, C. Dodgson (1872))

9.1 Introduction

We have suggested that one useful concept of virtual organization is that of an opportunistic grouping of collaborating organizations, each of which focuses on a set of core competencies or capabilities at which it excels (see Chapter 4). This opportunistic network of firms is fluid and changes according to circumstances and needs. Such a network of firms is likely to be created and sustained through the processes of outsourcing and partnering/alliance formation.

As the trend toward moving away from non-core activities intensifies, and indeed as the relationship between companies and their suppliers becomes less and less like the purchasing of the service and more and more like a partnership, so the trend toward virtual organizing will increase. Furthermore, as firms utilize IT and the Internet to expedite the information exchange elements of maintaining such relationships, we move even closer to the classically defined virtual organizational form.

In contrast to the position adopted in this book, in which we argue for the desirable existence of several different forms of virtual organization as strategic responses to give environments and opportunities, some writers posit the desirability of the new collaborating organization which uses alliance or outsourcing strategies as the complete means of component process fulfilment. It will help us now to look at these models or visions for the future, looking at the role of both outsourcing and partnering or alliances, and close relationship of both these to virtual organizing and the virtual organizational form.

9.2 The PriceWaterhouseCoopers e-business staged model

Consultants PriceWaterhouse present a model of contemporary and future business, taking account of and projecting developments concerning the Internet and e-commerce/ e-business. Their stages of growth, or maturity type, model is shown in Figure 9.1. This figure shows four stages of increasing business value resulting from the increasing leverage of e-business.

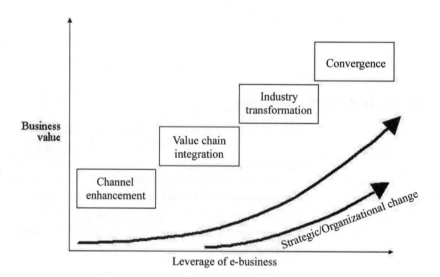

Figure 9.1

9.2.1 Stage one

In stage or snapshot one (as Martin Deise and co-authors call it), companies exploit the Internet as an alternative or additional marketing, sales and payment channel. This might resemble the virtual face model (introduced in Chapter 3) and a great variety of implementation forms might be expected. The chief characteristics of this model as a stage are that it is advanced as both a desirable starting point for most if not all organizations, and that it treats Internet tools as add-ons to be bolted on to pre-existing processes without question.

There is much to find fault with in this view, in our opinion, but this is not the place for refutation (our responses to this are distributed throughout this book – see in particular Chapters 3, 4, 5, 8, and 11).

9.2.2 Stage two

In the second stage, value chain integration, companies focus on their core value creating activities and integrate their value chains and information systems with the value chains of suppliers, logistics providers, distributors and retailers to maximize efficiencies and reduce costs. With the outsourcing of non-core activities and the integrating of business processes with efficient partners along the value chain, we have the creation of a virtual corporation consisting of the company and its value chain partners.

At first glance, this looks like a restatement of our value chain alliance (note that this implicitly, if not explicitly, assumes that there is a single player necessarily at the heart of this model who outsources functions) but in a weaker and less useful form. Let us merely note that there are organizations whose position with their business environments may make it advantageous to adopt this position, but it is not a recommended evolutionary stage for all.

9.2.3 Stage three

In stage three, industry transformation, a parting of the ways is reached as a consequence of e-business strategy adoption, it is argued. Some companies progress to the stage of focusing their core competencies on knowledge (knowcos) and others focus their core competencies on excellence in physical processes (physcos).

Knowcos focus on such activities as market strategy, product design, marketing and customer management. They also have well-honed skills in managing relationships in networks of collaborating firms, i.e. in virtual organizations or extended enterprises. Deise *et al.* (2000) call this capability value network management. Thus a knowco will have the agility to take on threats from competitors and respond with new products and services more quickly, because it does not need to factor in costs and utilization of physical assets, such as updating capital equipment, when making strategic decisions. Strategic networks of companies connected by high-speed 'backbone' computer networks will support the knowcos. Among these will be:

- *Strategic service partners* (SSPs) will supply knowcos with extensions of core business processes. If a knowco wishes to design a new product but not manufacture, warehouse or distribute that product, then the one or more SSPs may provide those functions. Thus for this product, product design and customer relationship management may stay with the knowco while manufacturing, warehousing and distribution are provided by the chosen SSPs. Communications with SSPs are over a high-speed backbone communications network. The business processes and information systems of the SSPs and the knowcos will be seamlessly integrated.

- *Value added suppliers* (VASs) would provide knowcos with engineered or configured parts or subassemblies unique to climb specific requirements.
- *Commodity suppliers* (CSs) will provide component parts and subassemblies commonly available on the market.
- *Non-strategic service partners* (NSPs) will deliver outsourcing capabilities for commodity type administrative and other business processes, including accounting and finance, human resources, indirect procurement, and travel – all processes integral to a company's ability to operate. Such companies may be similar to the business service providers (BSPs) that are emerging today.
- *Network operations partners* (NOPs) use a secure, high-speed backbone to connect companies with SSPs, CSs, VASs, and NSPs. It is believed that companies will turn to NOPs for full-service and applications-based information systems outsourcing.
- *Applications service providers* (ASPs) will use the Internet or alternative fast computer networks to deploy, manage, and lease packaged application software to customers from centrally managed facilities.

Thus, in this stage of industry transformation there is a differentiation of firms based on knowledge, and an even more extensive and significant use of outsourcing and partnering with efficient service and technology providers of all kinds.

9.2.4 Stage four

Stage four is a stage of what Deise calls convergence, the coming together of companies in different industries to provide goods and services to customers. Thus, finally, we not only have the blurring of organizational boundaries, but the blurring of industry boundaries. This comes about, not only as a result of the Internet and e-commerce, but also as a result of these developments together with other developments which are possibly just as significant change drivers for contemporary business, namely deregulation and globalization.

The above model is advanced by PriceWaterhouseCoopers as a helpful sense-making model of business today and in the future. It has been developed for consultants to use as a simple model when talking to business clients so that a common ground for action or advice can be established. The significance for this chapter is that it provides another lens through which to see the role and importance of outsourcing and partnering for contemporary business. As business moves to more effective and agile organizational forms, the practices of outsourcing and partnering will be vital ones to do well, and the capabilities associated with outsourcing and partnering, such as relationship management, will be increasingly valued in business.

The drawback of this model is that it tends to constrain thinking in a stage growth mode. It is too easy to see the four stages outlined above as necessary or optimal stages through which each enterprise should pass. This temptation should be resisted. While there is a stage growth model for the development of a butterfly not everything can, or should, turn into a butterfly. For this reason, we prefer the range of models introduced in Chapter 3, although it has not yet been determined whether there are optimal migration paths between these models for enterprises with specific characteristics.

9.3 The alliance for Converging Technologies Model

Another model for business in the Internet and internetworked world of contemporary business is that presented by Don Tapscott and his colleagues at the Alliance for Converging Technologies, an international research and consulting group. Tapscott sees the fundamental wealth-creating vehicle moving away from the integrated corporation of the industrial age toward fluid internetworked congregations of businesses called business webs (alliances of this nature were discussed in Chapter 4). Whereas the industrial corporation was ownership and power based, the business web is knowledge based and relationship based. Embracing this new organizational form to greater or lesser extent, Tapscott believes, is an essential part of business survival and success in the future.

Tapscott defines the business web as a distinct system of suppliers, distributors, commerce service providers, infrastructure providers and customers that use the Internet for their primary business communications and transactions. Several business webs may compete with one another for market share within an industry. In mature business webs, each business focuses on a limited set of core competencies, the things that it does best.

9.3.1 Key design dimensions

Tapscott gives a number of key design dimensions for effective and competitive business webs. Among the characteristics are the following:

- multi-enterprise capability machine
- coopetition
- customer-centricity
- bathed in knowledge
- value proposition innovation
- Internet infrastructure

By referring to business webs as 'multi-enterprise capability machines' Tapscott emphasizes that the business webs rely on a market model of partnering and alliances rather than the 'internal monopoly' of a build-or-acquire model. Thus the traditional corporation defines its capabilities as its employees and the assets it owns, whereas the business web marshals the contributions of many participating enterprises. The advantages of this mode of organization – cost, speed, innovation, quality and selection – typically outweigh the risks of partner opportunism.

9.3.2 Coopetition

Coopetition (introduced and discussed in Chapter 4) refers to the fact that business web participants simultaneously cooperate and compete with each other. Collaborative advantage is mixed with pure competitive advantage, and cooperative strategy becomes a focus alongside purely competitive strategy.

Tapscott, like others, argues that effective business webs function as highly responsive customer fulfilment networks. Members of traditional supply chains, such as the automobile industry, tend to focus only on the next link to which they ship their products. As competition moves from competition between firms to competition between supply chains, effective business webs encourage all participants to focus on the end customer.

9.3.3 Knowledge management

Knowledge is important for business webs. Knowledge sharing, particularly knowledge of business processes and operations, is important to establish competent, competitive and innovative supply chains that operate seamlessly across the boundaries of business web partners. The Internet is a vital low-cost tool in this knowledge sharing. (Note, however, the use of the Internet does not, of course, preclude or diminish the importance of personal relationships.) It is worth noting in passing that business web partners, of course, while sharing operational knowledge, are more cautious when it comes to strategic or competitive information or knowledge.

Tapscott and his colleagues believe that business webs are inherently innovative. They believe that business webs often deliver new value propositions to customers that tend to render obsolete old ways of doing things. An example given is the MP3 business web of commercial service providers, technology providers and content providers (musicians), which enables the downloading of music and infinitely expands the music community.

Internet infrastructure is another characteristic of business webs. The participants in the business web capitalize on the Internet's ability to lower transaction costs, using it as their primary infrastructure for interpersonal communication and business transactions.

Thus we have some idea of the characteristics of a mature business web. How then do such entities come about? Tapscott tells us that a process of disaggregation and reaggregation should take place.

In disaggregation, one first examines the end customer value proposition, looking for those aspects of the end-customer experience that really give value. Then follows the examination of the value chain of activities that ends in the delivery of that valued experience, including the analysis of the role of the particular firm and its partners in that value chain. We want to know what are the core competencies that the firm has, and how do they best contribute to the end customer's valued experience. We also want to know what are the core competencies of potential partners, and how they could contribute. Further we want to know what is the potential role of technology and the Internet in creating value in this value chain.

193

9.3.4 Questions arising from these models

Given the analysis above, including the new role of the Internet and technology, how could we reaggregate the value chain effectively? What things need to be done in what potentially new ways? What is the role of partners in this new enterprise? Thus to move away from the industrial age corporation towards the business web, new business partners and a careful outsourcing of business processes may be necessary. The business processes to be taken on by partners are likely to be different from the business processes in the original integrated firm. Tapscott gives a warning about attempting to move toward the business web organizational form by old-style outsourcing of the quick-fix cost-cutting style. That kind of outsourcing of problem functions or activities is dead, he maintains. The new partnerships or relationships are not the type of situation where both players are in a zero-sum financial game lacking openness and trust. This mindset should be replaced by well-aligned harmonious and mutually beneficial relationships.

Thus we have seen two models of the future of business – namely the PriceWaterhouseCoopers model and the Alliance for Converging Technologies model – in which outsourcing and partnering play vital roles. e-business models such as these graphically show the relationship between outsourcing, partnering, the business and the virtual organization. We will now examine in greater detail the important concepts of outsourcing and partnering in turn as they are currently understood in this context.

9.4 Outsourcing

Outsourcing is the contracting out of the provision of the business process, service or function to an external vendor. Taking a long-term view of outsourcing, the Corbett Group (www.Corbettgroup.com) defines outsourcing as the long-term results-orientated relationship with an external service provider for activities traditionally performed within the company. Outsourcing usually applies to a complete business process and implies a degree of managerial control and risk on the part of the provider.

Outsourcing is a practice that is transforming the face of business today, redefining the firm to be more agile and nimble, more concentrated around its core competences, while networked with best-in-class business partners. Starting out as an efficiency-driven cost-cutting tactic, outsourcing has grown into a vast trend of business practice that is now become concerned with redefining and redesigning the firm for increased adaptability, flexibility and competitiveness.

Starting as a small trend in the 1980s, outsourcing grew rapidly in the 1990s into a global phenomenon accounting for transactions priced at hundreds of billions of dollars. The Corbett Group's 1999 Strategic Outsourcing Study found that one-third of executive budgets are externally sourced today, and predict that that there is more external sourcing to come in the future. Dun & Bradstreet estimate that by 2001, global outsourcing will be worth over $1 trillion. As the size of the outsourcing phenomenon has grown, so has the scope. While the early trend tended to see outsourcing being undertaken for specific functions or activities (such as cleaning services, canteen services, IT services and so on) outsourcing now encompasses almost all business services. The major business services outsourced are IT, human resources, marketing and sales, and administration, with IT comprising 30% of the total, human resources 16%, marketing and sales 14%, and administration 9%.

9.4.1 Outsourcing and external sourcing

Outsourcing can be viewed as one of a number of external sourcing options, which include:

- Supplemental staffing – an external sourcing option in which non-company personnel are used, often at times of peaks in demand, to help carry out business operations. Such personnel could be unskilled or skilled temporary operatives or clerical workers, consultants or contractors.
- Selective sourcing – the outsourcing of aspects of a function or business process. For example, an IT department may decide to outsource computer systems development and retain other IT services internally. Or more selectively still, only certain computer systems development projects may be outsourced.
- Total outsourcing – the contracting out of an entire business process all function. However, often the term total outsourcing is used for a situation in which a large proportion, 80% or more, of a department or function is outsourced.
- Strategic alliance – a situation in which investments are shared between one or more business partners, each business partner focusing on their areas of competence. In a

strategic alliance, separate revenue streams are maintained for each organization.

● Joint venture – the creation of a new business entity with its own revenue stream. Investments in the new entity are shared between business partners.

Often, supplemental staffing, selective sourcing and the outsourcing of a business process or function are all collectively referred to as outsourcing. It is worth noting that when outsourcing is viewed as a long-term relationship with a provider of business services, this relationship gets very close to what we have referred to above as a strategic alliance. However, outsourcing is essentially a fee-for-service relationship based around a contract. In a strategic alliance, not only do the strategic partners share resources, they also share in profits and losses.

External sourcing then is sometimes taken to be more general than outsourcing in the sense that supplemental staffing is not taken to be outsourcing. In this chapter we will treat outsourcing as including supplemental staffing as well as selective sourcing. However, *we recommend that, with us, you distinguish between outsourcing and strategic alliances and joint ventures in which profits and losses are shared.*

9.5 Strategic outsourcing, transformational outsourcing and tactical outsourcing

There are three broad approaches to outsourcing, namely strategic, transformational and tactical. Strategic outsourcing is an approach in which the firm invests internally in those business activities from which it derives a competitive advantage and outsources the other necessary business activities to best-in-class providers of those activities. Essentially the firm concentrates on its core competencies and actively considers outsourcing its other business activities.

In transformational outsourcing the firm utilizes outsourcing to bring about innovative change. Relationships with world-class vendors of business operations and services are utilized to help move the firm to global best practice in all non-core business processes. Thus outsourcing helps in achieving the firm's strategic vision, and supports the management of organizational transformation.

Tactical outsourcing is the use of outsourcing to bring about operational efficiencies. In tactical outsourcing, internal business services and operations are benchmarked against the market-place of external providers of such services. If the costs and benefits of internal sourcing of such services do not compare well with external sourcing, the business service is outsourced.

9.6 Strategic outsourcing and core competencies

Strategic outsourcing rests on the proposition that resources and management time are focused on core competencies while considering non-core activities as possible targets for out-sourcing. But to be able to focus on, cultivate and grow core competencies, one must first identify them. However, given that organizational core competencies are rare, complex and embed-ded in organizational routines and practices, it can be difficult to identify and characterize them.

The core competence approach to outsourcing tells us that we may usefully see the defining characteristics of core com-petencies as:

- Skill and knowledge sets, not just products and functions.
- Broad areas subject to reassessment, adaptation and evolution.
- Limited in number.
- Unique sources of leverage in the value chain.
- Areas where the company can dominate.
- Elements important to customers in the long run.
- Embedded in the organization's systems and practices.

Core competencies are unlikely to be located in products or functions. Competitors too easily imitate these. Core com-petencies are likely to emanate from certain sets of skills and knowledge which are difficult to specify and imitate. The skills giving rise to core competencies are likely to cut across several functions, and knowledge is likely to be tacit rather than explicit. Core competencies, because of their importance in under-pinning the competitiveness and hence the survival of the firm, require intensity of focus and management dedication.

For these reasons core competencies in the true sense should be limited to two or three in number, and certainly do not number more than five. They are concentrated in areas where the firm can dominate. Since each company is really in competition with every supplier of every activity in its value chain, it is important that the activities in which it chooses to excel are areas in which it can really achieve preeminence. It is worth noting that at least one of these areas should be in the domain of understanding and managing the customer relationship, since this is so important to business competitiveness and survival.

Finally, core competencies are likely to be embedded in organizational systems, routines and practices thus not only rendering them difficult to imitate but also difficult to identify, understand and cultivate. Nonetheless core competencies are vital capabilities that are important to nurture, evolve and grow.

In common with the PriceWaterhouseCoopers thinking introduced in section 9.1 above, this thinking stays with traditional thinking that there must be a single dominant player leading or controlling the consortium. This thinking is at odds with the more flexible models introduced in Chapter 3 and tacitly assumed throughout this text.

9.7 Linking outsourcing to strategy

It is important that an enterprise's external sourcing decisions are aligned to its strategy. Insinga and Werle (2000) present a planning guide to help in this matter. The guide is structured around two basic dimensions. First, the activities of the firm are considered for their potential to yield a competitive advantage, and are assessed as either key to producing a competitive advantage, emerging towards being the key activity, basic to the firm or simply commodity activities. Second, the activities of the firm are rated in terms of the firm's capability at undertaking them, and assessed as activities in which the firm has a strong, moderate or weak capability. The planning guide is shown in Figure 9.2.

Generally speaking as one moves down and to the left of the matrix in the Figure 9.2 it is recommended that there be less investment in the activity, less knowledge of the particular business domain nurtured in the company, and less direct control over the day-to-day operations involved. Core competencies are thus located in the upper right of the matrix and commodity activities, suitable for outsourcing to a business service provider, are located in the lower left. However, when activities are examined in this way there may be significant differences between the recommended position of the activity in the company and its historical and present reality. Such differences require the attention of senior management, since these differences indicate other than the sensible and optimal allocation of resources.

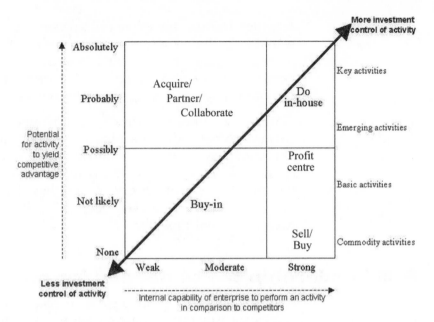

Figure 9.2

Cells 1, 2, 4, 5 indicate a need either to acquire the capability or to partner with an organization that has the capability. Partnering implies investing in the collaborating organization and positioning one's company to acquire more ownership if the particular activity emerges over time as more key or central to the competitive positioning of the company. As one moves to the lower levels of cells 4 and 5, and the activity is seemingly less critical to competitiveness, a collaborative positioning of pooling knowledge and sharing risk with less of an emphasis on ownership possibilities is recommended.

Cells 3 and 6 indicate activities which are critical to competitiveness or are emerging towards such status. They are also activities in which the organization has a strong internal capability. These activities should be being performed in-house under tight control. Where the activity is just emerging towards being important to competitiveness, and there is uncertainty about its future criticality, as in the lower part of cell 6, a suitable position might be to collaborate to share risk, thus economizing on resources expended in carrying out the activity, but remaining positioned to take the activity in-house if necessary.

Cells 7, 8, 10, 11 indicate both the weak or moderate internal capability in the activities, together with a low potential for yielding a competitive advantage. These characteristics of the activities indicate suitability for outsourcing to suitable external providers. As one moves towards the upper right of this set of activities, towards the top of cell 8, there is a likelihood that one would keep more knowledge and control of these activities and perhaps engage in a selective sourcing of sub-activities, or perhaps simply seek to reduce the dependency on internal capabilities by developing alternate sources of the activity.

Cells 9, 12 indicate a similar low potential for competitive advantage, but indicate a relatively strong internal capability. The planning guide recommends that a company should consider selling such a capability to the marketplace and invest the proceeds in more critical capabilities. The necessary activities and skills should then be purchased in the marketplace from competent providers.

9.8 Leadership traits needed for outsourcing

Once an outsourcing strategy is in place and the extent and significance of outsourcing increases, one must consider the management of the outsourcing relationships. Management in an organization with a significant number of outsourcing relationships requires a new blend of capabilities and talents. Useem and Harder (2000) claim that in the new organization, characterized by extensive and significant outsourcing, managers must concentrate on negotiating results rather than issuing orders. They must add to and to some extent substitute the skills for sending work downward, and gain skills in arranging for sending work outward. They need to exercise lateral leadership.

9.8.1 Four primary traits

Useem and Harder argue that the following leadership capabilities are required of managers, as outsourcing becomes significant in firms:

- Strategic thinking that links outsourcing considerations and decisions to issues of core competence and competitive advantage is a vital capability. Being informed by a strategic vision and perspective when deciding what to outsource and how to structure the outsourcing relationship is vital to future business competitiveness and survival, particularly when significant amounts of outsourcing are taking place.
- Deal making skills are important in securing compatible and high-quality providers of the outsourced business processes and activities. Deal making also involves obtaining buy-in

from those within the firm who must forge a seamless business process interface with the external provider. Thus, the dealmaker needs the skills to establish an effective and mutually supportive web of relations between the organization and the outsourcing provider that stretches seamlessly across the boundary of both organizations.

- Partnership governing – outsourcing to best in-class providers of business processes and activities will likely bring innovation and change to the organization.
- Managing change – as always, effective change management is required and is crucial to the success of the organizational change involved.

After a deal is secured with an appropriate outsourcing vendor, a good relationship must be established and sustained so that both partners in the relationship work together constructively. This is particularly important in today's business world where situations of turbulence, change and innovation pertain in so many markets since legislating vendor behaviour under such conditions with a contract is often difficult and suboptimal.

9.8.2 Overview

None of the qualities mentioned above, when taken singly, is unique to the management outsourcing, but their combination, Useem and Harder argue, is critical to managing organizations with important outsourcing relationships. In an extensive survey of US managers, the authors found that the skills mentioned were viewed as important. A large proportion of the managers surveyed reported that they would pay a premium for persons with such skills.

9.9 Summary

In this chapter we have introduced to you two models which you may have come across and placed them in the perspective of our thinking. We find that these models make much use of the concept of outsourcing, and we have tried to make sense of current uses of this term.

There are inevitable confusions arising in this context. When is a product or process outsourced? Do we speak of outsourcing water? Electricity supply? Buildings? Perhaps the answer will alter between cultures, but no matter wherever we are, there will always be things we expect to bring in from outside, and those which our current state of industrial development leads us to expect to supply from within. (For a great deal of insight on this see the work of Ronald Coase and his successors on transaction theory.)

At this stage, two-thirds of the way through this text if you are reading sequentially, we should pause to reflect that while the first half of the last century showed us that the most effective form of business enterprise was the hierarchical structure which subsumed suppliers and competitors horizontally and vertically as the (transaction cost-based) chance arose. During this time economies of scale were venerated, and in many cases realized, as firms organized into bureaucratic silos of divisions or functions. Information naturally flowed, like water, along the easiest paths – in this case determined by divisions and lines of authority. The coordination of power and responsibility was a central function of the apex of the pyramid, power being distributed from the centre in the form of resources.

By the 1980s it had become clear that enormous economic and social pressures had already effected great change to the previous beliefs about organizational structure and efficiency. Market convergence, the internationalization of competition and the advent of innovative information and communication technologies came together to produce restless marketplaces in which short-term shifts could easily destroy long-term survival. As well as strategy, firms were forced to rethink both structure and strategy to respond dynamically to change. The past hierarchies proved insufficiently responsive, and dynamic networks of organizations, or within organizations proved their worth. It is recognition of this that led to the positing of networks as novel, and the tired notion of the necessity of stage growth that has led to the PriceWaterhouse and Tapscott models introduced above.

Similarly it is the retention of thinking in terms of central authority and control that necessitates thinking in outsourcing terms. We have introduced these here for you, but caution reliance on these when they are failing to demonstrate their relevance in the e-business environment we are facing.

It is our contention that this text as a whole will encourage you to see emerging business forms as taking advantage of new technologies and increasingly adopt network postures. At the same time, middle management function will be less to worry about making in-house or outsourcing, but to replace internal administration task with the roles of information integrator and entrepreneur.

References

Deise, Martin V., Nowikow, Conrad, King, Patrick and Wright, Amy (2000) *PriceWaterHouse Coopers Executive's Guide to E-Business (From Tactics To Strategy)*, John Wiley & Sons,

Dyer and Singh (1998) The Relational View: Cooperative Strategy and Sources of Interorganisational Competitive Advantage, *Academy of Management Review*, Vol. 23(4), 660–679.

Insinga and Werle (2000) Linking Outsourcing to Business Strategy, *Academy of Management Review*, Vol. 14(4).

10   e-business strategies in the virtual organization

> In the future, highly qualified people will go on job interviews purely for recreation.
> (*The Dilbert Future*, Scott Adams)

10.1 Introduction

Much has been written in this book about the external drivers for e-business and how this concept will change how organizations work and the role of their employees. We have also noted the same phenomenon in large organizations where ERP systems have been introduced impacting greatly on the internal structures and processes for labour and work division. This combination of technologies offers established companies the opportunity to build interactive relationships with partners and suppliers, improve efficiency and extend reach, all at a very low cost. For example, GE estimates to save $500 million to $700 million of its purchasing costs over three years and cut purchasing cycles by as much as 50%. The Norwegian company Statoil processes more than 350 000 invoices annually, and awards over 40 000 contracts through web-enabled ERP commerce. The company expects a considerable improvement in the ratio of invoices to orders as well as a tangible contribution to revenue. Eventually, both companies expect to buy the majority of their purchases through web-based bidding systems. Faced with such e-business innovations companies are looking for effective solutions to marry the two technologies for strategic advantage.

Inevitably this will have a major impact on their employee workforce, the processes they have to perform and their skill requirements. The workforce has had to embrace a new culture as a knowledge-based community with far more flexible work

roles. Increasingly, we are seeing the large traditional organization breaking up and the emergence of new, networked
organizational forms in which work is conducted by temporary
teams that cross organizational lines.

In this new climate, organizations have to learn new approaches to managing a workforce of knowledge workers, yet little
information is available on how to implement this successfully
and how to ensure more effective personnel performance as a
result. Drucker (1998) suggests that the traditional role of
managers telling workers what to do is no longer viable and
instead managers must direct people as if they were unpaid
volunteers, tied to the organization by commitment to its aims
and purposes and often expecting to participate in its governance. As information technologies continue to permeate all
aspects of organizational life the role of the IT professional will
also change and they will have to embrace a set of shared
values and assumptions about how things work in the
organization.

Markus *et al.* 2000 suggest that organizations will have to seek to
harness the talents and energies of dispersed 'communities of
practice' and increasingly will face a workforce of volunteers as
more people choose periods of less than full-time work. This
obviously raises the question of how traditional management
tasks of motivating and directing employees will have to change
in the face of these new realities.

This chapter considers three important issues. First, we look at
B2B interactions along the value chain. Second we look at the
B2C interactions, taking the increasingly important area of
customer relationship marketing (CRM – shown as customer
interactions in Figure 10.1) as our focus. Lastly we look at
Business to Employee (B2E) relationships within the context of
ERP. In particular we look at the motivational factors influencing employees to initiate change in the face of these new realities
and the implications for management of both IT and non-IT
employees in the learning organization.

10.2 e-business and ERP

As reviewed in Chapter 7, a useful model for understanding the
adoption of e-business strategies for the learning organization
considers the organization as operating along three vectors –
customer/market interaction, asset sourcing and knowledge
leverage supported by a strong information technology

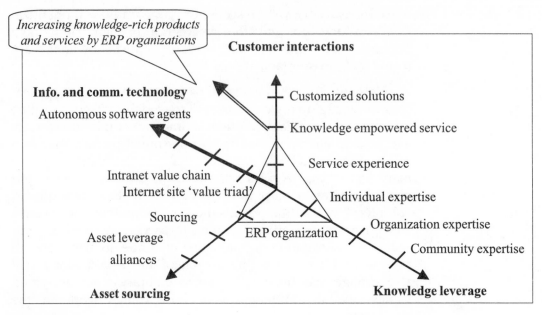

Figure 10.1
e-business and ERP

platform. Some see this as the virtual organizing model for the 21st century and as such a management strategy in itself.

Figure 10.1 gives a view of an organization using an enterprise resource planning (ERP) system such as SAP, as an integrated system to enable knowledge management across the three vectors of the organization.

Customer interaction (B2C) refers to the extent to which you virtually interact with the market defined at three levels of greater virtual progression:

- Remote product/service experience.
- Product/service customization.
- Shaping customer solutions.

Asset sourcing (B2B) refers to competency leveraging from:

- Efficient sourcing of standard components.
- Efficient asset leverage in the business network.
- Creating new competencies through alliances.

Knowledge leverage (B2E) refers to:

- Maximizing individual experience.
- Harnessing organizational expertise.
- Leveraging of community expertise.

This chapter focuses on the problems involved first in the B2B environment through supply chain management, then in the B2C environment with the use of effective customer relationship management (CRM) systems, and finally in the B2E environment through effective ERP integration with e-business.

10.3 B2B fulfilment and operations

10.3.1 Order fulfilment – what's virtual about trucking baked beans?

Fulfilment is the process of accepting an order, assembling the component in production or in transit, and then packaging, shipping, and delivering the order. The area we call e-business will look a lot more important a year or two from now. Somebody has to pick, pack, and ship until they figure out a way to squeeze baked beans down the phone line (which we aren't ruling out just yet). It's one thing to take an order, but the resources of the Vocan offer unprecedented levels of service in fulfilment areas such as:

- Accurate due delivery dates.
- Real-time product availability as opposed to what can be ordered.
- Coordination of multiple line items, maybe from different suppliers, to reduce shipping costs.
- Real-time shipping status – as popularized by Fedex.
- Pricing options for preferred production/delivery options.
- Available to promise – item made and delivery to order.
- Capability – product hasn't been made but production capacity can be reserved.
- Intelligent, automated, alternatives to fill demand and optimize for market share, fill rates, profitability, or customer satisfaction.
- Integrated orders that span multiple manufacturers but give one order status and price for the final component.

10.3.2 Curing the blind spots

Because the chain of commerce is fragmented, we are accustomed to many blind spots in the traditional fulfilment process. These cost money. All companies are are at the mercy of the varying efficiency of trading partners, but coordinating fulfilment across multiple supply chains is difficult to do manually.

And the problem is growing more acute. Raw competition is spawning more configurations and flavours of products with shorter life cycles. In 1981, 2700 new products hit grocery shelves in the US; that figure had ballooned to 20,000 by 1996. That variation poses big problems for supply chain management.

The first blind spot is end-market demand

Real-time demand is invisible to most companies because most sell through intermediaries or don't have any lead-time from their customers on demand shifts. Manufacturers may forecast with historical data but often don't have current information on shifts in demand. To avoid running out of stock and losing sales when demand escalates, companies build for all scenarios. Some makers require their suppliers to keep 90–150 days of inventory on hand and have resigned themselves to the cost of carrying this excess inventory in the supply chain. The US had a $1.37 trillion investment in inventory in 1998, and 40% of carry costs on this inventory was obsolescence! The better solution is to accept orders for things that haven't yet been built and deliver them quickly.

The second blind spot is through the supply chain

No company can tell what inventory and manufacturing capacity is available in their own supply chains: they're too complex, and anyway, until now the time taken to find out meant that the information was necessarily out of date and inaccurate. Their suppliers in turn can't see demand two or three levels up the chain. So they build inventory as well. Because manufacturers can't get real-time product availability from their suppliers, they assume fixed lead-times on all products, but life is variable. They can work to fixed lead-times if they require suppliers to carry excess inventory, but then the supplier has higher carrying costs and spoilage that show up in the final price.

Building to inventory yields higher defect rates

You can't see what's wrong with products sitting in a warehouse – they have to be used first. Tightening the link between production and consumption provides more frequent product feedback that can be rolled into production plans. Matching production to real-time demand is an obvious objective but difficult to achieve. Pretty quickly, one gets the picture of the massive inventory blowout that could be reduced if the entire supply chain had transparency of process and demand.

Virtual supply chains collaborating in real time represent the fastest return on the dollar

At stake are billions of dollars in inventory reduction, transport costs, and process improvement. The recent explosion of industry horizontal and vertical portals and hubs (e-hubs) reflect natural points of integration and coordination to facilitate the synchronization of demand and supply chains. The standard tradition is for companies to create build-to-order environments. Today the goalposts have been shifted: we see that the goal is to build fewer generic products for inventory (that has to be stored and handled) and more custom products for a known order – preferably being shipped right out the door, still warm from whatever production process that gave them birth. To do this, companies must create a global shop floor to link production more tightly to current demand.

10.3.3 Once commerce is online, every demand is an input into production planning

We know that marketing campaigns, configuration events, rebates, advertising, quotes, bids, partner campaigns, and negotiations all combine to drive production. Usually, production is the last to find out about these events because of the complexity and costs associated with sharing this information with all the relevant parties that lie along the route between a raw material producer and the consumer's point of purchase or consumption. e-commerce can help bring more precision to a historically imprecise process. The discontinuity between multiple parties in the chain of commerce, some within the same company, is immense and a small improvement could make a big difference. We introduced the value chain alliance as early as Chapter 3, and it should be clear by now exactly how and why some organizations will wish to adopt this organizational strategy.

Manufacturers need broad product lines to be competitive and meet a wide variety of buyer preferences. Yet you can't stay in business by offering all products in unlimited quantity all the time. You have to develop complex strategies for guestimating which portions of the product line will sell over a given production horizon. All that translates into stockouts and backorders or, conversely, excess inventory for the supplier.

As a result, buyers want to reduce their risk of getting a backorder or stockout. They would like to see detailed information about inventory and production capacity (available to promise, capable to promise). Instead of ordering and waiting for order status information, buyers would like real-time availability information and the ability to reserve products by serial and bin number.

10.3.4 Exchanges present and future

To date, exchanges have at best served as a rough and ready communications mechanism for shipment status. Typically, exchanges send the order to the supplier and leave the fulfilment and settling process to the trading partners working offline. Most exchanges cannot verify inventory before the order because they cannot see the supplier's back-end systems. And, of course, if suppliers post product listings on multiple exchanges without real-time inventory availability, they will end up selling products they haven't produced, and compound the problems of backorders and stockouts.

However, more advanced order management systems will accommodate the dynamic nature of web channels. All this isn't simple and won't happen overnight. Yes, companies have invested in supply chain software for years, but most of this has been inward looking and designed for internal planning and scheduling only. Today the Internet presents a platform for interenterprise optimization and planning with some exciting opportunities. Over the past two years hundreds of e-hubs have begun operations and their processes are evolving rapidly.

10.4 Customer orientation

The Internet and e-business technologies that are enabling our new organizational forms are radically changing the relationship between supplier and customer. Customer relationship handling is seen to be a strong asset as it brings the benefits of improved service, choice, and convenience to the customer and aids in customer retention and repeat orders for the organization. Today's electronic commerce isn't limited to shopping over the Internet. It's also not confined to supply chain transactions between large trading partners. Electronic commerce means doing business electronically – all of the aspects of doing business. It embodies the total business process – from advertising and marketing to sales, ordering, manufacturing, distribution, customer service, after-sales support, and replenishment of inventory – managing the entire customer and product life cycle.

When we look to apply e-business strategies, we are applying new technologies to streamline our business interactions. These technologies use the Internet as a backbone, but are increasingly looking to integrate advanced telephone systems, hand-held digital appliances, interactive TVs, self-service kiosks, smart cards, and a whole host of emerging technologies. All of these customer-facing technologies are supported, behind the scenes, by integrated customer databases, call centres, ERP and workflow systems, and secure transactional systems. They require sophisticated management so that systems communicate – seamlessly, reliably, and securely – across corporate and geographic boundaries.

10.4.1 Common customer management themes

When we look at how companies are looking to manage the customer experience in a new way, we can identify eight recurring themes. They are:

- Targeting the right customers.
- Owning the customer's total experience.
- Streamlining business processes that impact the customer.
- Providing an all-round view of the customer relationship.
- Letting customers help themselves.
- Helping customers do their jobs.
- Delivering personalized service.
- Fostering community.

10.4.2 Targeting the right customers

First, we need to ask whether we have identified the most profitable customer segment? Which people make or influence on purchasing decisions? Which group of desirable customers are defecting or choosing a competitor? Therein lies the first target market for your initiatives – to make it easy for the right customers to do business with you.

10.4.3 Owning the customer's total experience

How much control do you have over your end user's total experience. The customer's experience starts with learning about your products, then choosing an item, making a purchase, taking delivery, setup, installation, after-care, purchasing follow-on products, taking delivery, receiving accurate bills, and perhaps filing a complaint or resolving a dispute. If you deal through channels, you are ultimately responsible for the customer's entire experience with that channel partner. If you outsource delivery, service, or other operations, you still care about the quality of the experience the customer is having.

10.4.4 Streamlining business processes that affect the customer

Federal Express and United Parcel Service (UPS) are good examples of companies that have automated and streamlined the entire end-to-end business process that affects the customer. Each company needs to streamline the end-to-end business processes that affect customers in any way. Everything is a candidate for this process, from product design and manufacturing, shipment and delivery, pre-sales and post-sales service, billing, and credit-checking. Most large companies have reengineered internal operations to reduce cycle time or cut costs, but only a few companies have done this by focusing on the processes that impact customers the most. To be successful in e-business, you will need to streamline your business processes from the outside in – from your customers' perspective – rather than from the inside out.

10.4.5 Providing an all-round view of the customer relationship

Efficient call centre and customer management are built on the same seamless infrastructure that gives customers (and customer service reps) direct access to all accounts and functions across computer systems, business units, and departments. This means that account reps and customers helping themselves have immediate access to every service the customer has asked for, the service history for each, and his or her current account status.

10.4.6 Letting customers help themselves

We can all learn how industry leaders are making a success of letting customers help themselves. A stroll though the online customer interfaces of Dell Online and iPrint shows how customers who want to help themselves can do so. They not only simply find information, but also order products via the Web. These companies have thought through each step of the customer's decision-making and procurement process. It is time to measure your organization against this standard. How far can customers go in self-service? What happens when they reach a stumbling block? Can customers interact with your organization 24 hours a day from anywhere?

Once you get people to order online, or through any channel for that matter, you need to allow them to check what is happening to the order. The Web provides the cheapest and simplest way for customers to do this – and give them an empowered feeling of importance while saving the company money. In Cisco's case, as soon as they made online order status-checking available, calls to the call centre dropped to 10% of the former volume. Customers simply went to the Web, and liked it.

10.4.7 Helping customers do their jobs

Do you really understand your customers' decision-making process? Do you know how your product or service fits into your customer's job? Do you know what it would take to really integrate your product or service seamlessly into your customer's job?

10.4.8 Delivering personalized service

Dow Jones's *Wall Street Journal* Interactive and Liberty Financial's Stein Roe Farhnham websites are great examples of delivering cost-effective personalized service on the Web. Both build dynamic websites for each individual based on that person's profile. Personalization may mean tailoring the offer directly for each customer, as in the two examples above, or it may involve simply making account information available, or selectively alerting customers to items of particular interest to them.

What, we may ask, is the difference between handmade shoes made to measure by the local cobbler, and the kitchen made to order by an Internet design service? Both provide customized service, but the latter combines it with post-industrial revolution economies of scale. This is achievable because the design service can serve a widely spread geographical population, using the data transport provided by the Internet and the physical transport of our late 20th-century infrastructure, plus a data-base-driven manufacturing facility.

10.4.9 Fostering community

Why is fostering community a way to make it easier for customers to do business with you? At first, it seems like a 'nice to have', but not essential, characteristic of an easy-to-use website or a successful customer loyalty programme. But as the success of newsnet and online communities and chat-rooms of many types demonstrates, customers gain a lot of value from interacting with one another and often find the community aspect of a website is what makes them feel taken care of.

Cisco Systems' incredible success in electronic commerce (in addition to good products) has been built on a foundation of community – customers helping each other to solve highly technical problems. Each company now needs to ask what its customers have in common? Would they value the opportunity to learn from one another?

10.5 Getting close to customers within e-hubs

While companies like Dell and Amazon stay in the headlines, it is not surprising that many people believe that B2C e-business is a strong new business event. The reality is that, as many large (mainly US) conglomerates know, the real value to business e-business and virtual organization lies in B2B transactions. A survey by the US Census Bureau of the Commerce Department published in 2001 shows that in 1999 B2B activity accounted for US$485 billion, as against US$15 billion in B2C transactions. This means that 12% of manu-facturing shipments were made as a result of e-business transactions two years ago within the world's largest econ-omy. And the figure has been rising since then, particularly though industry portals and e-hubs. We therefore need to consider, as a matter of urgency, our strategy for managing the customers we have through these channels.

10.5.1 Online transactions – personal or impersonal?

Nobody, in their role as customer or supplier, likes being reduced to a line item in a catalogue. We value being treated as individuals and enjoy dealing with other people. But once we start to think about online opportunities, all sorts of possibilities open up. Replacing the static catalogue, sending an e-mail, or possibly speaking with an inexperienced sales representative, sellers can use online technology to present their wares precisely the way they want. Instead of describing a product, suppliers will be able to show the product in use, offer real-time education and training, and pop-up chat windows to speak with experts on the topic. Also, online-based sales methodologies are reliable. They aren't renowned for having a bad hair day, or leaving the office to play golf. Getting the best of both worlds, content gets presented in a consistent fashion and can still be customized for groups and individuals.

10.5.2 Profiling and segmentation will boom

Exchanges that help suppliers develop close linkages with their customers through the marketplace will find it a lot easier to attract suppliers. They don't want to treat every customer the same, and customers have different needs and differ in importance to the supplier. An intermediary represents a potential barrier between transacting parties. Exchanges that make that barrier as permeable as possible and provide technology infrastructure to foster relationship-building should have a good value proposition for suppliers.

Not surprisingly, a batch of specialist companies has emerged to provide the technology for profiling and segmenting customers by behaviour traits – both online (website traffic) and offline. Analytical technologies for customer profiling and segmentation from companies like E.piphany, Broadbase, and Hyperion will be converted into marketplace services over time. So while buyers can compare suppliers on price, suppliers can also compare different types of buyers. Suppliers will be able to discover the 20% of the customers that represent 60% of the profits. Buyers will see presentations created on the fly and addressing their specific needs.

One-to-one marketing

A notion gaining currency in the context of e-business, both for B2C and B2B marketing, is that of one-to-one marketing. This activity uses customer databases and interactive communications to sell to each customer on each occasion a bundle if as many products as are needed in that sales period. To happen, this marketing strategy is based on the combination of a deep knowledge of the customer's wants, and the company's ability to customize the delivery of products and services:

- serving the customer on the basis of lifetime worth, rather than single transaction-based profit opportunity. This requires a combination of information gathering, storage and retrieval; and
- the ability to customize production and probably cooperate with other companies.

10.5.3 Marketing automation

Despite all the fear that large trading hubs and the widening of electronic markets will drive prices down everywhere, forcing many companies out of existence, the potential for the digital medium to offer different customer segments different pricing, negotiated contracts, custom promotions, and related products and options, should counterbalance this. Suppliers will orchestrate marketing campaigns and promotions in the context of the marketplace. Suppliers have spent significant sums on marketing automation and aren't about to revert to one-size-fits-all marketing because of exchanges.

10.5.4 Personalization and interactive selling

Exchanges will have to offer much more sophisticated selling metaphors over time to offer context-based promotions, suggestions, and configurations. Moreover, buyers want more information and context around the transaction to make more intelligent procurement decisions. Advanced technologies such as streaming and interactive video will provide immediate information in context.

10.6 Cosset the customer – web-based call centres

Before the Internet, we saw two major call centre technologies in operation. The first was the interactive voice response (IVR) system which gave limited self-service to customers who used buttons on touch-tone telephones to navigate the customer service centre where they searched for answers to queries. By means of the other technology, computer telephony integration (CTI), the caller – as well as information about his or her account history – was directed by computer to the selected call centre representative.

Now, however, for many customers, the Internet is the preferred channel of interaction with a business. Because of this, and because of the efficiencies involved, it is time to consider web-enabled call centres to provide multiple contact points through which Internet users can access customer service at your company. The modern web-enabled call centre includes a variety of vital functions: in particular, call back; automated e-mail response; interactive chat; voice over IP; and shared browser sessions. Let's see how these work out in operation.

10.6.1 Interactive chat

The caller dials up the company website and uses a link on the browser to join up for an interactive chat session. The call is routed through the call centre to the appropriate service representative – identified by such factors as language, product/ model and/or history of site navigation. He or she then types into an appropriate chat session. Each service representative deals with many users, each of whom sees themselves as having a one-on-one chat with the representative.

10.6.2 Voice over internet protocol (VoIP)

Again dialling up the website, and linking through the browser, the caller indicates that they want to join a voice session and is equipped for this purpose with a microphone and headset plugged into the computer. This starts a voice over IP call (meaning that the cost of long distance rates is forgotten and the call is merely charged at local Internet link rates). Typically, information about the caller and the last web pages visited on the site are displayed on a screen to the receiving service handler. Replacing expensive dialup long distance, international or 1–800 numbers, this facility can be widely used.

10.6.3 Shared web browser sessions

To use this service, the caller dials in as above, using VoIP, and the service agent and user communicate by VoIP. The service representative then synchronizes the customer's browser so that both parties are seeing the same screen in front of them, and the service agent leads the user to specific website pages while communicating with him or her by voice.

How far a company chooses to put in place one or more of these solutions depends on business strategy, products and the needs/preferences of customers. These solutions are typically layered, with visitor call-back often occurring as the starting point. For example, a customer service function that offers automated e-mail response would want to offer call-back as an option as well. Companies that have resources to support shared web browser sessions also support the remaining four solutions.

10.6.4 The benefits

Moving to a web-based call centre is more a long-term decision than a tactical one for several reasons. It determines the face that an enterprise presents to the public. It needs an awareness and decision on the management strategy toward managing two of a company's most important assets – its prospects and its customers. A web-based call centre will have wide-ranging impact on the technology infrastructure. It should call for a broad segment of the organization to take part in serving customers. We suggest that this will certainly be used to competitive advantage – by you or your competitors.

The value proposition to be made for the web-enabled call centre and its major components include: minimizing lost sales, transforming information gatherers into shoppers, increasing the size of the average sale, and increasing long-term customer value.

Visitors arrive at your website to buy or to obtain information by which they can compare your product value to that of your competitors. There will be an increasing number of customers who prefer to interact with your company through Internet channels for speed, convenience and cost considerations. There will also be others who need help in navigating your site for information you have provided, but which they have been unable to locate.

10.7 A framework for e-business change management

The model in Figure 10.2 identifies a useful framework within which to identify facilitators and inhibitors of successful e-business change. The relationships presented in the framework are based on relevant work in organizational change, strategic management innovation, and information systems. The

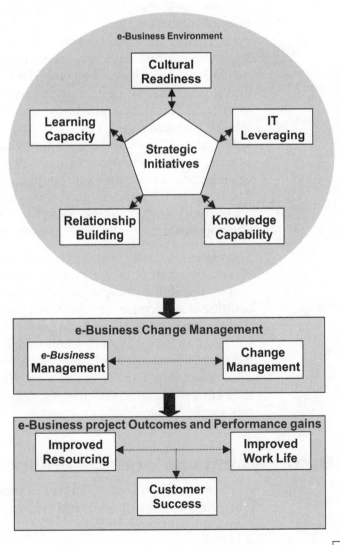

Figure 10.2
Framework for change management

general thesis of the framework is adapted from Guha's *et al.* (1997) work on 'business process change management':

Any significant business process change requires a strategic initiative where top managers act as leaders in defining and communicating a vision of change. The organisational environment, with ready culture, a willingness to share knowledge, balanced network relationships, and a capacity to learn, should facilitate the implementation *of prescribed e-business management and change management. Both of these are requisite for customer success and ultimately in achieving measurable and sustainable competitive performance. (p. 121)*

Kalakota (1999) states 'the creation and implementation of an e-business project is inextricably linked to the management of change' (Kalakota *et al.* 1999: p. 60). This requires systematic attention to learning processes, organizational culture, technology infrastructure, people and systems thinking. These gain even greater significance when considering the alignment of these dimensions with respect to ERP and e-business implementations. e-business change is defined here as an organizational initiative to design an e-business project 'to achieve significant (breakthrough) improvements in performance (e.g. quality, responsiveness, cost, flexibility, satisfaction, shareholder value, and other critical e-business measures) through changes in relationships between management, information, technology, organisational structure, and people' (Guha *et al.* 1997: p. 121). Planning and managing such systems requires an integrated multi-dimensional approach across the e-business and the development of new business process models.

Therefore, in any examination of outcomes, consideration should be given to (a) the environmental conditions for change and (b) the ability of the organization to manage change in those conditions. Outcomes of e-business change can be measured at various levels of the broad complex phenomenon of any e-ERP project. Previous studies by Guha *et al.* (1997) indicate successful e-business projects should tend to have facilitators over many dimensions but also failure is most likely to occur where too little consideration has been given to key factors such as cultural readiness or change management.

10.8 Analysing the change environment

A recent study of international organizations implementing e-business change through ERP found the following factors as critical to e-business success.

10.8.1 Change environment

- *Strategic initiatives* – this was frequently driven by user management rather than IT management and was generally initiated in a local unit rather than from centralized decision making.
- *Cultural readiness* – champions were typical of change and necessary to promote the change. Frequently interdepartmental rivalry inhibited change and further a culture of resistance to accept change was introduced from other business partner organizations.
- *Network relationships* – in all successful cases the e-business project demonstrated positive inter-agency cooperation and the beginnings of cross-functional cooperation. As one IT manager stated 'Our web-based solution assists the most casual user with global, personalized, and secure access to our corporate information on demand.'
- *Learning capacity* – in the most successful projects, learning by doing and learning from others helped improve the professional end-user IT skills. This enabled project managers to adapt to a quality decision-making procedure.
- *IT leveragability and knowledge capability* – generally, successful projects demonstrated positive local leadership, superior IT design for improved learning, and business-to-employee communication. To overcome resistance to change, knowledge capability must be aligned (along with the enabling technology) to the strategic e-business initiatives.

10.8.2 Change management

The pattern of change was reported to be a participative change tactic resulting in an evolutionary change. This was viewed as a 'waterfall' progression of change, starting with an alleviation of dissatisfaction by end users and eventually arriving at a well-managed process:

alleviation of dissatisfaction,
    ➔ vision for change,
        ➔ *evolutionary* change tactics,
           ➔ a well-managed process for change

10.8.3 Outcomes and performance gains

Outcomes of e-business change can be measured at various levels of the broad complex phenomenon of any e-ERP project.

More recently, leading firms that have begun to undertake e-business to meet strategic goals recognize that they only accomplish their objectives through people, therefore placing importance on improving the quality of work-life issues. If effectively managed, employees should ultimately be more productive in their work tasks and better able to serve customers, suppliers, and business partners. The key constructs that can be probed here are: gaps between effectiveness expectations (goals) and actual performance improvements, e.g. employee work satisfaction, efficient resourcing, and customer interaction (Venkatraman and Henderson 1998).

- *Outcomes* – it was found that where success was achieved, the project showed an improvement in one of the outcome constructs – the quality of work life from the outset thus motivating employees to support additional change processes.
- *Performance gains* – the performance gains were typically achieved from two sources; labour cost savings and greater operational efficiency through optimized resource allocation, and more effective decision making through access to more reliable real-time data frequently via mobile technology.

The intrinsic motivation and self-management of autonomous knowledge within the development teams played an important role in the successful implementation. The emphasis was very much more on collective performance rather than individual but at the same time development and maintenance of personal and professional reputations was a significant driver.

10.9 Successful management of change

The findings from our study found that a successful project had facilitators in all components of the business framework shown in Figure 10.2, including the change environment and project management. It was also found that the least successful e-business projects had inhibitors in several dimensions, especially in the area of cultural readiness and change management. This highlights the need to encourage the balancing of conflicting organizational knowledge, when contemplating the adoption of e-business solutions.

In the future, as e-business activities become commonplace, corporate portals for empowering employees will be considered as an economic necessity. The next wave of economic advantage lies in revenue generation from new business opportunities in other business-to-business models, such as business-to-consumer for customer satisfaction. These are complex problems that can never be solved with technology alone. They require leadership, appropriate problem solving skills, lots of hard work and executive commitment, and a culture that embraces the ideals of the learning organization (a team and community orientated work process). The organizational design, learning environment, and human-to-human communication and collaboration must be aligned to the enabling technology. One should always keep in mind the balance between people, business processes, and technology. In a labour force of cross-functional virtual teams management will be more about motivation and governance may be largely a question of self-regulation rather than traditional managerial control. IT professionals may well be better equipped for this change given the large 'community of practice' with a strong, shared culture of technical professionalism and their extended use of technology for communication and decision making.

10.10 Summary

We began this chapter by inviting you to consider how ERP systems, introduced in Chapter 7, and e-business tools complement and integrate with each other.

We went on to introduce a model of organizational activity which displays three vectors along which e-business tools are introduced to meet business ends, and in the process, adding degrees of virtuality to an existing company.

Along the vector of asset sourcing and relationships with other firms, we considered emerging trends in customer relationship management as they apply both in B2C and B2B activities. We went on to spend rather more time on the implications of being within B2B online trading groups, and extending our view of customer relationships into this area. We came back full circle by considering how both B2C and B2B e-business operations can integrate the emerging Internet technologies within a modern call centre for customer and business partner satisfaction.

The third vector is the complex area of knowledge management as a corporate resource, and this topic has been introduced here as the third vector of our organizational activity model. We have looked in particular at the role and practice of change management with companies undergoing the adoption of e-business strategies, although this topic in itself warrants a separate book.

References

Drucker, P.F. (1998) Management's New Paradigms, *Forbes*, Oct. 5, 152–177.

Guha, S., Grover, V., Kettinger, W.J. and Eng, J.T.C. (1997) Business Process Change and Organisational Performance: Exploring an Antecedent Model, *Journal of Management Information Systems*, Vol. 14, No. 1, 119–154.

Kalakota, R. and Robinson, M. (1999) *e-Business: Roadmap for Success*, Addison-Wesley Longman, MA, USA.

Markus, M.L., Manville, B. and Agres, C.E. (2000) What makes a virtual organisation work? *Sloan Management Review*, Vol. 42(1), 13–26.

Venkatraman, N. and Henderson, J.C. (1998), Real strategies for Virtual Organising, *Sloan Management Review*, Fall '98, 33–48.

Creating virtual cultures for global online communities

Japanese and American Management is 95% the
same and differs in all important respects
(Adler, Doktor and Redding 1989: 27)

11.1 Introduction

Culture operates at many levels of aggregation: group, firm, industry, profession, region, group, country, group of countries. Regardless of groupings culture remains the means by which non-genetic information is transmitted either within a given generation of agents or from one generation to the next. Technological practice forms an integral part of such information transmission but usually combines universal theoretical knowledge with more practical, local and culture specific application. This has particular implications for the management of communication within multinational, multicultural organizations and for the specific form of virtual organization which comprises technology-based alliances over several cultures operating in an even broader cultural environment.

Information and communication technology (ICT) is, by definition, the technological foundation of e-business consisting of a number of business-centric categories such as business-to-business (B2B), business-to-consumer (B2C), and business-to-employee (B2E). As discussed in previous chapters, e-business has been extended to allow for the systematic integration of an organization's internal and external systems, via the Web, both up and down the supply chain. This in turn will result in today's business-centric e-business topologies evolving into customer-centric e-communities.

In this chapter we review cultural influences on organizations and information technology applications. This is expanded into the development of online communities where a shared culture of common practices is a key factor in effective development and maintenance. Finally, the whole issue of global expansion is placed under the spotlight and the implications for the future examined.

In future, an organization's success within the global e-community will require culture-focused organizations where communities allow for:

- Differentiation and the creation of attractive communities.
- Creation of unique value propositions.
- The ability to be a 'good citizen' and to enter into engaging dialogues with other members of the e-community.

11.2 e-business cultures

11.2.1 Organizational cultures

Schein (1996) defines culture as a set of basic tacit assumptions that a group of people share about how the world is and ought to be; it determines their perceptions, thoughts, feelings, and to some degree, their overt behaviour. Culture manifests itself at three levels:

- the level of deep tacit assumptions that are the essence of the culture;
- the level of espoused values that often reflect what a group wishes ideally to be and the way it wants to present itself publicly; and
- the day-to-day behaviour that represents a complex compromise among the espoused values, the deeper assumptions, and the immediate requirements of the situation.

Overt behaviours cannot be used alone to decipher culture because situational contingencies often make us behave in a manner that is inconsistent with our deeper values and assumptions.

11.2.2 Culture and IT

The impact of information and communication technologies (ICT) has extended far beyond organizational boundaries and permeates almost every aspect of daily life around much of the globe. Many of the changes which ICT has brought about were foreseen and have been well documented. The concepts of the information society, virtual organizations, networked communities and home offices have all been touted as the result of the information explosion and the advancements in technology. However, many of these IT-based applications have unlooked-for consequences which relate directly to cultural mismatches between the philosophy of the system application or methodology and the cultural philosophy in which it is expected to operate. ICT innovations generally bring about greater user empowerment and help to promote flatter organizational structures, all of which are now held to be positive outcomes in the North American dominated management literature. The same attitude may not be held true in Southeast Asian societies where high power distance and rigid hierarchies are the preferred organizational model and low individualism but high social interaction is the preferred personal role.

The division between subjective culture (referring to values, behavioural norms, attitudes and religion) and objective culture (referring to infrastructure, technology and other material objects) is important since it is the unique combination of the two which defines how information is communicated in a society. The United States and Japan both have access to the latest communication technologies but whereas electronically mediated communication is heavily used in the US. Japan relies more on face-to-face or oral communication than the written or typed mode. In studying the effect on the use of e-mail and fax in Japan, significant differences have been found between Japanese and US knowledge workers in both perception and use of ICT. The determining factor appears not to be the degree of industrialization but whether the country falls into a low-context or high-context culture which will give a relative emphasis to written or oral communication respectively.

Boisot (1998) suggests that technology is itself an expression of culture and by institutionalizing an organization through ICT an organization is redefining a culture within certain boundaries. In current times the results are often seen through the repercussions of downsizing and outsourcing. Just as each society strikes a balance between individual separateness and interdependence, between authority and freedom, between achievement and compassion, between rigidity and uncertainty, so the virtual organization must tailor its global systems to reflect cultural values and enhance performance without disrupting societal norms.

11.2.3 Culture and change

Senge (1998) states that 'the trouble with most business relationships is that they work like dysfunctional families. Everybody is basically concentrating on just pleasing the boss and avoiding getting their ass kicked, rather than on building real relationships'.

To survive crises and change there needs to be a deep level of trust and regard, yet change induces stress and under stress people revert to their most primitive behaviours which in an organization means management control, time pressure, do it faster, do it cheaper. The irony is that this is the antithesis of all that is preached about the virtual organization and the development of a change culture. In order to be more adaptable and resilient, faster and more responsive, organizations have to be more reflective and encourage people to really think together. An effective virtual organization needs to be a learning organization and this represents a significant shift in culture over the norm for Western models of management and organizational development. This new mental model permeates through the organization through different leadership styles, community behaviours and individual beliefs.

Four core attributes of this new mental model for the 'individualized' corporation are:

- companies as collectors of people;
- developers of horizontal knowledge flows;
- builders of a trust-based culture;
- the organization as an integrated network.

Whereas people are social animals and innately curious, interacting and learning from each other, the modern organization has been constructed in such a way to constrain, impede and sometimes kill this. Unlearning these behaviours and 'learning to forget' are perhaps the most difficult challenge that management face. In most organizations the 'forgetting' curve is flat and takes an enormous amount of effort to shift.

One solution is the adoption of 'vulnerability management' approaches and the use of vulnerability audits. For example, during reengineering, vulnerability analysis can be used to predict how cutback of resources will be distributed, what disappears, what survives and what prospers. Organizations may be resilient against spending cuts but be highly vulnerable to staff cuts, marketing strategy, IT adoption or management training. Identifying and learning from these can assist the corporation to be prepared for the unthinkable. There is a need for the organization to shift design and culture from one that suppresses unpalatable news to ones that actively seek different viewpoints, opinions, and contradictory information.

Nevertheless, culture has become a concept thrown around by consultants as if it can be changed as easily as donning a new set of clothes or a radical hair restyle! Culture is not easy to change and in times of change people will cling to culture for their stability. The organization must consider whether gradual change is an acceptable solution or whether a complete culture change is the only route and possibly accompanied by a complete change of personnel. Certainly the development of a one-company culture needs to be closely tied to reward systems aligned with learning-driven goals and objectives. Frequently the real target group should be the middle management level who can effectively act as a sink to prevent upwards and downwards flows of information.

11.3 Culture and the virtual organization

11.3.1 Virtual culture alliances

In conventional organizations, shared assumptions typically form around the functional units of the organization, and are often based on members' similar educational backgrounds or experiences. This assumes, however, that we define the boundaries of the organization as the population of employees – what if we also include suppliers and customers? Developing a single culture of reliability in virtual organizations is very much more difficult because of such extended boundaries (including subcontractors and other alliance members along the supply and demand chains) often encompassing several cultures. The existence of shared deep tacit assumptions and values across all members of the alliance, or of similar educational backgrounds or experience, is unlikely in such organizations, particularly if crossing cultural lines. The various cultures represented in the different members of the network will almost surely introduce dysfunctionalities and miscommunications, as communication and functionality take place across organizations that do not share common values, assumptions, or perceptions. Japanese firms, for example, typically exhibit cultures that extend well beyond the normal legal boundaries of an organization.

Virtual organizational strategies need to meld the varied cultures that comprise the system into a cohesive whole in which the deep assumptions and espoused values of each of the member organizations can be built around the need for reliability. This is extremely difficult in distributed, multicultural systems aligned by temporary linkages that may dissolve as business opportunities and requirements change. Virtual organizations may also be plagued by vulnerabilities that make the development of a melded culture of reliability very difficult: a proliferation of different languages and cultures; different power structures and organizational politics; communication between units and members of comparable stature, but non-comparable experience and training; rivalry between alliance members; a reluctance to listen and ask questions; an eagerness to 'get the job done'; and ethnocentrism, a tendency to discredit members or individuals not of the same background or experience.

These characteristics are present in traditional multinational corporations, but are exacerbated in virtual alliances because of the distributed interdependence and amorphous nature of such networks. As Schein (1996) emphasizes, too often behaviour is unwittingly in place that is dysfunctional to the system. For example, many organizations – virtual and otherwise – espouse teamwork and cooperation, but the behaviour that the incentive and control systems of the organization reward and encourage is based more on a shared tacit assumption that only individuals can be accountable and that the best results come from a system of individual competition and rewards. If the external situation truly demands teamwork, the group will develop some behaviour that looks, on the surface, like teamwork by conducting meetings and seeking consensus, but members will continue to share the belief that they can get ahead by individual effort and will act accordingly when rewards are given out.

Attention to incentive and control systems can help prevent situations where shared cultures of deep and espoused values are required for success, but are undermined by the individual members' reward and control systems, or by competing business opportunities.

11.3.2 Impact of culture on virtuality

One of the many challenges in virtual organizations is deciding where a unified culture is essential and where 'one thousand flowers' may be allowed to grow. Some of the questions that need answering in relation to culture are:

- Are virtual cultures industry dependent or business model dependent?
- Is the relationship between culture and the virtual organization one of diversity exploitation or controlled manipulation?
- Does the extent to which there are shared goals, synchronicity of work, co-locations and reciprocity of risk and responsibility define shared culture yet inhibit the extent of virtuality that can be exploited in the organization?
- Are stronger cultures required at the interfaces of virtual alliances to ensure reliability enhancement?
- Where member goals, roles, and responsibilities are more carefully articulated in a virtual organization does this imply the greater need for a unified culture?
- How can the virtual organization manage a diversity of cultures?
- Will a desirable diversity of cultures be supported only under conditions of high trust and open communication?
- To what extent should incentives and control systems be used in virtual organizations to develop unified cultures?

Four areas should be considered as part of a basic framework for reconstructing the organization:

- investment in extensive socialization: managers need to be able to cope with diversity of race, gender, culture and intellect;
- development of language skills;
- extensive documentation for common understanding;
- extensive commitment to training, both analytic and experiential.

The future belongs to the imaginative.

11.3.3 Success in cultural change

An example of successful cultural change is described by Buckman (1998) at Buckman International Laboratories as they designed a system and built a culture that facilitates the communication of whatever is needed across all the organization's boundaries (1200 people, 21 countries location, 90 countries for customers). The cost has been estimated at US$7500 per person (3.5–4.5% of revenue) but they believe the results justify every cent. Their philosophy has been to move the entire organization to wherever it is needed at the time. This has been achieved by expanding the span of communication and influence for each individual. This work anywhere, anytime at your most efficient mode of operation is both a consequence of and a driver for the further globalization of the e-community. Globalization is not necessarily a strategy to be embraced lightly, however, since it carries with it many more implications above and beyond the obvious cultural ones. Virtual organizations entering global markets need to learn from the experiences of long-term global players.

11.4 Community building

11.4.1 Development stages

Venkatraman and Henderson (1998) (as described in Chapter 7) outline three stages in the development of an e-community. These are summarized in Table 11.1.

ICT, particularly systemic (ERP-style) integration of the organization's ICT infrastructure and applications, is seen as the foundation of this model.

Increasing levels of e-community involve greater usage of ICT to increase the richness (particularly in terms of value adding knowledge) and complexity of the relationships between the

Table 11.1 Three levels of e-community (after Venkatraman and Henderson 1998)

Vectors and characteristics	Stage 1	Stage 2	Stage 3
Customer interaction (virtual encounter)	Remote experiences of products and services	Dynamic customization	Customer communities
Asset configuration (virtual sourcing)	Sourcing modules	Process interdependence	Resource coalitions
Knowledge leverage (virtual expertise)	Work-unit expertise	Corporate asset	Professional community expertise
Target locus	Task units	Organization	Interorganization
Performance objectives	Improved operating efficiency (ROI)	Enhanced economic value added (EVA)	Sustained innovation and growth (MVA)

organization and its supply chain partners, customers, and sources of expertise.

Clearly, one would expect to see considerable differences in the communications networks, and particularly in how those networks are used, in organizations that are at different stages of development.

11.4.2 Shifting locus of core competencies

Prahalad and Ramaswamy (2000) suggest that organizations need to 'create their future by harnessing competence in an enhanced network that includes customers'. They also present a three-stage model that is summarized in Table 11.2.

Table 11.2 shows that the idea of extending the organization's ICT network and changing the nature of its usage to improve core competencies is a central component of their model.

11.5 The customer as king

In the past, most practitioners and scholars have had a company-centric focus and have been primarily concerned with 'alliances, networks, and collaborations among companies'. The old idea of the 'extended enterprise' (i.e. a central organization supported by a constellation of supply chain partners) should give way to the idea of an enhanced network of traditional suppliers, manufacturers, investors and customers. Managers need to recognize that consumers are a source of competence forces. Managers and researchers must focus on developing relationships with the consumer as the agent that is most dramatically transforming the industrial system as we know it rather than just their supply chain partners. Table 11.3 summarizes the changing role of customers.

Competence now is a function of the collective knowledge available across the whole of the enhanced network and the market has become a forum in which consumers play an active role in creating and competing for value. The Internet is given as one of the main reasons that consumers have been increasingly engaging themselves in active and explicit dialogue with manufacturers of products and services and dialogue is no longer being controlled by corporations.

Table 11.2 Locus of core competencies

	The company	Family/network of companies	Enhanced network
Unit of analysis	The company	The extended enterprise: the company, its suppliers and its partners	The whole system: the company, its suppliers, its partners, and its customers
Resources	What is available within the company	Access to other companies' competencies and investments	Access to other companies' competencies and investments, as well as customers' competencies and investments of time and effort
Basis for access to competence	Internal company-specific processes	Privileged access to companies within the network	Infrastructure for active ongoing dialogue with diverse customers
Value added of managers	Nurture and build competencies	Manage collaborative partnerships	Harness customer competence, manage personalized experiences, and shape customer expectations
Value creation	Autonomous	Collaborate with partner companies	Collaborate with partner companies and with active customers
Sources of managerial tension	Business-unit autonomy versus leveraging core competencies	Partner is both collaborator and competitor for value	Customer is both collaborator and competitor for value

11.6 The increasing power of the connected consumer

Community and conversation are fundamental to human society. They maintain that in the past giant bureaucracies were able to use their special knowledge, the power of advertising and public relations and their sheer size and power to distance themselves from their customers and to suspend true market

Table 11.3 The evolution and transformation of customers

	Customers as a passive audience			Customers as active players
	Persuading predetermined groups of buyers	**Transacting with individual buyers**	**Lifetime bonds with individual customers**	**Customers as co-creators of value**
Time frame	1970s, early 1980s	Late 1980s and early 1990s	1990s	Beyond 2000
Nature of business exchange and role of customer	Customers are predetermined	Seen as passive role	Buyers with specific patterns of consumption	Customers are part of the enhanced network; they co-create and extract business value as collaborators, co-developers, and competitors
Managerial mindset	The customer is an average statistic; groups of buyers are predetermined by the company	The customer is an individual statistic in a transaction	The customer is a person; cultivate trust and relationships	The customer is not only an individual but also part of an emergent social and cultural fabric
Company's interaction with customers, and development of products and services	Traditional market research and inquiries; products and services are created without much feedback	Shift from selling to helping customers via help desks, call centres, and customer service programmes; identify problems then redesign products and services	Providing for customers through observation of users; identify solutions from lead users, and reconfigure products and services based on deep understanding of customers	Customers are co-developers of personalized experiences. Companies and lead customers have joint roles in education, shaping expectations, and co-creating market acceptance for products and services
Purpose and flow of communication	Gain access to and target predetermined groups of buyers. One-way communication	Database marketing; two-way communication	Relationship marketing; two-way communication and access	Active dialogue with customers to shape expectations and create buzz. Multilevel access and communication

conversation. They show how the rise of the Internet has enabled people to restart conversations in a global world. The basic message of this book is that the balance of power is rapidly moving away from giant impersonal corporations and shifting toward well-informed and articulate consumers. One of the main reasons behind the increase in power of the consumer is the fact that the Internet provides a means whereby they can group together into powerful virtual communities. One of the messages in this book is that the large suppliers who try to ignore this change will do so at their own peril.

One could argue that the balance of power, at least on the Internet, moved away from the giant corporations to articulate, well-informed and above all, well-connected consumers several years ago. This argument is supported by the 1994 Pentium fiasco. In June 1994 Intel engineers discovered a division error in their new Pentium chip. Intel managers decided not inform anyone outside the company on the grounds that the division error could only affect a very few customers. On 24 October Dr T.R. Nicely, a math professor in Virginia (who double-checked all his work by computing everything twice, on two different computers), detected the error and contacted Intel technical support to report the error. Intel did not get back to Dr Nicely and so on 30 October Dr Nicely e-mailed a few people to inform them of the bug he had discovered. On 3 November Terje Mathisen of Norsk Hydro posted a message entitled 'Glaring FDIV Bug in Pentium' on the Internet newsgroup comp.sys.intel. By 24 November the story had been reported by the *New York Times*, more than 200 other newspapers as well as on the radio and TV news networks.

At this stage Intel made an offer to replace a Pentium processor only after Intel had determined that the processor would cause a problem in the application in which it would be used.

On 12 December IBM issued a press release announcing that it had halted shipments of Pentium-based PCs and Intel stock had dropped by $3.25 that week.

By 20 December Intel finally agreed to replace all flawed Pentiums upon request. Intel had to set aside a reserve of $475 million to cover costs of the Pentium recall.

On 18 January 1995 the *Wall Street Journal* (cited in Hoovers-Online 1994) reported that Intel's flawed Pentium chips resulted in their profit falling 37% in the fourth quarter of 1994.

Another mistake made by Intel, back in 1994, was to underestimate the power of, and fail to monitor the discussions of, their end-users who had become welded into a powerful virtual community by the Internet.

Today, Intel posts all known flaws on the Internet to avoid a recurrence of this problem. It also provides a number of both technical and non-technical support forums for its user community. As Intel now say:

The support that Intel provides with electronic messaging (email and support forums) provides the same technical expertise that can be found on the telephone as well as the instant documentation that can be found with self-help services. With publicly accessible forums, you have all of the benefits of email technical support, with the added benefit of the option of viewing previous messages written by other participants, and participating with pertinent suggestions and tips that can help others (Intel 1999).

These forums also allow Intel to engage in conversation with their user communities and become a member of those communities.

However, we are not just concerned with the increasing power of virtual groups of consumers. We are also very much concerned with the nature and role of markets and how they should be regarded as communities.

11.7 Community building through ICT

Returning to Venkatraman and Henderson's concept of e-communities we might expect to see ICT vendors starting to market products aimed specifically at virtual community building. This has in fact happened. Indeed, in the ERP software arena product developments have taken place almost exactly in accordance with the model.

Consider the developments in SAPs, the premier ERP software vendor, product line (R/3) since the mid-1990s. Prior to the launch of release 3.1, in 1997, R/3 provided comprehensive and highly integrated functionality for virtually all of an organization's internal business processes. However, it had no real facilities for interconnecting with either business partners or customers. Even traditional EDI was only supported if third party products were bolted onto R/3.

The launch of release 3.1H, in 1997, was the addition of a basic Internet transaction server layer to the traditional three-layer client–server architecture but, very little additional B2B or B2C functionality was provided with release 3.1. However, the launches of versions 4.5 and 4.6 in 1998 and 1999 included a massive new range of EC and EB functionality. SAP now provides a whole range of Internet ready EC (front-end) and EB components providing linkages to the internal ERP components.

Since the release of 4.5 SAP has refocused on providing products that are designed to facilitate what Venkatraman and Henderson refer to as VO-ing and what Prahalad and Ramaswamy refer to as enhanced networks of traditional suppliers, manufacturers, investors and customers.

There major product groups are now labelled 'marketplaces', 'workplaces', and 'business applications' – and significantly they are presented in that order.

Marketplace products are primarily concerned with the creation of electronic marketplaces and include components such as portal management, auction systems, web casting, forums, chat services and even a community management service.

The workplace products provide a one-stop, web-based enterprise portal that lets the employee or any other authorized person access the applications, information, and services available on the enhanced network.

The business applications include:

- E-commerce (including the usual electronic catalogues, shopping carts, payment systems, etc.).
- Customer relationship management.
- Supply chain management.
- Strategic enterprise management.
- Business intelligence.
- Knowledge management.

All these are in addition to the original core internal functions of human resources, logistics execution, manufacturing, product life cycle management, and financials.

SAP's new outward focus is characterized by their own corporate portal. This has been re-branded 'mySAP.com' and when accessed opens a window that displays:

Share Your Thoughts About SAP's Web site

SAP values your opinion about all its products and services, and we would like to know what you think about our Web site. Our goal is to make SAP.com a truly customer-led site, and your comments are a critical part of our ongoing efforts to reach this goal.

Another vendor, NetSage, has developed customer relationship software agents, called 'sages', that integrate media with business and social rules. The software agents know when to intervene, what to say, and which product or recommendation is appropriate for a particular customer on the basis of what the customer has already done and the context of that customer's actions. The 'sages' are claimed to be socially intelligent and able to interact with particular customers throughout the entire spectrum of the customer relationship.

NetSage state that the design of their software agents is based upon the psychological studies of Byron Reeves and Clifford Nass who have demonstrated convincingly, in their book *The Media Equation*, that interactions with computers, television and new technologies are identical to real social relationships and to the navigation of real physical spaces.

However, it is possible for a business to create a virtual community without having to use extremely sophisticated extended ERP software or intelligent social agents. This is demonstrated by the following case.

11.8 Community building: the ActionAce.com case

ActionAce.com is an online retailer that retails pop-culture (e.g. Batman, Star Trek, DragonBall etc.) products, including toys, action figures, video games, movies and music. In addition to toy sales, ActionAce's website provides toy-related content. It has an online magazine called *ActionZine* which provides reviews of movies, toys and games as well as polls, trading posts and auction message boards.

The online toy retailer grew out of the idea of Casey Lau and John Wong, the managers of a Hong Kong web design company, to build a website for selling action figures and comic books. Wong and Lau started the company, then called ComicPlanet.com, with just three employees in January 1997. In mid-1998, David Haines, now ActionAce.com's chief executive officer, joined the company, brought in some venture capital, and renamed the company ActionAce.com. (Lombardo 1998).

By mid-1999 ActionAce had a total of 24 employees in Hong Kong and the US. Although it takes orders from around the world most of ActionAce's customers are from the US. This is one of the reasons it opened its distribution centre in the US in September 1998. Most of ActionAce's products are now shipped from the US. The Hong Kong office is ActionAce's headquarters and is mainly responsible for strategic planning, administration and sourcing. The office in Richmond, California, is responsible for creative design as well as distribution (Hong Kong Trade Development Centre 1999).

Another major reason for incorporating in the US was to gain access to a suitable financial services infrastructure. In 1998/9 no local bank could provide ActionAce with suitable electronic transaction settlement service (*Economist* 1999). According to Claire MacDonald of *Asiaweek* Asia still lacks basic systems allowing consumers to purchase and easily pay for goods and services electronically, whereas in the US, transaction settlement is handled through a clearinghouse network connected to nearly every financial institution in the country. Although E-tailers could get online transaction-processing services, they were very expensive, because of the perception that the Internet business is rife with 'charge-backs', credit purchases where the buyer refuses to pay. Card-processing services charged up to 15% per transaction, roughly three times the typical fees paid by brick-and-mortar stores for settlement. According to David Haines, managing director of ActionAce, the lack of credit facilities 'is the biggest thing holding back e-commerce in Asia'.

ActionAce currently keeps inventory on about one-third of the items it carries, which are the more popular ones. Its information system monitors the inventory and will issue notice for reordering in respect of items that fall below a preset inventory level. If the supplier concerned has established an EDI link with ActionAce, the order will be issued electronically.

For the remaining two-thirds of the items, ActionAce relies on the inventory kept by its suppliers. By electronically linking its website with the suppliers' inventory system ActionAce is able to sell on the basis of what its suppliers have in stock. When ActionAce receives an order, it immediately passes the order to its suppliers who are required to deliver the products to ActionAce by the next day. ActionAce then ship the goods to the customers.

When ActionAce launched its website in June 1998 the site carried around 300 product items and had about 15 000 visitors in its first month. By August 1999, the site carried more than

1000 items and attracted more than 2 million visitors (Hong Kong Trade Development Centre 1999).

In the second half of 1999 it expanded its product line significantly and invested heavily in advertising in the US market to build up its brand name there. Its aim was to build a pop-culture community around its website. It already published a weekly magazine on toys, comics and movies at its site, and launched an auction market for collectible toys/action figures in quarter three of 1999.

By November 1999 the site had become one of the web's premier action entertainment portals with over 65 000 toys, action figures, video games and anime titles in stock, daily entertainment news and original episodic anime.

According to NCompassLabs:

Actionace.com is raising the online experience to a new level – combining original content, a passionate community and e-commerce to create an all-inclusive action entertainment experience. (NCompass-Labs 1999)

In the second quarter of 2000 ActionAce launched its new 'NeoGlyphix' service which provided:

exciting webisodic animated shows that play through your PC or MAC on Netscape and Explorer, using the Macromedia Flash plug-in.

They plan to introduce online gaming in the summer of 2000 so that virtual community members can game together over the Internet.

When one visits the ActionAce portal, and the services that lie behind, it creates an experience more like visiting a club than a retail outlet.

11.9 Global communities

The increasingly widespread use of the Internet means that corporations can no longer 'control' the information and knowledge available to their customers as was shown by the Pentium fiasco. Instead corporations should be leveraging the knowledge their customers possess in order to co-create value for the wider community as well as the organization.

The ICT required to do this is now readily available. Whether or not companies will make use of this technology to create their own customer communities remains to be seen.

However, success within the global e-community will require:

- Differentiation and the creation of attractive communities.
- Creation of unique value propositions.
- The ability to be a 'good citizen' and to enter into engaging dialogues with other members of the e-community.

Truly global markets now produce and consume about 20% of world output – about $6 trillion of the planet's $28 trillion gross domestic product. Within 30 years, as that GDP expands to $91 trillion (assuming an overall real growth rate of 4%), global markets could multiply 12-fold, reaching about $73 trillion, more than 80% of world output.

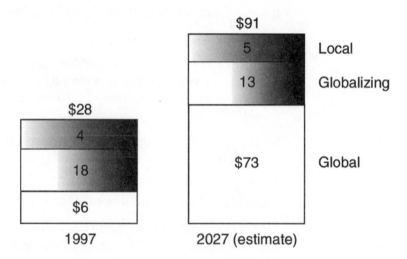

Figure 11.1

Economic integration, the force driving this expansion, will promote the formation of global markets in almost every industry (including service based such as education) and, more integration will take place in the next 30 years than occurred in the previous 10 000 or more. In a world without economically significant geographic boundaries, the rules are going to change. The good news is that companies will have access to the world's finest resources: the most talented labour, the largest markets, the most advanced technologies, and the cheapest and best suppliers of goods and services. The bad news is that the risks will be high because every business will have to compete against the world's best, and integrating markets are volatile and uncertain.

Global companies are looking to emerging markets for growth. Companies in emerging markets are searching for ways into the burgeoning global economy. Alliances can seem the obvious solution for both sides. Yet alliances between global and emerging market players are hard to get right, and often highly unstable. Many have failed to meet expectations, required extensive restructuring, or been bought out by one of the partners. Differences of size, ownership structure, objectives, culture, and management style can all prove stumbling blocks. Alliances also need to recognize that there are four stages of market evolution and each stage of this will be driven by each partner's shared strengths and weaknesses and by the relative importance of each contribution in shifting the balance of power (Figure 11.2).

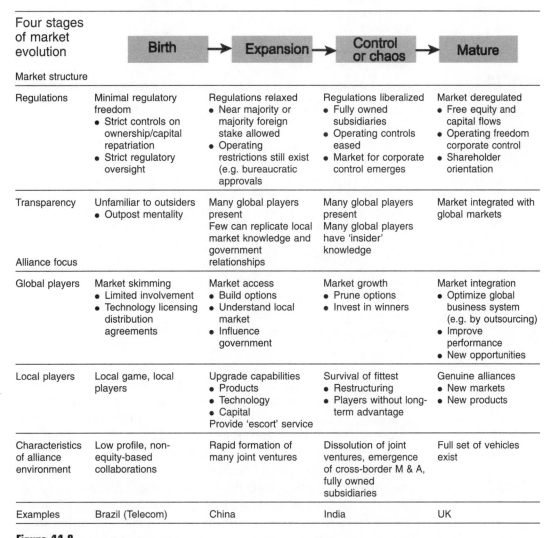

Four stages of market evolution	Birth	Expansion	Control or chaos	Mature
Market structure				
Regulations	Minimal regulatory freedom • Strict controls on ownership/capital repatriation • Strict regulatory oversight	Regulations relaxed • Near majority or majority foreign stake allowed • Operating restrictions still exist (e.g. bureaucratic approvals	Regulations liberalized • Fully owned subsidiaries • Operating controls eased • Market for corporate control emerges	Market deregulated • Free equity and capital flows • Operating freedom corporate control • Shareholder orientation
Transparency	Unfamiliar to outsiders • Outpost mentality	Many global players present Few can replicate local market knowledge and government relationships	Many global players present Many global players have 'insider' knowledge	Market integrated with global markets
Alliance focus				
Global players	Market skimming • Limited involvement • Technology licensing distribution agreements	Market access • Build options • Understand local market • Influence government	Market growth • Prune options • Invest in winners	Market integration • Optimize global business system (e.g. by outsourcing) • Improve performance • New opportunities
Local players	Local game, local players	Upgrade capabilities • Products • Technology • Capital Provide 'escort' service	Survival of fittest • Restructuring • Players without long-term advantage	Genuine alliances • New markets • New products
Characteristics of alliance environment	Low profile, non-equity-based collaborations	Rapid formation of many joint ventures	Dissolution of joint ventures, emergence of cross-border M & A, fully owned subsidiaries	Full set of vehicles exist
Examples	Brazil (Telecom)	China	India	UK

Figure 11.2
Evolution of market alliance

	Importance of factor		Balance of power			
			Now		Future	
Determining factors	High	Low	Us	Partner	Us	Partner
Product or process technology						
Brand ownership						
Channel control						
Manufacturing capacity						
Ability to invest in the business						
Local relationships (e.g. regulators)						
Global relationships (e.g. global suppliers; global customers)						
Management control						

Figure 11.3
Checklists for power shifts

To assess whether an alliance will evolve the partners in the alliance should plot how contributions are likely to shift as shown in Figure 11.3.

Likely evolution is along four paths:

- sustainable power balance;
- power shift to global partner;
- power shift to local partner;
- competition, dissolution or acquisition;

as shown in Figure 11.4.

These vulnerabilities are all inherent within global virtual alliances and must be recognized when global partnerships are formed. It is especially important to recognize that emerging market alliances pose different challenges to those faced by alliances in mature markets and are generally far less stable. Structural change in an industry is usually the result of cumulative processes leading to large-scale discontinuity. A virtual organization that wishes to take advantage of such discontinuity must have the ability to see it coming earlier than their competitors and to react more quickly and so require a focused strategy for change.

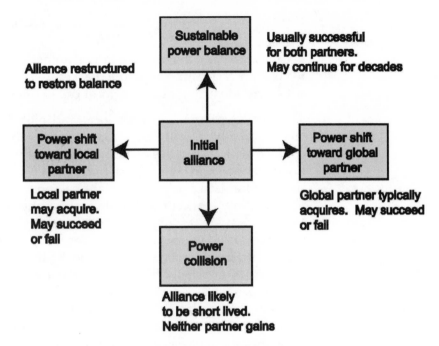

Figure 11.4
The four paths of
evolution

11.10 Strategies for global change

The evolutionary models suggested for global expansion can be likened to the management of metamorphoses. A dynamic resource system view is recommended where destruction as well as construction is a necessary strategy. The following steps should be taken:

- Know your resource system.
- Look for leading indicators.
- Anticipate shocks.
- Identify resources that must be built to contribute to a future sustainable advantage.
- Identify resources that must be destroyed.

In selecting alliances you also need to develop a strategy to build power. What is the organizational goal – is it to become the global hub as the main competitor? is it as a defensive measure to retain a share of the global market against predatory attack? is it to develop a sustainable home-market-based alliance to build a global entry point? Strategies for maximizing power include:

- Invest today for tomorrow's power base.
- Think twice before allying with a global leader.
- Consider alternative partners.

- Protect your future by securing access to key intangible assets.
- Create world class alliance opportunities.
- Position early and shape the market.
- Clearly identify global and local capabilities and focus.

This power balance between local and global is not clear cut since globally distributed organizations obviously have to contend with disparities of culture within as well as without the organization. A recent report from the OECD would suggest that an alternative approach might be appropriate and cites the 'learning city' concept as an alternative approach. Europe has led the way in establishing the learning city concept with examples in Poitiers in France, Jena, in Germany, Oresund region of Scandinavia, Andalusia in Spain and Kent Thames-side area of London, UK. These purpose-built cities or regions have advanced communications infrastructures but also a commitment to place innovation and learning at the core of the development. Firms and knowledge institutions clustered in the same location have greater opportunities to share a culture and understanding that facilitate the process of social interaction and learning where no institution has a monopoly on knowledge. Virtual organizations may need to reconsider the extent to which embedded globalization will leave them at a disadvantage.

It may well be that such strategies are only appropriate for organizations with Western-based strategic management concepts. In Singapore the development of an information society based on virtual organizations may well be restricted by the political control over information flow and the current stage of democracy at this stage of Singapore's development. Similar issues and concerns have been raised by the World Bank in their 2000 report and frequently by groups such as OECD. This whole area of socio-economic change and the impacts of globalization merits discussion in the world arena.

11.11 Summary

For the virtual organization playing in a global world there are no rules but many lessons to be learned from multinational and cross-cultural organizations around the world. Those that survive accept a much broader portfolio of concerns and apply constant reappraisals to their marketplace. The virtual organization which does not realize this should be renamed the vulnerable organization.

References

Adler, N.J., Doktor, R. and Redding, S.G. (1989) From the Atlantic to the Pacific Century, in: Osigweh, C.A.B. (ed.) *Organizational Science Abroad: Constraints and Perspectives*, 27–54, New York: Plenum Press.

Boisot, M. (1998) *Knowledge Assets – Securing Competitive Advantage in the Knowledge Economy*, Oxford Press.

Buckman, R.H. (1998) Knowledge Sharing at Buckman Labs, *The Journal of Business Strategy*, Vol. 19, No. 1, 11–15.

Economist (1999) E-commerce Asia online; Singapore and Hong Kong. 2000. http://www.economist.com/editorial/freeforall/17-4-99/wb9911.html

Hong Kong Trade Development Centre (1999) Electronic Commerce in Hong Kong: Reference Case: ActionAce.com, Hong Kong Trade Development Centre. 2000. http://www.tdctrade.com/sme/ecommerce/general.htm

Prahalad, C.K. and Ramaswamy, V. (2000) Co-opting Customer Competence, *Harvard Business Review* **78**(1), 79–87.

Schein, E.A. (1996) Three Cultures of Management: the Key to Organisational Learning, *Sloan Management Review*, 9–20.

Senge, P. (1998) Sharing Knowledge, *Executive Excellence*, Vol. 15(6), 11–12.

Venkatraman, N. and Henderson J.C. (1998) Real Strategies for Virtual Organising, *Sloan Management Review*, **40**(1), 33–48.

| Appendix 1 | Case: Little River Winery Co.

Introduction

The company is a family-run winery business located in the booming wine industry region of Swan Valley in Western Australia. It was established in 1972 and owned by two members of the management. The company cultivates a total acreage of 12.5 in addition to supplies from contract growers. West Wines Co. produces a variety of Australian choice wines with main markets in Australia, Japan, Singapore, Malaysia and Taiwan. Its annual level is 10 000–15 000 cartons. It established its first online site in June 1995 as a virtual face model, focusing on providing an additional outlet for the firm's operations and to support its strategy to reach international clients. The site has subsequently been redesigned twice to reflect the changes in operation as the organization expanded virtual operations, linkages and strategic alliances and took advantage of a growing e-market for wine.

e-business infrastructure

The company's online shop focuses on marketing products, and providing corporate and industry information to its clients. The site also provides information about its key agents and sales outlets. There are a total of six permanent staff including three members of the Simpson family. The company also employs approximately 15–20 part-time staff who perform a variety of tasks (e.g. cellar door wine tasting, wine sales and café activities).

The site features an electronic ordering facility enabling customers to purchase with their credit cards and provides information about wine production, price lists, Company Vintage Report (Swan Valley Vintage Report 1999), information about the Swan Valley Region and recent visitors to the winery.

Linkages and relationship management

LRW maintains extensive linkages with key players in the local, national and international wine industry: Japan (3), Singapore (1), Malaysia (1), Taiwan (1), Australia (14) – Western Australia

(1), Victoria (1), Sydney (6 + 5 NSW restaurants), Darwin Agent (1). The site also features a page with links to 32 or so wine sites worldwide. There are also links to key local industry players in Western Australia, e.g. Wine Industry Association of Western Australia Inc., and Australian Wine Online.

LRW has joined the London Wine Clearing House – a facility allowing international wine producers to stock their produce in the UK without incurring import tax and sales tax until such time as actual sales of wines are made. Integrating the company's online ordering facilities with the clearing house had enabled LRW to realize huge cost savings and effective management in inventory, export, staffing and product delivery. Now the CEO can manage all sales in the UK over the Net from the home base in Western Australia. Without the online facility, the company would need to have at least a sales representative in the UK to take care of orders and arrange delivery from stocks in the warehouse. According to the CEO, James, the UK market is a premium market representing very competitive pricing and very small profit margins, which makes such the cost savings crucial.

The integrated online ordering clearing house system also enable the company to monitor stock levels in order to plan future productions. Easy and real-time stock levels means the company can engage in selective strategy to push sales through its gift services – a new product line aimed at customers who would like to place orders for choice wines for delivery to friends or loved ones.

Virtual organizing e-business strategy

The core feature of managing a business on the Internet is to consistently review the entire business value chain to identify opportunities for adapting and redefining core operations while looking to exploit emerging capabilities of the Internet for creating enhanced business value. This is essentially a virtual organizing strategy. The strategy continually reviews the strategic agenda and the appropriateness of the business model and how these align with the relevant product markets, demands of the stakeholder community and existing and/or available infrastructure capabilities.

At LRW, there are indications that they are moving the e-business to a *virtual alliance* model where other wineries in the Swan Valley region would participate in some form of common brand marketing. Such an alliance may be implemented as common web space featuring common facilities for the participating group of firms or just provide visibility for the alliance and its objective with smart links on the company's website which would be reciprocated on the sites of participating SMEs. Given the fact that LRW is already a major supplier of wine production related services to many of the other Swan Valley wineries, it is easy to see the company's adaptation as a way to add on new product lines especially in the business-to-business category targeting the other wineries

There is an ongoing commitment to improve online systems as a way to improve the company's marketing strategy. Since 1995 the company has undertaken two major upgrades of its e-business infrastructure. A review of the company's initial website, developed in 1995, shows that LRW has an active strategy for enhancing its online infrastructure.

Comparison of the three versions of sites shows radical improvements to the design. One key difference is that the older site attached significant importance to clients visiting the physical location of the winery. At that time physical awareness (as associated with traditional marketing strategies) was considered key to image building and brand loyalty by the company. This emphasis has become reduced in the current version of the site. The online ordering facility has remained simple in layout but the new hyperlinks emphasize stronger alliances along the value chain and a broader commitment to the global marketplace. This has resulted in a considerable increase in national and international sales. The LRW site encourages visitors to join the company's electronic mailing list on wine and health to learn about developments in the industry and the company's products as well as communicate directly with the company. This is aimed at building brand loyalty.

Success factors

A group discussion on LRW e-business led by the company's CEO revealed a number of insights about some of the factors which influence its success. These are reviewed below.

Technical knowledge about e-business environment

This was described as an important factor for LRW e-business success, and supports a common finding of the review of a host of e-business sites where information on company statements suggests that e-business success depends on the knowledge about the e-business environment help by the CEO or manager–owner. This included the appreciation of capabilities of e-business facilities, and an understanding of the potential of the Internet for creating business value. In the case of LRW, the CEO of the company mentioned that he has been involved in computers 'since the days of CPM/DOS operating systems'. The CEO, with the help of his daughter – an employee with a bachelor degree in commerce – takes care of the day-to-day management of the website. According to him, his technical knowledge helps him in negotiating good deals with his chosen ISP and that he had to scan the market and compare prices before settling on the present ISP. Although the website redesign was outsourced, the company considers the ability to make changes on a routine basis in-house very important and the CEO expressed his eagerness to receive input from clients and visitors in aspects of site usability.

Virtual organizing within the Internet requires a continuous reorganization of business processes, infrastructure components as well as product mix in order to respond to changes in markets. Translating strategic decisions into product features, marketing information and online presentation, and introduction of new online facilities require changes to site content and format on a routine basis. This also involves appreciation of the soft issues of the Internet environment, such as customer perception of value online, brands management, and how to capture and sustain the interest of visitors and ensure revisits.

An alternative to the existence of in-house knowledge about the e-business environment is to form a strategic alliance with external sources of the requisite knowledge base, for example with a local ISP or e-business solutions provider. Dstore.com, an Australian online retail business, provides a typical example of such an alternative where the company has formed a techno-logical alliance with the national telco, Telstra, to develop state-of-the-art e-business infrastructure. Dstore.com's technology alliance with Telstra represents one feature of virtual organizing aimed at adding to the limited scope of an SME and to provide a competitive edge for its e-business operations.

Strategic visioning for the internet

The ability to articulate a strategic vision about the company's use of the Internet is another important factor of success. This would depend on the knowledge base about the e-business environment and is the basis of selecting an appropriate e-business model. In the case of LRW there is a clear vision to adopt the Internet infrastructure to support the company export strategy, especially since the local market in Western Australia is very small. The company sees the Internet as a means to market and advertise its products to other Australian states and to its international targeted markets especially the UK and Japan. According to the CEO, Western Australian, through its commissioned retail agents, represented only 5–10% of the total, while NSW provide up to 40–50% of sales.

Appropriate choice of e-business format

Employing a virtual face business model enabled the company to reach the potential clients in other Australian states, especially in Sydney, NSW. In the UK, the company's online ordering facilities enable it to effectively manage orders from its customers of its premium product range. Participation in the online wine clearing house is further facilitated by the ability to check and process orders electronically and relay purchase information directly to the clearing house for fulfilment. Recent developments within the entire Swan Valley region point to a potential reorganization of its e-business around a virtual alliance in the long term.

Questions

You have been asked to advise the owner and managing director of Little River Winery in the Swan Valley with regard to a strategic plan for e-business. What advice would you offer and how should he proceed to develop his business on the Web?